DATE			

The Democratic Muse

THE
DEMOCRATIC
MUSE

Visual Arts and the Public Interest

A TWENTIETH CENTURY FUND ESSAY

Edward C. Banfield

Basic Books, Inc., Publishers New York

Library of Congress Cataloging in Publication Data

Banfield, Edward C.
   The democratic muse.

   "A Twentieth Century Fund essay."
   Includes bibliographical references and index.
   1. Art patronage—United States. 2. Art and state—United States. I. Twentieth Century Fund. II. Title.
   N5207.B36   1984   707'.9   83–45250
   ISBN 0–465–01598–0

CONTENTS

Foreword by M. J. Rossant   vii

Acknowledgments   xi

Introduction   3

Chapter 1   *But Is It Art?*   18

Chapter 2   *Making the Law*   38

Chapter 3   *Administering the Law*   63

Chapter 4   *Art versus the Museum*   92

Chapter 5   *Art versus the Public School*   117

Chapter 6   *Collectibles versus Art*   139

Chapter 7   *"Fine" versus "Applied" Art*   155

Chapter 8   *Art versus Welfare*   178

Chapter 9   *Art and the Public Interest*   195

Notes   207

Index   237

FOREWORD

IN the confident climate of economic growth that prevailed in the 1960s, Americans began thinking in terms of their nonmaterial needs. President John F. Kennedy played host at the White House to artists and writers, and the idea that the federal government ought to be supporting individuals and institutions involved in cultural activities began to take root. These developments led to the establishment of the National Endowment for the Arts (NEA) and the National Endowment for the Humanities (NEH), overcoming a good deal of resistance from those who had long held that public subsidies for the humanities and the arts were not a proper use of public funds or who voiced the view that such subsidies would result in a politicization of our culture.

The Twentieth Century Fund played a role in this debate. August Heckscher, my predecessor as director of the Fund, served as special consultant on the arts to President Kennedy, and favored the involvement of the government in such activities. He took the lead in seeing to it that the Fund sponsored the first thorough economic analysis of the performing arts; the result, *Performing Arts: The Economic Dilemma* by William J. Baumol and William G. Bowen, had an important part in making the case for federal support of the arts.

Once public subsidies for the arts were accepted, they grew at a rapid rate, even under presidents who had had no previous affinity for the arts. Since the Fund had been involved since the inception, it seemed to the trustees and to me that we should mount a series of studies dealing with public policy and the arts to determine how well this new venture was faring. Thus, we sponsored Dick Netzer's *The Subsidized Muse* on the effects of subsidies on the arts; Karl E. Meyer's investigation of *The Art Museum*; and *Patrons Despite Themselves*, the analysis of indirect government subsidies to the arts by Alan L. Feld, Michael O'Hare, and J. Mark Davidson Schuster, all of whom, despite their critical approach, supported public funding of the arts.

When Edward C. Banfield, a distinguished political scientist at Harvard University, came to the Fund with the idea of questioning whether the government ought to provide subsidies to the arts and under what conditions, it was agreed that his proposal had merit. Banfield wanted to make use of the techniques of economic theory to weigh the various economic justifications for government "intervention" in the marketplace for the visual arts; but his chief purpose was to determine whether increased access to the visual arts was in the public interest. Although few Fund trustees could see themselves allied with Banfield, they agreed that he should be given the opportunity to have his independent say.

He has not let us down. In his study he evaluates the primary beneficiaries of government funding—the NEA, the art museum, and the public schools—in an effort to clarify what government intended in providing support. Banfield's answers are set forth on the following pages, and, like everything else he has written, his responses are critical, insightful, and provocative about the role of government in the arts. Banfield's views are likely to inflame passions among fervent supporters of the arts in government and out. But he also should lead other advocates of public subsidies of the arts to take up his challenge and think of ways to better the per-

Foreword

formance of government in the arts. Either way, I believe
that he has made a useful contribution, and the Fund is
grateful to him for it.

M. J. ROSSANT, *Director*
The Twentieth Century Fund
December 1983

ACKNOWLEDGMENTS

BECAUSE their number is so large, it is impossible for me to acknowledge properly all who helped in the making of this book. I must limit myself to thanking those who made some special contribution: Elliott Banfield, whose views about the nature and importance of art gave me an initial perspective from which to form my own; Martin Meyerson, who, as on previous occasions, provided encouragement of a sort that only an old friend and collaborator can give; Rosemary A. Hartman, who presided over the initial fact-gathering efforts while making a unique contribution of her own; and four patient and perceptive critics of early drafts—Christopher C. DeMuth, Constance (Mrs. Robert L.) Hoguet, Gabriella D. Mills, and Michael Straight. It goes without saying that none of them is in any way responsible for the shortcomings of the book, and it cannot be presumed that they necessarily agree with the views expressed. I should like also to acknowledge the stimulation that I received from discussion with the diverse specialists brought together by the Liberty Fund in cooperation with Brigham Young University in seminars on "The Visual Arts in a Free Society" in the summers of 1982 and 1983.

I wish to record my entire satisfaction with the Twentieth Century Fund: it gave me the absolute freedom that a scholar requires, and it was remarkably patient when I failed to meet the deadline to which I had agreed. Carol Barker, associate director of the Fund until recently, was a wise and steadfast friend. Brenda Price, a skillful and painstaking editor, has left her improving marks on almost every paragraph. I also owe a substantial debt of gratitude to Lori Ohliger, a copy editor for Basic Books, and to Michele Millon, a Basic Books project editor.

Finally, I want to mention with gratitude, affection, and respect my friends Daniel and Joanna Rose.

E. C. B.
Cambridge, Massachusetts
June 1983

The Democratic Muse

Introduction

To the Editor:
  I am sorry that Martha Wilson is "shocked" by the President's recommended cuts in funding for "the arts," which she believes would be "dealt a heavy blow" affecting "the quality of life in America" (letter Feb. 14, 1981).
  The worst blow—the unkindest cut—is inflicted when officials and those with a stake in approved high culture decide what "arts" my tax dollar is to support. I am tired of having people confiscate my movie money to buy what they consider esthetically preferable. I welcome the Reagan move toward restoring my right to define what constitutes quality in my life.
  No matching funds needed, thanks.
                                —Leonard Rubin
        New York Times, March 1, 1981

THIS BOOK is an evaluation of public funding of the visual arts. It assesses the three principal institutions through which such funding is provided—the National Endowment for the Arts (NEA), the typical art museum, and the public

3

schools, which provide art education—and considers two policy options that these institutions, and the art world generally, have rejected. The book goes on to evaluate the case for subsidy of visual art, first in the light of the increased satisfaction that might accrue to individuals, and then from the standpoint of the public interest.

Art Subsidies

Contrary to public opinion, taxpayers have given substantial support to the arts for at least a century. Until 1965 it was almost entirely indirect, first in the form of gifts of land, later in tax exemptions to "educational" institutions and tax advantages for private giving. In 1965 Congress added direct support with the National Foundation on the Arts and the Humanities Act, which created the foundation that was in effect a holding company for two endowments—the National Endowment for the Humanities (NEH) and the NEA.[1]

The NEA, whose concerns include the visual arts—the focus of this book—was given wide powers to make matching and other grants to states, not-for-profit organizations, and individuals. Its aim was to encourage productions of "substantial artistic and cultural significance" and to make the arts more accessible to the public. By 1980 total spending by the NEA was well in excess of $1 billion. Nine federal departments were then spending an additional $500 million annually for the arts and arts-related activities, all state legislatures (except one) were making appropriations to arts agencies, and there were some 720 municipal arts agencies, a few of which received local tax money along with grants from public and private sources.[2] At the same time, support of the arts through tax exemptions continued, yielding several times as much revenue as direct appropriations.[3]

Support of the arts, of course, is only one of many activities that has been added to the federal agenda in the past two or three decades. Since the mid-1960s, federal domestic spending more than doubled as a percentage of gross national product, much of the increase due to support of activities that had hitherto been considered state or local responsibilities (see table I.1). Although the amount spent on the arts is picayune as a percentage of total government spending, the arts programs nevertheless raise questions that ought to be asked of all government spending: Is the activity one that is properly within the sphere of government, especially that of the national government? Does it have a purpose that was arrived at by deliberation and with an understanding of the situation? Are the means employed for the attainment of the purpose effective? Does the activity entail no unintended consequences that offset or perhaps more than offset the value of the ends sought? Are the means employed more likely to achieve the purpose, or to achieve it at less cost, than some other means?

With respect to all of these questions, the answer is an unequivocal no. The American regime exists for purposes that are not served by art, and the support of art is not among the powers that were given to the federal government. None of the arts agencies under study—not the NEA, the art museum, or the public school—has a defined purpose in any proper sense of the word, let alone one arrived at with knowledge and deliberation. What passes for purpose with each of them is a set of vague and conflicting statements of good intentions based on gross misperceptions of the nature of art and of the amount and character of the public demand for it—the precipitate, so to speak, of competitive struggles among interest groups and of adaptations by administrators endeavoring to maintain and enhance their organizations in the face of changing circumstances. Although accompanied by constant invocations to public interest, the proponents of public support of the arts have not offered a justification for it that bears examination or analysis. Chapters 2 and 3 de-

5

TABLE I.1

Selected Federal Programs Dealing with Traditionally
Local Problems

Arson Control
Meals-on-Wheels
School Security
Solid Waste Disposal
Rat Control
Bridge Replacement and Rehabilitation
Noise Control
Urban Gardening
Education of Gifted Children
Home Insulation
Urban Park Facilities
Snow Removal
Police Disability Payments
Alcohol Abuse
Homemaker Services for the Elderly
Bikeways
Museums
Runaway Youth
Pothole Repair
Adolescent Pregnancy

SOURCE: Advisory Commission on Intergovernmental Relations,
An Agenda for American Federalism: Restoring Confidence and Competence,
Washington, D.C., June 1981, Commission Report A–86, p. 41.

scribe in some detail how the NEA's program was shaped first in the legislative process and then in the administrative one. Program formation in the typical art museum is described briefly in chapter 4 (most museums are private organizations, but with rare exceptions get some support from government), and art education in the public schools is discussed in chapter 5.

These chapters support the conclusion that public funding encourages arts agencies to emphasize activities that have little or nothing to do with art properly understood: instead of making aesthetic experience more accessible, they turn attention away from it in order to present art as entertainment, psychotherapy, material for historical studies, and so on. By misrepresenting the nature of art, they contribute to widespread public confusion and indifference to it.

The agencies under study have not seriously tried to evaluate their programs. Nor have they tried to examine the potential benefits of programs very different from those to which they have more or less accidentally become committed. Chapters 6 and 7 discuss two plausible alternative approaches—separation of aesthetic from other values (e.g., investment and antiquarian) by use of near-perfect copies of works of art, and de-emphasis of fine art (paintings and sculpture) in favor of improving the appearance of ordinary things. From time to time, thoughtful people have proposed both options; however, neither has ever been seriously considered by the publicly funded agencies because, whatever their merits, acting upon either option would jeopardize the standing of the agencies with their supporters in the art world.

Public funding of art is sometimes said to be justified by the increases in the number of people viewing art. Subsidies have not been the reason for the larger art public of recent years, nor have they attracted more of the poor. The art public is now, as it has always been, overwhelmingly middle and upper-middle class and above average in income—relatively prosperous people who would probably enjoy art about as much in the absence of subsidies. Indeed, they might enjoy it more, for subsidies tend to create and perpetuate institutions that are relatively unresponsive to the tastes of those whom they exist to serve.

Affording enjoyment to people is not a proper function of organizations serving the common good, whether they be private—foundations, for example—or public. Government agencies constitute a special case because, among other things, anything they do involves an exercise of force—or what amounts to the same thing, the threat of it. In order to be justifiable, the action of a public-serving body must benefit the public in some significant way—something that public funding of art does not do.

The Proper Sphere of Government

The conclusions drawn here do not rest entirely on the facts revealed by the study of the arts agencies, but depend also on judgments that are in some degree, but by no means altogether, arbitrary.

The principal assumption made with regard to the proper sphere of government is that the appropriate criteria are those that distinguish the American regime, which in the words of Josiah Lee Auspitz, is one of "natural law liberalism."[4]

One belief upon which the American regime was founded —a belief most eloquently stated in the Declaration of Independence—is that all men are endowed by their Creator with certain inalienable rights and that it is to secure these rights that governments are instituted. "Individuals entering society," Washington wrote in his letter accompanying the draft Constitution to Congress, "must give up a share of liberty to preserve the rest."[5] Paraphrased from the philosopher John Locke, these words imply that the preservation of liberty is the only justification for infringement upon it.

Locke's philosophy is no longer fashionable, but the principle that force can legitimately be used only to protect the individual is still strenuously affirmed by widely respected political thinkers. Robert Nozick, for example, maintains in *Anarchy, State, and Utopia* that the sole legitimate function of the state is the protection of its citizens against force and fraud:

The moral side constraints upon what we may do, I claim, reflect the fact of our separate existences. They reflect the fact that no moral balancing act can take place among us; there is no moral outweighing of one of our lives by others so as to lead to a greater *social* good. There is no justified sacrifice of some of us for others.[6]

In his view, "Taxation of earnings from labor is on a par with forced labor."

Another contemporary philosopher, John Rawls, arrives at similar conclusions by an altogether different route in *A Theory of Justice:*

There is no more justification for using the state agencies to compel some citizens to pay for unwanted benefits that others desire than there is to force them to reimburse others for their private expenses. . . . [T]he principles of justice do not permit subsidizing universities and institutes, or opera and the theatre, on the grounds that these institutions are intrinsically valuable, and that those who engage in them are to be supported even at some significant expense to others who do not receive compensating benefits. Taxation for these purposes can be justified only as promoting directly or indirectly the social conditions that secure the equal liberties and as advancing in an appropriate way the long-term interest of the least advantaged.[7]

The liberal principle is not the only one upon which the American regime rests, however. The Founders were heirs to the thought of Aristotle as well as Locke, and personal liberty did not enter into the classical conception of the political good. "What the statesman is more anxious to produce," Aristotle wrote, "is a certain moral character in his fellow citizens, namely a disposition to virtue and to the performance of virtuous actions."[8] John Adams, in his draft of the Massachusetts Constitution of 1780, inserted a provision making it the duty of magistrates and legislators to "cherish the interests of literature, the arts and sciences, and commerce" and to "inculcate the principles of humanity and general benevolence, public and private charity, industry and frugality, honesty and punctuality, sincerity and good humor, and all social affection among the people."[9] It is noteworthy that, when his draft was submitted to the people of the various towns, there was some objection to a requirement that the towns provide schools, but none to the limitless charge placed upon lawmakers.[10]

Other state constitutions did not go this far. Most, however, contemplated the improvement of men as well as their protection. This is evident from the provisions they contained for the promotion of religion, morality, and education.[11]

The drafters of the federal Constitution did not make similar provisions for the improvement of men. James Madison and others believed that in constitution making it was necessary to take men as they were rather than as they should be; this meant designing institutions that would divert predominantly self-serving impulses into activities that would be relatively harmless from a political and moral point of view: to wit, the acquisition of wealth and creating a political structure that would cause ambition to counteract ambition. This emphasis upon institutions represented a deliberate rejection of the claim of the much-admired French philosopher Montesquieu that the cultivation of civic virtue was indispensable to popular government. James Wilson, a signer of the Declaration of Independence who was a principal figure in the Convention of 1787, was moved to protest that property was not the sole or primary object of government and society—that "The cultivation of and improvement of the human mind was the most noble object."[12] The convention nevertheless ruled out projects for the regulation of private life by the national government.[13]

Natural law liberalism, the amalgam of more or less opposed principles in proportions that differed in the national and state governments, places great value on the protection of the individual in the exercise of his rights; at the same time, it allows a large sphere for such intervention by government as the people deem necessary to establish preconditions for the development of a competent citizenry. This, Auspitz says, was the rationale for the wholesale provision of western lands to homesteaders, the public education movement, the enactment of wage protection and welfare entitlements during the New Deal, the Civil Rights Act of 1964, and the provision of legal and safety net services to the poor during the Great Society.[14]

This conception of the proper sphere of government allows for support of art only if it can be expected to have significant consequences for public, as opposed to private, interests. To borrow from Auspitz, the public interest clearly requires that there be a courthouse. But does it also require that there be a statue in front of the courthouse?

In the American regime the federal government is limited in a way that the state governments are not. The powers of the national government, James Madison wrote in *Federalist* 45, are "few and defined":

Those which are to remain in the State Governments are numerous and indefinite. The former will be exercised principally on external objects, as war, peace, negotiation, and foreign commerce. . . . The powers reserved to the several States will extend to all the objects, which, in the ordinary course of affairs, concern the lives, liberties, and properties of the people; and the internal order, improvement, and prosperity of the State.

In fact, eighteen powers are enumerated in the first article; few can properly be called "defined." The framers were well aware that terms like "necessary" and "proper" are open to a variety of interpretations; nevertheless, there is no doubt that they intended to limit sharply the new government's powers. Lest there be doubt, the Tenth Amendment asserted, redundantly, that powers not delegated to the United States were reserved to the states.

Support of art and culture is not among the enumerated powers. To find any warrant for it one must interpret the "general welfare" clause in a way that Madison called absurd.[15] This, however, is the interpretation that has prevailed. In 1936 the Supreme Court declared that "the power of Congress to authorize appropriations of public moneys for public purposes is not limited by direct grants of legislative power found in the Constitution."[16] This was not the understanding of the people who ratified the Constitution in the state conventions. It is safe to say that, if it were, the Constitution would not have been ratified.

The composition of national and state powers now being exactly the opposite of what the Founders intended—the powers of the national government being "numerous and indefinite" and those of the states "few and defined"—it is clear that a fundamental principle of the American regime has been abandoned. (If there is doubt, it arises from the fact that the change has occurred in the absence of any deliberative process involving the public; practice has certainly changed, but this does not imply abandonment of principle.) However this may be, the principles that define the proper sphere of government—those of "natural law liberalism"—remain as they were. The functions of government are not unlimited; they are to protect the individual in the exercise of certain inalienable rights and to establish preconditions for the development of a competent citizenry. Although the national government now exercises powers that were once reserved to the states, the question must still be asked whether a particular exercise of its powers—the funding of art, for example—is a proper one.

Not all activities affecting the public interest properly merit governmental action. Indeed, there is near-universal agreement that government is inherently unsuited to deal with some of them. Religion is a conspicuous example. Most Americans, including unbelievers, would agree that it is in the public interest for religious belief to be widespread. Very few, however, would favor the creation of a National Endowment for Religion; even those who did not fear that this agency would infringe upon religious freedom might well expect its activities to be ineffective at best or even counterproductive. On similar grounds, some democratic socialists oppose governmental efforts to promote culture. The political theorist Michael Walzer, for example, in *Radical Principles: Reflections of an Unreconstructed Democrat,* after stressing the socialist aspiration for governmental expansion of the public sphere, goes on to say that it is beyond the competence of the state to promote culture. "Culture control [by the state]," he says, "has nothing to do with socialism or a meaningful common life."[17]

One may also oppose governmental intervention in certain matters of public interest on the grounds that it is all too easy for government to bite off more than it can properly chew; that, unfortunately, it must forgo doing some things that it would be nice to have done in order that it may more effectively do other things—national defense, for example—that are absolutely essential. In the mid-1950s, when the federal government was administering about 130 grant-in-aid programs, a presidential Commission on Intergovernmental Relations (the so-called Kestenbaum commission), warned that the existence of a national interest in an activity "is not in itself enough to warrant national participation." "Substantial evidence," it said, should be required to show that national participation is necessary.[18] A quarter of a century later, the number of grant-in-aid programs had risen to about 500, and the federal government was deeply involved in many matters that had always been considered of purely local concern. The Advisory Commission on Intergovernmental Relations, established by Congress in 1959 to monitor the federal system, urged the president to hold a debate on "What is a 'national purpose'?" The outcome, it thought, might be agreement on a set of categories ordering national purposes according to their relative importance, including "paramount" (defense, foreign relations, and the economy), "primary" (e.g., the postal system), "secondary" (e.g., lesser regulatory programs), "tertiary" (state and local responsibilities that warrant a modest federal involvement), and "of no real concern" (activities having no real impact and whose purpose is trivial).[19]

Welfare versus the Public Interest

Although Americans have never agreed upon the proper mix of the two great ends of government—the protection of the individual in the exercise of his rights and his improvement as a citizen—they *have* agreed that government ought to serve public as opposed to private interests. The Vermont Constitution of 1793 contained a typical provision: "That the government is or ought to be instituted for the common benefit, and not for the particular emolument or advantage of any single man, family, or set of men, who are only part of that community. . . ." To Madison and others of the Founders, nothing was more obnoxious than "faction," by which they meant an organized interest that was opposed to the interest of the whole society.

In the present century the concept of "the public interest" has fallen into disrepute. The predominant view now is that, however useful it may be for rhetorical purposes, it can have no concrete content (is any interest shared by *every* member of the public?), and it is highly unrealistic to view the political process other than as a competitive struggle among private and partial interests.[20]

These criticisms have substance. Policy with regard to the support of art is made by special interest groups almost always in the name of public interest. This, however, does not warrant the conclusion that the concept of public interest should be jettisoned; even though it be honored much more in the breach than in the observance, the concept is indispensable not only for normative but sometimes for descriptive studies. Because they live in a society, individuals must share some guiding conceptions of right and justice. Moreover, from time to time they must collectively deal with various problems; in doing so, they must be conscious of the need to preserve their ability to act together in response to potential problems. They must, in short, feel that they constitute a community that has an interest apart from and sometimes opposed to their private interests.

A person acting in the role of citizen decides, directly or indirectly, what is and what is not of public concern. In the American tradition there is a presumption that the public interest will be served by leaving people free to pursue happiness, each in his own way. In principle, however, "welfare" —what individuals acting in their private capacities consider good for themselves—is subordinate to "public interest"— what citizens consider good for the community. Thus, for example, the market operates within a framework of laws: most things one may buy and sell as one pleases; one may not, however, engage in transactions that are deemed contrary to the public interest—trafficking in narcotic drugs, for example.

That an activity—the making and viewing of art, for example—increases or decreases welfare does not in and of itself make it a matter of public interest. Whether it is universally admired or universally detested, a statue in front of the courthouse cannot be justified in the way that the courthouse itself can be justified.

What Is Art?

In much usage art is almost any activity involving the materials—paints, canvas, modeling clay, and so on—that are usually associated with the work of artists. Thus, a person who shows a second-grade child how to hold a crayon is an "art teacher," one who does the same thing in a mental hospital is an "art therapist," and one who tells when and how artists began to draw in perspective is an "art historian."

Arts-related activities are sharply distinguished in the present study from art itself. Art is what engenders in the maker or viewer the special state of mind called aesthetic. Conceivably, some or even most arts-related activities serve the public interest and deserve public funding. However, because the purposes of these activities could be served as well or perhaps even better by means not involving art, public support for them ought to be justified on grounds other than the value of art. Thus, even though pictures may be useful in teaching history, the case for public support of picture making (in this situation) should rest upon the fact that the teaching of history is in the public interest.

The assumption is that a justification for public support of art must depend upon the existence of a public interest in a value—aesthetic experience—that can only be supplied by art. It is often assumed that this experience has profound and beneficial effects upon society, that society cannot have too much of it. Yet some philosophers—Plato and Rousseau, for example—have taught that art is subversive of moral and political values.[21] Whether in given circumstances the aesthetic experience is beneficial or injurious to the society is of course an empirical question, albeit one that, for lack of good evidence, can rarely if ever be answered conclusively. However, if the public interest may sometimes justify the support of it, it may also sometimes justify its suppression.

From the standpoint of public interest, it is therefore critical to ask, What are the consequences of aesthetic experience for the individual and indirectly for the society? It then becomes evident that aesthetic experience is by no means all the same: the experience produced by Michelangelo's *Pietà*, for example, can hardly have anything in common with that produced by a work of art consisting of the reintroduction of grasses, shrubs, and trees to make a block of lower Manhattan look as it did several hundred years ago.[22] Obviously

16

for policy purposes it is necessary to distinguish among the varieties of aesthetic experiences. The next chapter describes four kinds of aesthetic experiences, each deserving separate evaluation from a policy standpoint. Very possibly the distinctions made are inappropriate for purposes such as the study of art history. They should be studied, however, for their usefulness in making judgments about the wisdom and justice of public intervention to encourage or discourage one or another kind of art form.

1

But Is It Art?

... it is necessary for a society in which works of art arise and are supported, to find out whether all that professes to be art really is art, whether (as is presupposed in our society) all that which is art is good, and whether it is important and worth those sacrifices which it necessitates.

—Tolstoy, *What Is Art?*

DOUBTS filled the mind of Michael Straight, the deputy chairman of the NEA, as he confronted a pile of grant applications awaiting his signature. The chairman, Nancy Hanks, was home ill that day and he was acting chairman. The fifty or so applications he was facing that June in 1974 had been winnowed from among several thousand by one or another of several panels of consultants chosen by the staff for their professional competence and representativeness.

The panel's choices had then been approved by the National Council on the Arts, which met three or four times a year to advise the chairman. The acting chairman was now expected to "sign off" on the list of awards.[1]

Straight had grown up with the arts. Born into a family of great wealth (his father was a banker, and his mother, Dorothy Whitney, was a philanthropist), famous works of art and famous artists had been a part of his everyday life since childhood. While still a youth he bought a Picasso. In later life, as editor and publisher of *The New Republic* (which his parents had founded), he was a vigorous advocate of "enlightened" and sometimes "advanced" opinions on political and cultural matters. He was a man who could be expected to make informed and sympathetic judgments about cultural matters.

Straight was perplexed by some of the applicants' brief accounts of what they proposed to do. He gives examples in *Twigs for an Eagle's Nest,* a small book that he published after leaving office:

—My project is a series of paintings, ten to fifteen layers of paint deep, consisting entirely of extremely subtle gradations of grey.
—The project I propose will temporarily manipulate the Chicago skyline for the period of one year.
—My project is to introduce taxidermy as a sculpture media by using painted plywood construction, dirt, sand, gravel, and animals to create different environmental situations.[2]

After reflection, Straight signed these along with some other applications that he found puzzling. They were, after all, the choices of the professionals; besides, they "probably would not harm the Endowment."[3] Certain other proposals, however, were "more questionable":

—A loop tour of Western U.S. . . . dripping ink from Hayley, Idaho to Cody, Wyoming—an event commemorating the birthplaces of Ezra Pound and Jackson Pollock.
—I will rent a ground level studio with high ceilings and a cement floor, adjacent to a lush meadow. And to this place I will bring Pigme, a full-grown sow (whom I have known since her ninth day), two female rabbits (who know each other and me), a buck (stranger), two ring-necked doves (strangers), a wooley monkey, Georgina (who knows me slightly). . . . We will all move together.

19

I will also bring those things necessary for a comfortable survival, including food and materials to use for building and maintaining nests. All of us will contribute to the creation, maintenance and change of such an environment. Once settled, we may discover that there are others who would like to join us even if just for a short time (birds, mice, people, etc.). I will record our activities so that those unable to visit and experience our situation directly will know something of what it is like. This will best be done by using portable video equipment.

Sometimes, we will leave our place and go together to another, or bring others to us. For these events, we will need a vehicle, preferably a motorbike with a large sidecar. Perhaps this communal way of life will be quite difficult. However, the educational value, for all of us will be extraordinary.[4]

Straight refused to approve these grants, along with about twenty others. He was happy to concede that the artists were sincere, but he could not defend supporting these projects with public funds. Presumably, he believed that Congress, in giving the chairman sole authority to approve grants, intended that in cases of conflict the judgment of politically responsible officials should prevail over that of civil servants, representatives of the art world, and other advisers. He also believed that these grants would make the NEA appear ridiculous in the eyes of the press, the public, and Congress.

By refusing to sign all the applications approved by the staff, Straight created a crisis. The chairman was called from her sickbed. In a two-hour conference, the director of the Visual Arts Program defended the projects. They were, he explained, in styles much admired by the contemporary art world. Some of the applications that Straight was questioning reflected the influence of the great Marcel Duchamp, who, when he moved to New York, had brought with him a bottle labeled "Paris Air." Others were closer to the work of a well-known Italian painter, Piero Manzoni, who had bottled his own excrement and sold it as "Artist's Shit."

Straight, now speechless, steadfastly refused to sign. The

grants were made, but over the signature of the chairman. And the rules were changed to circumvent similar crises in the future: hereafter, applicants were not to say what they intended to do with the fellowship. Thus there could be no public criticism of the NEA's choices, no matter how bizarre they might sometimes be.

Defining Art

Highly civilized people can define art in profoundly various ways. Here, art will be defined as that which has the capacity to engender in a receptive viewer an aesthetic experience. This definition, of course, is helpful only if it is possible to show that there is such an experience and to describe its nature.

The aesthetic experience is not universal as is, say, the experience of fear. Admittedly, it is probably impossible to point to a culture, past or present, in which people have not lavished effort far beyond what was needed for purely practical purposes on all sorts of things, especially objects connected with religious observances, but also on weapons, clothing, tools and utensils, and their own bodies. The marvelous drawings prehistoric men made on the walls of their caves tempt one to conclude that an impulse to create art has always and everywhere been a part of human nature. This, however, is a mistaken view. What we experience aesthetically could not be experienced in the same way by people whose culture—perceptions, thoughts, feelings—vastly differs from our own.[5]

"Admiring as we do the art of the ancient Greeks," R. G. Collingwood writes, "we naturally suppose that they admired it in the same kind of spirit as ourselves. But we admire it as a kind of art, where the word 'art' carries with it all the subtle and elaborate implications of the modern

21

European aesthetic consciousness. We can be perfectly certain that the Greeks did not admire it in any such way."[6]

The point is elaborated by Johan Huizinga, who says that for the Greeks the visual arts belonged to a different and lower order of experience than did music, poetry, and dance —"play forms" that were closely related and that were presided over by Apollo and the Muses. The mechanical and plastic arts, if they were under divine guidance at all, were the concern of lesser gods and not of any Muse.[7]

In most primitive societies, according to Richard L. Anderson, the concept "art" does not exist in native thought, and in those in which it does ". . . there is only an approximate correspondence between their notion of art and our own." Of the few hundred methodologically sound accounts of art in other societies, none, he says, contains systematically gathered information on the affective response to art.[8]

Even within a culture—say, the western European since the Renaissance—there are from time to time and place to place very marked differences both in what is responded to as art and in the subjective state that constitutes the response. It is interesting that the word "aesthetic" did not appear until the early eighteenth century and that the concept itself is not much older. The word "art," used in its modern sense and without any qualifier, does not appear in any English dictionary before 1880.[9]

In *Art as Experience* (1934), John Dewey maintains that art is making or doing something in a way that produces an aesthetic emotion, by which he means the feeling that one has when one perceives an intended action as running to its fulfillment by virtue of its internal integration:

Man whittles, carves, sings, dances, gestures, molds, draws and paints. The doing or making is artistic when the perceived result is of such a nature that its qualities as perceived have controlled the question of production. The act of producing that is directed by intent to produce something that is enjoyed in the immediate experience of perceiving has qualities that a spontaneous or uncontrolled activity does not have. The artist embodies in himself the attitude of the perceiver while he works.[10]

The spectator also experiences art when he perceives that the action of the artist was directed in the appropriate way.

For Dewey the distinction between "fine" and other art is one of degree rather than of kind. Any conceivable activity is art if carried on (or perceived to have been carried on) in the right manner. "The intelligent mechanic," he writes, "engaged in his job, interested in doing well and finding a satisfaction in his handiwork, caring for his materials and tools with genuine affection, is artistically engaged."[11]

A difficulty in Dewey's position—and in any that makes the intention a defining characteristic of art—is that one can rarely if ever know the intention of the maker of a work and therefore whether or not the result is a work of art. Suppose, Dewey writes, that a finely wrought object believed to be the product of some primitive people is proved to be an accidental product of nature: "As an external thing, it is now exactly what it was before. Yet at once it ceases to be a work of art and becomes a natural 'curiosity.' It now belongs in a museum of natural history, not in a museum of art."[12]

Which museum should house a manmade object when the nature of its experience or intention is unknown? The object is not art unless it was the intention of the maker to produce something to be enjoyed in the immediate experience of perceiving. The fetishes of the Negro sculptor, Dewey remarks, were more useful to his tribal group than spears or clothing. They were not intended for enjoyment. But the fetishes, he says, are now "fine art," inspiring artists in the twentieth century "only because the anonymous artists lived and experienced so fully during the process of production."[13] Presumably, if it were discovered that the sculptor was merely following a routine prescribed by tribal custom, the fetishes would cease to be fine art and would be exhibited in a museum of ethnology.

For the philosopher Eliseo Vivas the aesthetic experience consists essentially of perceiving things and events—and their symbols—in a way that engages the mind without referring to anything beyond them. An aesthetic object is interesting in itself because of meanings and values that pertain to it, not to something suggested by it. "I take the perception of aesthetic objects," he writes, "to be a rare kind of attention that is intensely directed to an object's imminent meanings as they present themselves immediately to the mind."[14] As an example, Vivas tells of a moment when his attention was entirely absorbed at the sight of a panther pacing in a zoo. The value of the experience, he writes, cannot be compared to that of listening to Bach or Mozart or of seeing a canvas of Cézanne or Renoir:

Held by the pacing animal, the affective rush that flooded me was not an object of direct awareness and a few moments later, when I turned away from the rail I could not have been able to tell, any more than I am now, what its components were: fear and wonder, admiration, joy, were present with other emotions, the nature of which I could not then have discriminated. I asked no questions when the beast held me, passed no judgment. I looked and saw, for a moment only; but for that brief moment it was a fascinating experience which in retrospect allows me to assert with confidence how little do I see ordinarily; what I usually do is look.[15]

Vivas defines the artist as one who deliberately and successfully makes something that elicits this intense rapt attention. The majority of human beings, he says, do not see paintings as aesthetic objects; for them a painting "must be a painting of something and that something must be external to the painting and perceivable independently of it." There is a kind of mind, he adds, that is apparently incapable of aesthetic response; for such minds, experience is always cognitive.[16]

Another influential theory is that of the philosopher George Dickie, who says that a thing is art if a member of

24

the art world confers upon it "the status of a candidate for appreciation." Members of the art world include not only artists but museum directors, museum-goers, art historians, art theorists, and all others "who keep the machinery of the art world working."[17] Dickie's view is that art is what people connected with arts institutions say it is. This is, of course, a circular definition, for what is an arts institution and what is an art world? The assumption is that there exist standards of some sort that define an arts institution or art world. But *are* there such standards? And if there are, why should it be assumed that what they define has anything in common with what is ordinarily called art? Vito Acconci is said to call the *New York Times* regularly to announce that his breathing is art.[18] Ought his claim to be taken with greater seriousness now that he has been awarded a Guggenheim Fellowship, something that would not have happened had not members in good standing in the art world written letters endorsing his application?

Perhaps the most influential theorist of recent years is Nelson Goodman, whose *Languages of Art*—a development of ideas put forward by Cassier, Collingwood, Langer, and others—describes art as a "language," albeit nonverbal, of symbols.[19] The real question, Goodman says, is not "What objects are (permanently) works of art?" but "When is an object a work of art?" His point is that an object functions as a work of art only when viewed in the right context:

Indeed, just by virtue of functioning as a symbol in a certain way does an object become, while so functioning, a work of art. The stone is normally no work of art while in the driveway but may be so when on display in an art museum. In the driveway it usually performs no symbolic function; in the art museum it exemplifies certain of its properties—e.g., shape, color, texture. The digging and filling of a hole functions as work insofar as our attention is directed to it as an exemplifying symbol. On the other hand, a Rembrandt painting may cease to function as a work of art when used to replace a broken window or as a blanket.[20]

25

This is not the place to attempt a critique of Goodman's very complicated theory. It is necessary to point out, however, that the visual art worlds do not agree on what objects are "exemplifying symbols." Claes Oldenberg, an artist mentioned by Goodman, thinks that digging and filling a hole in Central Park would be a work of art if done with artistic intent.[21] But surely there are other eminent members of this same art world who would say that it would be a silly waste of time.

Recently, a skinned rabbit was hung in a gallery of the Art Institute of Chicago.[22] Was it a work of art? Dewey would say yes if putting it there and seeing it produced aesthetic emotion. Vivas would agree if it elicited rapt attention. Dickie would say yes if, but only if, it were put there by a member of the art world who intended to offer it for appreciation, but not if it were put there as a prank. Goodman would say that it was art no matter who hung it there or why, provided that it functioned as an exemplifying symbol to at least some of those who viewed it.

It would be easy to multiply the number of these very different theories as to the nature of art. It is not surprising, then, to learn from the sociologist Howard S. Becker that "Art worlds typically devote considerable attention to trying to decide what is and isn't art, what is and isn't their kind of art, and who is and isn't an artist."[23] Despite their doctrinal and other differences, Becker says, members of an art world characteristically produce "reliable judgments about which artists and works are serious and therefore worthy of attention."[24] If by "reliable" he means that judgments tend to agree, then it is my impression that he considerably overstates the case as respects the world of contemporary visual art.[25]

The Role of Art in Society

As this brief sampling of views suggests, any conception of the nature of art has implications for policy making. A follower of Dewey, for example, would encourage ordinary people to do ordinary things—and to perceive them when done by others—in an artistic manner. It may be evidence of Dewey's influence on policymakers that in 1969 the authors of the first official publication of the "social indicators" movement wrote:

There is art not only in museums, theaters, opera houses, and books but in every aspect of life—in cooking, dress, and industrial design. Although this . . . concentrates on the conventionally most professional and "highbrow" forms of art, we must not forget that this is only a small part of the total and *may not be the most important.* (Emphasis added.)[26]

A follower of Vivas, by contrast, would see no artistic value in something made by an intelligent mechanic who was interested in doing his job, except in the unlikely event that it would elicit rapt attention without reference to its use or other associations. Although the Vivas-minded policy maker would attach great importance to art ("it is art that creates culture, that creates the values and meanings by which men in society fulfill their destiny"[27]), he would not think it possible to universalize the art experience in its non-trivial forms.

A Goodmanite would keep the finely wrought object in the art museum, but only if it functioned as a significant symbol, which would be much more likely if it were made by an artist (i.e., one who uses a symbolic language that viewers can understand). Because the experience of art is cognitive as well as noncognitive, making and viewing art would be closely integrated into any educational process.

Whatever is taken to be its defining function, art obviously

27

has other functions as well. Monroe C. Beardsley distinguishes between the *incidental* value of a work (he gives as an example the use of the *Winged Victory* as ballast) and its *inherent* value—its capacity to produce aesthetic enjoyment.[28] Collingwood identifies seven forms of "pseudo-art" according to the purposes for which they are created. He renames them as follows:

> Where an emotion is aroused for its own sake, as an enjoyable experience, the craft of arousing it is *amusement;* where for the sake of its practical value, *magic.* . . . Where intellectual facilities are stimulated for the mere sake of their exercise, the work designed to stimulate them is a *puzzle;* where for the sake of knowing this or that thing, it is *instruction.* Where a certain practical activity is stimulated as expedient, that which stimulates it is *advertisement* or . . . *propaganda;* where it is stimulated as right, *exhortation.* (Emphasis added.)[29]

Confusion arises, Collingwood says, because art may be combined with pseudo-art: for example, art and religion (magic) in which the artistic motive, although genuinely present, is subordinated to the religious. "What happens," he writes, "is that a combination of art and religion is elliptically called art, and then characteristics which it possesses not as art but as religion are mistakenly supposed to belong to it as art." He concludes, "The various kinds of pseudo-art are in reality various kinds of uses to which art may be put."[30]

Vivas makes a similar point and lists some "non-residential" functions of art, that is, functions that are extrinsic or secondary in that they can be performed—some of them more efficiently—by other means (unlike those that he terms "residential," "intrinsic," or "primary").[31] Although less systematic, Vivas's list has elements in common with Collingwood's:

> Socially, art has been conceived as a means of inculcating morality or the proper political beliefs and attitudes. Today it is widely held that its function is to impart knowledge. And sometimes it is thought to be capable of imparting so high, or so deep, a wisdom,

that what it imparts is taken to be sacred and ineffable. At the individual level, art is held to offer us the healing illusion or escape, to be a means of exciting emotions, or of purging them, or of arousing vitality, or of saying yes to the terrible aspects of existence.[32]

Art must be justified by its inherent (as opposed to incidental) values. Thus it is necessary to describe the nature of the aesthetic response: its worth, to the individual and to society, must be the basis for its justification. Aesthetic response, however, is rarely the same from time to time, place to place, and person to person. In an effort to deal with this complication, four principal modes of aesthetic experience are here outlined in ideal-typical form; that is, as logically improved-upon versions of reality, useful for analysis.*

The *ideational* mode of response engages the mind (and therefore in greater or lesser degree the feelings) by its subject matter and content. "Content," as opposed to the subject matter, Erwin Panofsky writes, "is the basic attitude of a nation, a class, a religious or philosophical persuasion—all this unconsciously qualified by one personality. . . ."[33]

Consider the response of John Adams to a collection of paintings he viewed in London in 1786. There were, he writes in his diary, "the pleasures of imitation" in looking at pictures of landscapes, flowers, game; however, a million such pictures could be seen "with much indifference," for the things themselves were to be seen in nature at any time. "[T]here must," he says, "be action, passion, sentiment, and moral, to engage my attention very much. The story of the prince, who lost his own life in a bold attempt to save some of his subordinates from a flood of water, is worth all the paintings that have been exhibited this year."[34]

In the eighteenth century this was a common response to

*For expository convenience, references are made to historical figures. The reader should keep in mind, however, that the intention is to provide tools for analysis, not to say anything about art history. In the hope of avoiding confusion the types have been given names that do not suggest art-historical styles.

art. Sir Joshua Reynolds in his *Discourses* comes close to making it orthodox, as does Diderot, who criticized Boucher for filling his pictures with nipples and buttocks. It was not the *only* mode then or later. "The greatest picture," John Ruskin declared in the nineteenth century, "is that which conveys to the minds of the spectators the greatest number of the greatest ideas."[35] Although this is far from being the most common response to art today, some contemporary works are intended to—and do in fact—engage the attention with action, passion, sentiment, and moral.

The *romantic* mode of response differs in that subject matter is irrelevant; style or form produces the response, which is one of feeling. Historically, this mode can be traced to Edgar Allan Poe's essay "The Poetic Principle," in which he compares Beauty and Truth to oil and water. The contemplation of Beauty, he writes, produces "a pleasureable excitement of the soul," which is easily distinguishable both from the response to Truth (the satisfaction of the Reason) and from Passion (the excitement of the Heart).[36]

As developed by Baudelaire and others in France and by Walter Pater and Oscar Wilde in England, the romantic concept holds that art exists solely to give pleasure, cannot be associated with moral or other meaning, and is transient by nature. A great picture, Pater writes, "has no more definite message for us than an accidental play of sunlight and shadow for a few moments on the wall or floor. . . ." Art comes to you "frankly proposing to give nothing but the highest quality to your moments as they pass, and simply for those moments' sake."[37]

The *transcendental* mode is responded to with "disinterested intensity of contemplation."[38] Art created to evoke this response is sometimes explained on the theory that there are two orders of experience: the ordinary experience of the real world, which is radically incapable of giving rise to aesthetic feelings, and the categorically different order of experience that does give rise to those feelings.

This mode is historically associated with "modern art," that is, art free of any representational elements (abstract) and art representing the internal world of feeling (expressionist) as opposed to the external or objective world. "This art," writes Wassily Kandinsky, whose abstract works consist of bright patches of color in asymmetrical arrangements, "creates alongside of the real world a new world which has nothing to do with *external reality.*"[39] Piet Mondrian, whose works consist of geometric lines and large, empty spaces, writes that the ultimate goal is the expression of "pure reality" by means of "pure plastics."[40]

The *nihilist* mode is experienced as relief from boredom; it fills an "infinite emptiness of [the] soul" and affords an escape, however brief, from the "dreary length of . . . existence," according to the poet Friedrich von Schlegel, in whose late eighteenth-century work a recent writer has found a "theory of modernism."[41] As Karsten Harries explains:

The world assigns man a place: it tells him what to do. Nature, society, religion, and art fetter him by making demands. Defying these demands, the romantic nihilist posits freedom as his ideal. His conception of freedom is negative: to be free is to be free from the place which the individual has been assigned, to act other than one is expected to act, to enjoy what one is not expected to enjoy. The interesting serves this ideal. It dislocates man by presenting him with something unexpected or novel. Its appeal depends on certain expectations which are then disappointed. Thus the normal is boring, the abnormal interesting.[42]

Although different in intent, art created for the nihilist response often resembles art created for the transcendental response. Both seek to confront or escape from the ordinary world in order to enter the aesthetic one—a world that *must* be strange, even unintelligible. Art in both of these modes must therefore continually jolt the viewer out of his accustomed ways of seeing and feeling. Taking a familiar thing out of context is one way of doing this. A can of Campbell's soup presented as a work of art, Harries remarks, is interesting: "To stress the unimportant, giving it great importance, can be interesting."[43]

There are other strategies for inducing these modes of aesthetic experience. The work of art may shock ordinary sensibilities with something disgusting, loathsome, or obscene. ("Funk's lumpy, varicose limbs, droopy, deformed breasts and gargantuan genitals in sadistic fantasies and sexist fixation take us beyond supposed vulgarity to matters of humanity and inhumanity.")[44]

It may present a puzzle that is unsolvable by ordinary ways of seeing, thinking, or feeling. ("When the most ordinary, reliable materials of our experience—such as those reassuringly uniform brands found in supermarkets—are torn from their context to be strewn like boulders in the placid stream of our consciousness, the definitions both of art and of life become subject to doubt.")[45]

The viewer may be bored to a state of vacuity that constitutes or produces a new kind of awareness. ("The knot of attention is untied [by Andy Warhol's six-hour movie of a man asleep], and its strands are laid out before us anew. . . . [T]he audience's participation in the image is never allowed to fall into the slot of that *other* temporal reality. . . .")[46]

Finally, it may jolt the viewer by exhibiting the absurdity of things. ("He was literally crucified with nails driven through his palm, on the back of a Volkswagen . . . replacing the cross with a Volkswagen effectively transformed a religious cliché into a diabolically droll, nightmarish masque: Jesus indeed.")[47]

Implications of these Modes of Aesthetic Experience

Beauty. In ideational art, beauty is a value insofar as it leads the mind to thoughts and feelings that are beautiful. In romantic art, what delights the eye is the only value. In transcendental art, beauty is highly suspect because it distracts from disinterested contemplation. "There is no excuse for a china pot being ugly," writes Roger Fry, but "there is every reason why Rembrandt's and Degas' pictures should be, from the purely sensual point of view, supremely and magnificently ugly."[48] From the standpoint of the transcendental and nihilist modes, decoration is altogether valueless. As Curt Ducasse remarks, what is agreeable, pleasant, and charming *therefore* cannot give the jolt required to transport the viewer into the realm of aesthetic emotion or pure feeling.[49]

Art responded to in the nihilist mode need not necessarily be of visual interest; it may be "conceptual," having existence only in the mind of the artist and, perhaps, of a few persons to whom he has described his "idea." Or it may be a "happening"—an event not sharply distinguishable from theater.

Cognitive Content. Because it has subject matter and content, ideational art must explicitly appeal to the rational (cognitive) faculty and therefore to what is most distinctively human. When subject matter is subordinated to form and emphasis is shifted from thought to feeling, as in romantic art, this appeal is reduced or lost. Rodin, a realist, was absorbed, Edgar Wind remarks, in the subrational: *The Thinker*'s feet, he said, look more intelligent than his face; moreover, in some of the best figures by Braque and Henry Moore ". . . the heads are vestiges that look like knobs." It may not be irrelevant, he goes on, that among the compounds of man and animal in the repertory of Greek fable—

33

centaur, faun, siren, harpy—modern painters have shown a marked preference for the Minotaur, the only one of the monsters whose face is not human.[50]

The artist who intends his work to be experienced in the transcendental mode suppresses his rational faculty by adopting the naive simplicity of a child, or a primitive, or by putting himself in a trancelike state, and he often relies in some degree upon chance processes, such as throwing or flicking paint, in order to add an element of unintelligibility.[51] One who aims at the nihilist response gives himself up entirely to chance and accident, which is a path to the interesting.

Moral and Political Significance. Art that addresses the rational faculty must have meaning in the usual sense of the word, and therefore moral and political significance. Romantic art, in which subject matter is irrelevant, has nothing to do with morality or politics. "To art's subject matter," writes Oscar Wilde, "we should be more or less indifferent. We should, at any rate, have no preferences, no prejudices, no partisan feelings of any kind. It is exactly because Hecuba is nothing to us that her sorrows are such an admirable motive for a tragedy."[52] The transcendental and nihilist modes also have nothing to do with morality or politics, except as these may be treated in a shocking way in order to jolt the viewer into the aesthetic realm or out of his boredom.

Art as Play. When art is experienced other than cognitively—that is, as "excitement of the soul," "disinterested contemplation," or relief from "the infinite emptiness of the soul"—it is a sort of play.[53] The modern artist, remarks José Ortega y Gasset in *The Dehumanization of Art,* by repudiating reality, places himself above it. "Being an artist means ceasing to take seriously that very serious person we are when we are not an artist." The new art, seeing itself linked not to dramatic social or political movements or to philosophical currents, recognizes that it is "a thing of no consequence." To the mind of the modern artists ". . . the kingdom of art commences where the air feels lighter and things, free from formal fetters, begin to cut whimsical capers."[54] To the nihilist, the air feels lighter still: often absolutely weightless.

Fine and Applied Arts. The ideational and romantic modes of aesthetic experience involve a sharp, but not a categorical, distinction between fine and applied art. The transcendental mode does not allow for a useful art. Use, like beauty, distracts from pure aesthetic contemplation, and useful things necessarily pertain to the ordinary world, which must be transcended in order to enter the aesthetic realm. "It is only when an object exists in our lives for no other purpose than to be seen that we really look at it . . ." Fry remarks, and so adopt "to some extent the artistic attitude of pure vision abstracted from necessity."[55]

The difference disappears entirely when, as in the nihilist mode, whatever is interesting is artistic. "It matters little if differences seem to exist between the artist and the craftsman," says a maker of purely decorative ceramic objects. "The success of both [art and craft works] depends upon the creative act, its intensity and its revelation of eternal knowledge."[56]

A portrait, drawing, or photograph may be experienced in the ideational mode because it is a good likeness. In the other modes its being a good likeness is at best irrelevant: to have aesthetic value, the work must arouse feelings that are largely or wholly independent of any objective reality.

Nature of Appeal. Ideational and romantic art, both of which offer visual beauty and subject matter (although only in the former is the subject matter essential to the art), make an appeal to which everyone can respond if only at a rudimentary level. Transcendental and nihilist art, by contrast, are "difficult"; often they are entirely inaccessible except to the few who can and will put aside their normal perceptual habits. As Ortega y Gasset notes, most people see art as a means of entering into contact with human affairs; all modern art, he infers from this, is unpopular, even antipopular, "and it is so not accidentally and by chance but essentially and by fate."[57] Nihilist art in some of its forms—a giant hamburger, soft telephone, or nylon fence eighteen feet high and extending over more than twenty-four miles of farmland—is doubtless interesting to a great many people. But it may be doubted that the interest of most is related to the relief of boredom, which is the appropriate aesthetic response to this kind of art. When the Serpentine Gallery in London exhibited inflatables, they were an enormous public success. The critic Edward Lucie-Smith writes:

When we did them over public holiday weekends people kept on coming back during the week with their kids and asking why they weren't still there. But it was also quite clear that if those inflatables, or anything else put on at those holiday weekends, had deep philosophical implications the public was absolutely determined to ignore them. They weren't interested at all in that kind of thing. In fact, the deeply philosophical, poker-faced, serious conceptual artist doesn't meet with rage and incomprehension any more from the public in the kind of democracy we have in Britain. He meets with a kind of cheerful trivialization. The public accepts him, pets him, but is determined to take him at a valuation quite other than the one which he puts upon himself. The artist, because he walks on stilts, is regarded as a public jester.[58]

Originality. Novelty (or originality) is not essential to the production of aesthetic experience in the ideational mode. It has its uses in stirring the "excitement of the soul" that is the defining quality of the romantic mode. The transcendental mode, because it must escape from the world of ordinary experience, cannot do without novelty; for the nihilist mode it is not only necessary but sometimes sufficient: something strikingly new—better yet, bizarre—is sure to be "interesting."

The modes that need novelty need it in ever-increasing doses. Each jolt must be stronger than the preceding one. The most characteristic feature of contemporary artistic life, writes Leo Steinberg, is the "rapid domestication of the outrageous." The time lapse, he says, "between the shock received and the things returned gets progressively shorter. At the present rate of taste adaptation, it takes about seven years for a young artist with a streak of wildness in him to turn from *enfant terrible* to elder statesman—not so much because he changes, but because the challenge he throws to the public is quickly met."[59]

Technical Skill. A high degree of technical skill, notably in draftsmanship, is a necessary but not a sufficient condition of creating art in the ideational and romantic modes. The transcendental and nihilist modes, by contrast, depend little or not at all on any technical proficiency: to be able to draw is unnecessary, although some artists working in these modes are excellent draftsmen.

CHAPTER

2

Making the Law

It is in the neighborhoods of each community that a nation's art is born. In countless American towns there live thousands of obscure and unknown talents.

What this bill really does is . . . to make fresher the winds of the arts in this great land of ours.

The arts and the humanities belong to the people, for it is, after all, the people who create them.

—President Lyndon B. Johnson[1]

WITH the passage of the National Foundation on the Arts and the Humanities Act of 1965 the United States assumed responsibility for the support of a cultural policy. That is what the act said. In fact, the new NEA could not support a medium-sized museum or orchestra, let alone a "cultural policy." Its appropriation for fiscal 1966 was $2.5 million, about one-quarter of what the Ford Foundation had been giving the arts annually for several years. Nevertheless, NEA's appearance upon the scene was an important event.*

To those who helped bring the bill to passage, its signing marked the end of a long and difficult road: with skill and patience they had prevailed; they were the Davids who, with nothing but a slingshot, had slain a Goliath—or so it seemed to them and their allies.

It had indeed taken ten years of listening to scores of witnesses and of reading (or not reading) thousands of pages of argument. In retrospect, however, it is clear that from the beginning there was never any doubt that something very much like the NEA would eventually be created. The fundamental fact was that some people stood to gain much from the passage of such an act, whereas no one stood to lose (even if Congress were to appropriate lavishly for support of the arts, the cost to the average taxpayer would be no more than a dollar or two a year).

Yet the ten years it had taken for the ayes to have it was not evidence that there was a Goliath in need of slaying. Some of that time was needed for the proponents of the legislation to reach agreement among themselves as to what and how much to aim for. And at the same time, there were countless other interest groups seeking to secure passage of countless other laws. The torrent of legislation emerging from Congress could not flow fast enough to accommodate all groups simultaneously; some waiting was unavoidable, but the arts supporters knew their turn would surely come.

---

*The act authorized annual appropriations for three years of $10 million jointly to the NEA and the NEH, and it provided a "Treasury Fund" of $5 million to be drawn upon to match donations from nonfederal sources. (In 1978 the endowments were administrated separately; appropriations were no longer made jointly.) The initial appropriation was half the amount authorized. NEA's Treasury Fund for fiscal 1966 was $34,308.

An Overview of Arts Policy in the United States

From the nation's earliest days there were those who favored public support of the arts. Almost without exception, however, the supporters of the arts agreed that the federal government had no power in the matter except in the District of Columbia, where its powers were plenary. It was understood that Congress could exercise only the powers that were enumerated in the Constitution; all other powers were retained by the states and the people thereof. Among the enumerated powers there was one authorizing Congress to provide for the seat of government; there was none, however, that authorized the support of the arts elsewhere.

In his first and again in his second inaugural addresses President George Washington proposed the establishment of a national university, presumably, where civil servants could be trained. He seems to have thought the federal government's authority to provide for the seat of government was sufficient. James Madison apparently disagreed, for when as president he made the same proposal he said he thought a constitutional amendment would be necessary in order to implement it. Thomas Jefferson was an enthusiast for the arts: "It is an enthusiasm of which I am not ashamed, as its object is to improve the taste of my countrymen, to increase their reputation, to reconcile to them the respect of the world, and to procure them its praise."[2] But he was also the strictest of strict constructionists and believed art should be a matter of state, not federal, concern.

President John Quincy Adams held unorthodox views concerning the powers of the national government. In his first annual message to Congress, after acknowledging that the Constitution is one of limited powers, he went on to say that if the powers granted to Congress could be used for (among other things) "the cultivation and encouragement of the mechanic and of the elegant arts, the advancement of literature, and the progress of the sciences" to refrain from exercising these powers "would be treachery to the most sacred of trusts."[3] Congress refrained from exercising the power Adams supposed it to have, and when Andrew Jackson succeeded him, any possibility of its being exercised ended abruptly. In the remainder of the century there was no serious effort to put support of the arts on the national agenda.

Within the District of Columbia, where Congress has exclusive authority, commissions for the embellishment of the Capitol and other government buildings, some of them lavish but most of them frugal, were awarded by Congress until after the Civil War. President Jefferson, who had pledged strict economy and who might have been expected to resist even symbolic aggrandizement of federal power, insisted that the Capitol have "rich Corinthian capitals, based on those of the Choragic monument of Lysicrates in Athens."[4] Congress was less enthusiastic. An Ohio representative who said that he had been brought up a backwoodsman in tents and camps declared that money spent to make the Capitol magnificent was "in great measure, money thrown away."[5] This was an opinion that others shared.

In response to a memorial signed by almost one hundred artists and friends of art, Congress created a Select Committee in 1858 to consider complaints against the awarding of commissions to foreign artists and the claim that a developing national art required "a liberal, systematic, and enlightened" encouragement of American artists. An Art Commission, whose members were appointed by President James Buchanan in 1860 in compliance with an act of Congress, issued a year later a seven-page report that dealt mostly with the decoration of buildings; it greatly disappointed those who had hoped that it might have called for establishment of a national museum and perhaps a national art school. The commission was quickly abolished.[6]

In 1846, the Smithsonian Institution was established "for the increase and diffusion of knowledge among men" with money willed to the United States by James Smithson, an Englishman.[7] Eventually, the Smithsonian became the official curator of all of the government's art. In its first years, however, it housed only a few works, most of them portraits, and even these were lost in a fire in 1865. The privately supported Corcoran Gallery, which opened in 1874, was the only art gallery in Washington until 1906, when the Smithsonian established, with a bequest of Old Masters, what is now the National Collection (not to be confused with the National Gallery of Art).

In 1910 the National Commission on Fine Arts was established with an annual appropriation of $10,000 and was authorized to "advise generally upon questions of art when required to do so by the President"; the advice it gave, however, had mostly to do with the location of statues, fountains, and other works in the District of Columbia.

The manner in which the federal government had been supporting art did not attract much notice. Religious, educational, and charitable organizations were exempted from the federal income tax under the law enacted in 1894. It was declared unconstitutional, but a new law passed in 1913, when the Constitution was amended, restored the exemptions.

In 1916 a federal inheritance tax law gave wealthy people an incentive to make bequests to educational and charitable institutions, among them art museums, and in 1917 the Internal Revenue Code was amended to allow tax deductions for charitable purposes.[8] Someone proposed in 1921 that there be a secretary of fine arts; although President Warren Harding "expressed interest," it was never realized.

It took the Great Depression and the New Deal to bring the national government to center stage as a supporter of the arts. The New Deal produced two national arts agencies, neither of which was permanent. Three months after he took office, President Franklin Roosevelt was urged by the artist George Biddle, a Groton and Harvard classmate who had been much impressed by Mexico's support of the decoration of public buildings with murals, to do something similar here. This was the beginning of what became in 1933 the Section of Fine Arts in the Treasury Department, then the custodian of federal buildings. The section's mission was to expose the public to "good" art; "We have nothing to do with relief," its chief declared. By 1943, when it was disbanded, the section had employed well under 1,000 artists, most of whom had won commissions in competitions.[9]

The other agency, the Federal Art Project of the Works Progress Administration (WPA), gave work relief to artists (as well as to a good many who simply called themselves artists); it employed at least ten times as many artists as the treasury's section. Although "fastidiously faithful to the rhetoric of relief," writes historian Richard McKinzie, the WPA art project established a higher priority for itself—"raising the level of national taste and making art a part of daily life (and perhaps of perpetuating [its] own existence in the process)."[10]

The heads of both agencies (Edward Bruce of the Section of Fine Arts and Holger Cahill of the Federal Art Project) expected their agencies to outlast the Depression. Government, Harry Hopkins said to a conference of state WPA administrators in 1937, "is in the subsidy of arts once and for all time." In 1938 Congress heard debate on bills intended to establish permanent arts organizations. Representative William I. Sirovich of New York proposed a cabinet-level Department of Science, Art, and Literature, and Representative John M. Coffee of Washington joined with Senator Claude Pepper of Florida to sponsor a bill to absorb the WPA's art functions into a Bureau of Fine Arts. The hearings, McKinzie writes, revealed a deep division between the supporters, who "seemed to envision awakening and stimulating folk arts when they spoke of cultural development," and the opponents, who "predicted that the works produced by the new agency would be so inferior as to degrade the arts."[11]

President Roosevelt withheld support from all proposed arts legislation then and later. He spoke privately of the "importance of continuing the projects in some form," but he also remarked that the opposition of legislators reflected the views of their constituents. "The American government and the American people," McKinzie concludes, "never decided whether the support of the arts was a legitimate and desirable function of government."[12]

The Drive to Create a National Arts Foundation

After World War II a fresh effort to secure federal support for the arts began. In 1948 leaders of twelve national organizations—among them, the American Association of Museums, the American Federation of Artists, and the American Institute of Architects—formed the Committee on Government and Art, whose objective was to get the president to appoint a commission "to consider the whole question of Government's relation to art, to study existing governmental agencies and methods, and to submit recommendations for their improvement."[13] Bills to establish a bureau of fine arts were once again in the congressional hopper.

In 1951 President Harry Truman met with the Commission on Fine Arts, at its request, and asked for recommendations for a U.S. arts policy. Having no money for expenses, it heard testimony from federal agency heads, state and local government officials, embassy representatives, and interest groups, including the Committee on Government and Art. After two years and four volumes of testimony, the commission recommended—to President Dwight Eisenhower—that it continue to act in an advisory capacity. One member, George Biddle, who had prodded President Roosevelt to establish the Treasury's Section of Fine Arts, urged in a separate statement that the government "give more encouragement to and have a more active participation in the cultural life of the nation."[14]

While the commission's report was discouraging to advocates of federal support, the report of a three-man special subcommittee of the House Committee on Education and Labor must have been even more so. In 1954, after noting that all of the witnesses in two days of hearings had endorsed the idea of federal encouragement and promotion of fine arts, the majority reported unfavorably on all of some fifteen bills. "We cannot conceive it our duty," they said, "to dip even further into his [the American worker's] threadbare pocket to indulge in the luxury of subsidizing an endless variety of programs and projects supposedly related to the so-called finer arts." The majority's views took two and one-half pages of the report; thirty-four pages were given over to a summary by the minority members of testimony given in support of the bills, one of which would have authorized the new Department of Health, Education, and Welfare (HEW) to make grants to the states for the development of fine arts programs.[15]

An important development was the election in 1954 of Frank Thompson of New Jersey to the House. He soon became a leading activist on behalf of arts legislation, although he did not care for the arts but very much enjoyed mixing with people who did. When Thompson entered Congress, a journalist friend had advised him to specialize in something, and his district, consisting mostly of Trenton (and therefore a safe seat for a labor man like himself), included Princeton. Whatever his reasons, Thompson soon made himself, in the opinion of McGeorge Bundy, when president of the Ford Foundation, "the most interesting and best-informed person in Congress on the subject of the arts and humanities."[16] To have such a man in the House was of the greatest possible importance to the arts advocates' cause.

Meanwhile, other events were giving them hope. Nelson

Rockefeller, who had campaigned for Eisenhower, was appointed undersecretary of HEW in 1953 and a year later was named special assistant to the president. It was probably no coincidence that in his State of the Union Message in 1955, President Eisenhower (an enthusiastic painter, but otherwise without interest in the arts[17]) declared that "the Federal government should do more to give official recognition to the importance of the arts and other cultural activities" and said he would recommend establishment within the HEW of a federal advisory commission on the arts to find ways to encourage artistic and cultural endeavors and appreciation.

Appearing before a House subcommittee in July 1955, Rockefeller was careful not to alarm the opponents of federal aid. He proposed the creation of the advisory commission, consisting of twenty-one citizens, that would be an organ for study and planning and for making recommendations. Implementation of its proposals would depend on congressional approval. The administration's bill was "an important first step" to open the way for "gradual but steady progress toward more adequate Federal policy." It stated "three fundamental beliefs":

a) That the growth and flourishing of the arts depend upon freedom, imagination, and individual initiative.

b) That the encouragement of creative activity in the performance and practice of the arts, and of a widespread participation in an appreciation of the arts, is inseparable from the general welfare and the national interest.

c) That the encouragement of the arts, while primarily a matter for private and local initiative, is an appropriate matter of concern to the U.S. Government.[18]

The bill passed the Senate in July 1955. But given a public for art that was concentrated in a few big cities, it failed in the House. The same thing happened the following year with a bill introduced by Senator Herbert Lehman of New York and Representative H. Alexander Smith of New Jersey. And it continued in this fashion for the next three years.

Despite these defeats, the outlook for eventual passage was growing brighter. The arts advocates were encouraged when Rockefeller, having been elected governor of New York in 1959, succeeded the next year in creating the New York State Council on the Arts. The state, he said, should "act as a catalytic agency to stimulate and encourage participation"; it should not, however, in any way limit freedom of artistic expression.[19] In 1961 he persuaded the legislature to appropriate $450,000 for the council. At about the same time, Michigan also created a state arts agency. Proponents of national legislation could point to two working models.

Talk was now of subsidy, not advice. The financial crisis of cultural institutions was dramatized for the public in 1960, when a wage dispute caused the Metropolitan Opera Association to cancel its season. After ending the strike by an arbitrator's award so generous to labor, some thought, as to put the association in jeopardy, the secretary of labor, Arthur Goldberg, declared that "the question before the nation" was how to restore the financial viability of cultural institutions. The federal government, he said, should help state and local governments and private not-for-profit groups to build and maintain the physical plants required by arts organizations and, on a matching-grant basis, make up their operating deficits.[20] Goldberg's statement drew enthusiastic praise from many sources. "I've never had such a response to anything I've done," he said.[21]

There were indications of coming success. Both candidates for president in 1960 supported arts legislation. As senator, John F. Kennedy had opposed creation of a department of culture on the grounds that it would have a stultifying effect on the arts; as a presidential candidate, he supported the Democratic platform's call for an advisory committee, but he opposed direct support: "I do not believe Federal funds should support symphony orchestras or opera companies, except when they are sent abroad in cultural exchange programs."[22] Richard Nixon, after pointing out that the arts were thriving in the United States, said that he supported an advisory council and also "indirect" assistance: scholarships, exchange programs—"encouragement rather than subsidy."[23]

Kennedy's opposition to subsidies did not deter cultural leaders from supporting him. At the suggestion of one of them—Katherine Halle, a Washington hostess—they were invited en masse to his inauguration. Afterward he wrote them asking their views on what government should do for the arts, and his letter brought more than one hundred responses, which accumulated in a White House file. Under pressure to do something and aware that a bill to support the arts could not get through the House, Kennedy did what he could: in February 1962 he endorsed the current, ill-fated proposal to establish an advisory council, saying that the government should confine its efforts to "broad encouragement" and that the area was "too new for hasty action."[24] The next month he appointed a special consultant on the arts, August Heckscher, a wealthy New Yorker who was director of the Twentieth Century Fund and who had written (but not yet published) *The Public Happiness*.[25] Heckscher, who favored government support of contemporary art, had been chairman of the cultural panel of the Eisenhower Commission on National Goals, and had written a chapter for its report.[26]

Heckscher occupied an office in the White House and for more than a year surveyed federal activities relating to the arts and traveled around the country exchanging views on cultural policy. His thirty-four-page report, published as a Senate document, dealt with a wide range of matters: acquisitions by the National Gallery, the Smithsonian Institution, and the Library of Congress; funds for the embellishment of new government buildings; design of posters; changes in the tax laws to encourage gifts to cultural institutions. In its last two paragraphs the report addressed what was *the* issue for arts advocates: the establishment of an arts foundation to

. . . administer matching grants to States setting up arts councils. It might make available grants for demonstration projects proposed by particular cultural institutions. Thus it could consider helping support experiments designed to increase attendance, to foster creativity and introduce contemporary works to new audiences, or to offer services on an experimental basis.[27]

There was by now a great deal of support in both houses of Congress for a gesture, such as the creation of an advisory council, in the direction of federal support for the arts. At least forty bills had been introduced, one of them with one hundred co-sponsors. If a bill could have been brought to the floor, it could probably have been passed. But the chairman of the House Rules Committee, Howard Smith of Virginia, was determined that no bill would be brought to the floor. Heckscher and two other presidential advisers, Arthur Schlesinger, Jr., and Richard Goodwin, urged Kennedy to issue an executive order. Kennedy was, Heckscher said later, "skeptical of any idea that government could do more than sometimes stir things up, and sometimes give recognition and support to what had strangely or wonderfully occurred."[28] Fearful of being accused of bypassing Congress, Kennedy told Heckscher to "clear it with John Lindsay."[29] The Republican representative from New York's 18th ("silk stocking") District, Lindsay had made arts legislation one of his principal concerns; Kennedy thought him the congressman most likely to make a fuss about their being bypassed.

With Lindsay's agreement assured and Heckscher's report in hand, Kennedy issued an èxecutive order in June 1963 creating an Arts Commission (he avoided Advisory Council because so many bills using this term had failed in Congress). After many discussions, in some of which Kennedy participated, the membership of the commission was decided upon. The first intention was to appoint as chairman Michael Straight, whose name was put forward by Arthur Schlesinger, Jr., and William Walton, head of *The New Republic*'s Washington bureau until he quit it to become a painter. The

49

expectation was that sooner or later an endowment would be created and Straight would be its chairman. Straight, however, had recently told the FBI of early associations with and later knowledge of Soviet espionage activities. Thinking the appointment inappropriate under the circumstances, he asked not to be appointed.[30] Kennedy then decided upon Goodwin for chairman of the commission. The announcement of this appointment was scheduled for the day that he was expected to return from Dallas.

President Johnson put Kennedy's list of commission appointments aside and sent his friend and adviser Abe Fortas to tell Heckscher, who now wished to stay on the job in order to ensure continuity, that he was to turn his files over to the Kennedy archives at once.

Johnson appointed Roger L. Stevens as an adviser in 1964. A highly successful New York real estate operator—he had once bought and sold the Empire State Building—Stevens was a former chairman of the Finance Committee of the Democratic National Committee who was now a principal promoter of the National Cultural Center (which was renamed the John F. Kennedy Center for the Performing Arts).

Stevens's job was to salvage what he could of a bill that was now waiting only for House approval, which would create a national council of the arts and a national arts foundation. Stevens succeeded by having provision for a foundation dropped from the bill, thus saving the council. The National Arts and Cultural Development Act of 1964 passed in the House and then in the Senate with a voice vote. Two weeks later it was approved by the president, who named Stevens chairman of the new National Council on the Arts. His job now was to secure passage of the part of the bill that had been sacrificed.

The Creation of a National Endowment for the Arts

The election of 1964 gave President Johnson the largest Democratic majorities in Congress since 1937. The creation of a National Arts Foundation would be easy if, but only if, the president would agree to make funding the arts a part of the Great Society program. "Somebody had told him it wasn't a good idea," Goodwin later recalled. But when he gave his State of the Union Message in 1965, Johnson read the indispensable words Goodwin had slipped in: "To help promote and honor creative achievements, I will propose a National Foundation on the Arts."[31]

The chairmen of the appropriate subcommittees (the House Select Subcommittee on Education and the Senate Subcommittee on Arts and Humanities) introduced identical bills and in March 1965 held joint hearings. The chairman of the House subcommittee, Frank Thompson, and the chairman of the Senate subcommittee, Claiborne Pell, could not have had more different backgrounds. Thompson came from a working-class family and, after being refused admission to Princeton, went to an obscure college on an athletic scholarship; Pell, a member of a wealthy and distinguished Rhode Island family, had graduated from Princeton. They had in common, however, a determination to distinguish themselves as the principal congressional supporters of the arts.

Almost all of the witnesses in the joint hearings were favorable, and some were enthusiastic; it was a good beginning.[32] But it would take pressure from the president, who had other bills taking priority, to overcome the obstacles in the way of passage.

One obstacle, which was responsible for the repeated failures in the House, was that the public for art was in a few big cities, especially New York, which was the nation's cultural capital. The important art galleries, theaters, publishing houses, and television networks were all headquartered there. New York is the home of some of the greatest of the cultural institutions—the Metropolitan Opera House, the Metropolitan Museum of Art, the New York Philharmonic —as well as some 1,200 other nonprofit arts organizations. Tourism depends heavily upon these cultural attractions. By one estimate, the gross income of the cultural industry was about $3 billion a year for 1972–74.[33] New York would get the lion's share of any appropriation for the arts, with most of the rest going to a half dozen other large cities. Most congressional districts would get practically nothing.

Another serious obstacle was a bill to establish a foundation for the support of the humanities. "We are in trouble," Stevens said when he learned of this bill, which had eighty co-sponsors and made no mention of the arts.[34] The humanities advocates were mainly professors who taught literature, languages, history, and other cultural subjects, and especially the deans and presidents who had to find money to pay their salaries. For years the humanists had suffered in income and prestige in comparison with colleagues in the sciences, whose cups overflowed from grants from the National Science Foundation, the National Institutes for Mental Health, and a multitude of other federal agencies; the humanists got foundation grants or nothing at all.

They believed there was an imbalance that threatened the national well-being and that they had to organize to impress upon Congress the gravity of the problem. The American Council of Learned Societies, which had been refurbished in 1957 with a grant from the Ford Foundation, took the lead. In collaboration with the United Chapters of Phi Beta Kappa and the Council of Graduate Schools, it created in 1963 a National Commission of the Humanities under the chairmanship of Barnaby C. Keeney, president of Brown University. Its report, a 222-page hardcover book published the next year, gave the stern warning: "The state of the humanities today creates a crisis for national leadership." The panel

reported that "there is no room for debate": the humanities
were in the national interest and deserved financial support
from the federal government.[35]

The humanities advocates did not have the problems facing the arts advocates: every congressional district had a
college that might benefit from federal grants, and of course
there were universities in all states. Obviously, the arts
would gain the strength that they lacked in the House by
joining forces with the humanities. The humanities would
also gain, for there was grave danger that legislation on their
behalf would be administered by the Office of Education,
which "would only serve to accentuate the status distinction
between the natural sciences and the humanities and deepen
the schism in higher education," warned Gustave O. Arlt,
the president of the Council of Graduate Schools.[36]

Both interests would gain from a merger. But when Stevens put the idea to him, Goodwin, the president's adviser,
was at first opposed: the political base of the humanities was
so much broader than that of the arts, the arts would get little
when it came to dividing up the appropriations. Keeney and
Stevens had no trouble, however, persuading Senator Pell
and Representative Thompson. Pell depended heavily on the
advice of a legislative assistant, Livingston ("Liv") Biddle,
who had been his roommate at Princeton and had remained
his close friend. After writing four novels with Philadelphia
settings, Biddle had come to Washington in 1963 to write a
political one. Working for Pell gave him a good opportunity
to gather material, and when Pell asked him what subject
matter interested him most, Biddle, who had been impressed
with the wartime efforts of the British Arts Council, decided
to become a specialist on arts legislation. His job now was to
help draft a bill that would pass.

Goodwin, Stevens, Keeney, along with Pell and Thompson, eventually agreed upon an ingenious arrangement
whereby a foundation would be created to serve as a "holding company" for two endowments, one for arts and the

other for humanities, each with its own chairman and its own appropriations. Early in March the president sent Congress a bill to establish such a foundation. The arts, Pell said, were to be piggybacked on the humanities.

In June Pell's committee reported on the administration's bill with amendments, and the Senate passed it at once by a voice vote. A month later the House Committee on Education and Labor reported on its very similar version. It went to the Rules Committee, whose chairman refused, as he had year after year, to "give a rule" enabling it to come before the House. This year, however, procedure had been changed; it was possible by petition to force discharge from the committee of a bill that it had held for twenty-one days. To get the needed petitioners, help might be needed from the White House, and this was feared to be impossible. President Johnson, it was said, was furious because some of the celebrities invited to a White House Festival of the Arts, which had been held a few days before to draw attention to the new National Council on the Arts, had used the occasion to protest the Vietnam War.

Furious or not, the president did intervene. The bill reached the House floor in September 1965; after a lively debate, a motion to recommit failed.[37] The bill then passed on a voice vote. Two weeks later the National Foundation on the Arts and the Humanities came into being with funds authorized, but not yet appropriated, for three years.

The Justifications for Federal Support

In the thousands of pages of testimony and debate that preceded passage of the 1965 act remarkably little is said about the material benefits some supporters expected. A report that took a distinguished panel two years to prepare for the Rockefeller Brothers Fund elaborated the warning of impending crisis that had been made by Arthur Goldberg.[38] Even in this, however, the financial well-being of New York's "culture industry" did not seem to be the main concern.

The claims made by the arts advocates were mostly about the general welfare and the public interest; they were of course well aware that special interests had a great deal at stake, but they talked and wrote, however, as if these were of only incidental importance. The arts advocates believed, perhaps, that it was more dignified, or more becoming, to use the language of statesmanship rather than that of politics, and they may have also sensed that (as Richard Posner has suggested) the rhetoric of the public interest was useful as a kind of screen that would take opponents some time and trouble to remove.[39] The five principal public interest arguments elaborated by the arts advocates are discussed below.

Recognition. Of particular significance was the belief that the establishment of a federal agency and a "national cultural policy" would give "official recognition" to the arts, thus "improving the image" and "raising the prestige" of the government of the United States and also of the people of the United States. President Eisenhower, in his message proposing the creation of an advisory council on the arts, had said it would give "official recognition" to art and culture. In 1961 Congressman John Lindsay told the House that this was *the* purpose of the bill before it:

Let me remind the House that this is not a grant-in-aid bill. This is what you might call a status bill. What it does is to give status and recognition to the importance of culture in the United States.[40]

Earlier that year John Kenneth Galbraith, participating in a televised debate, declared that arts legislation "is the final step now that recognizes that the artist is a first-class citizen, that he is as worthy of being taken as seriously as the scientist, the businessman or even the economist. And that art is seen as one of the great and respectable resources of our society."[41] When President Kennedy solicited suggestions from cultural leaders, the one most frequently made, according to Heckscher, called for Congress and the president to "recognize" outstanding contributions to culture by the award of a medal.

In 1964 Senator Pell began the presentation of his bill by saying that its passage would be a "famous 'first' ": "For the first time . . . we will give recognition to the arts."[42] The manager of the House bill, Adam Clayton Powell of New York, said that "by giving statutory recognition to culture, we will place greater emphasis on the finer things in life."[43]

Recognition was symbolically important: it showed democracy's regard for the higher things. In 1965 the president of Yale University, Kingman Brewster, told a House subcommittee:

It seems terribly important to me that the people's representatives in the Houses of Congress should visibly and concretely declare their sense of the importance of the intellectual, the aesthetic, and the moral aspects of life and declare it in a way in which everyone can see and hear.[44]

Prestige. The preamble of the bill asserted that "The nation's prestige and general welfare will be promoted" by federal support of the arts. Senator Jacob Javits of New York, in listing what he considered to be the major reasons for creating an arts agency, put national prestige first: the United States, he told the Senate, was the only great nation not to have given recognition to the arts, where ". . . the grandeur and dignity of our nation are at stake."[45]

What future generations would think was also a matter of much concern. The Eisenhower Commission on National Goals made this point in its report:

In the eyes of posterity, the success of the United States as a civilized society will be largely judged by the creative activities of its citizens in art, architecture, literature, music, and the sciences.[46]

Senator Pell amplified the point by putting hard rhetorical questions to his fellow senators:

How will history eventually judge us as a Nation? Will some group of historians in the future say that somehow the United States faltered?
Do we remember ancient Egypt by its list of Pharaohs—or for its Pyramids?
Do we remember Greece for its phalanx of soldiers—or for its Parthenon—for Plato, for Aristotle, for Socrates?
Do we remember Rome for its catapult in battle—or for the orations of Cicero, the poetry of Ovid and Virgil?[47]

President Johnson, when he sent his bill to Congress, wrote that its passage would "help secure for this Congress a sure and honored place in the story of the advance of our civilization."

International Understanding. Another line of argument asserted that federal support of the arts would contribute to international understanding and world peace. "It is only through a Nation's arts and literature that other nations discover it has a soul," wrote Clare Booth Luce, a former ambassador to Italy, in her magazine column.[48] The report of the Rockefeller panel said that the arts could make a distinct "if not precisely measurable" contribution to international understanding.[49] Heckscher, as President Kennedy's special consultant, went as far as to say that the outcome of the cold war might hinge on the "total picture" the world formed of the United States, an important part of which would be the attitude of Americans toward the arts:

It is significant that in the worst days of the Berlin crisis of 1961 General Clay sent back word urgently requesting that a first-rate exhibition of art be sent over to the beleaguered city. And it may be worth remembering that during the tensest hours of the recent Cuban crisis, Mr. Khrushchev was reported as spending four hours at the opera.[50]

Jimmy Carter, in his campaign for the presidency, charged that the Nixon and Ford administrations had never fully understood the potential of the arts as a means of improving relations with other nations: "More effectively than weapons, more effectively than diplomacy, the arts can communicate, people to people, the spirit of America."[51]

The Culture Boom.   Another line of argument asserted that a cultural explosion had created a crisis of culture that could only be dealt with by federal subsidies. Art museums and other cultural institutions were serving unprecedented numbers of people, but their financial position was meanwhile becoming steadily worse. Some museums, even though they were closed two days a week, were rapidly using up their endowments. Musicians, actors, and dancers were underemployed and underpaid, although popular demand for them was higher than ever. The cultural explosion, Senator Hubert Humphrey said, was an expression of unsatisfied desires and therefore an indication of the need for federal legislation.[52]

It was somewhat surprising that an increase in the demand for the services of cultural institutions should have put them in difficulties, especially as changes in the Internal Revenue Code had increased the percentage of individual income that might be given to cultural institutions with a tax exemption. Essentially, the problem was that increased demand for service added to operating costs, where gifts, which were almost entirely of capital (especially paintings and buildings), far from relieving operating costs, increased them. Even so, since the national income was growing steadily, the crisis should have been temporary. This, however, was not the opinion of leading arts advocates. John D. Rockefeller III told a Senate subcommittee in 1963 that it seemed "obvious that only by enlightened government action at the municipal, State, and National levels, can the gap between the inevitable needs and present resources be appreciably narrowed."[53] Francis Keppel, the U.S. commissioner of education, estimated that it would take $320 million to fill that gap.[54]

Rockefeller, it may be noted, thought in terms of needs—what people *should* have, as opposed to what they might be willing to pay for. If cultural organizations raised their prices or reduced their costs (or both), most of them would prosper. The Rockefeller panel came close to acknowledging this in its report. The highest-priced seats at concerts of both the New York Philharmonic and the Boston Symphony Orchestra were then $7.50, and both orchestras almost always played to full houses. It was probable, the panel allowed, that tickets could be priced higher. This, however, "would defeat their [the orchestras'] purpose as a cultural resource."[55] Accordingly, the panel, while favoring federal subsidies, made no recommendation pertaining to pricing. This was the attitude with which the trustees and directors of most cultural institutions faced the crisis. Some museums made a nominal admission charge; others made none at all.

The Benefits to the Poor. The managers of cultural institutions maintained (possibly for public relations reasons) that free or subsidized admissions benefited the poor. At a time when the war on poverty was in the headlines, it was another useful argument justifying public support. It was the democratic right of all people, no matter what their circumstances, to have access to all of the arts; the fact that many people lived far from museums and concert halls was not a misfortune but an injustice that government should rectify. President Kennedy, in a statement accompanying the Executive Order creating his arts commission, expressed dismay that "children are growing up who have never seen a professionally acted play." Congressman Powell called sparsely settled states "cultural dust bowls."[56] The Rockefeller panel declared the ideal of "cultural democracy" would be achieved only when every American could enjoy arts of very high quality.[57]

Some arts advocates (Powell, whose district was Harlem, was not among them) thought the arts could be important in relieving tensions in the ghettos of large cities. Addressing the first session of the Business Committee for the Arts, David Rockefeller, president of the Chase Manhattan Bank, made this his main theme. Projects involving the arts, he said,

are not just a kind of fluffy periphery of American life. They are essential to the root problem that faces our country today. We have, at the present time, the most serious crisis in our cities that we have ever faced. We are asking Congress and the people to make sacrifices to deal with these basic, serious urban problems. But I wonder if the problems of the arts are separate from those. I believe that unless we can give the people who live in our ghettos, who are the under-privileged of our rich country, a hope to be able to enjoy the better things in life and not just the bare necessities—unless we can convince them that they, too, can share in beauty and creativity, are we really going to satisfy their wants?[58]

Congressman Hugh Carey of New York went a good deal further. He told the House that the NEA, by stimulating "an outpouring of creativity," would ". . . do far more than even the Civil Rights Act to bring them [the ghettos] into the mainstream of American culture."[59]

The Case Against Federal Support

A few voices were raised from within the world of high culture in opposition to federal support of the arts. Some expressed fear of censorship, but the main concern of most opponents was that government, by reflecting popular taste, would lower artistic standards. Few, if any, of the critics saw a moral problem in the further extension of government power.

What worried Russell Lynes was not creeping socialism but creeping mediocrity. An arts council, he said, would consist of political appointees who represented—in the eyes of those who appointed it—"expert" opinion. A council appointed by President Kennedy would doubtless include some "progressives," but, even so, it would have a conservative influence on the art world. The best that would be hoped for was a "safe, sane, and moderate committee with a tolerance of experimentation, an uncle-like interest in the aspiring young, and a suitable regard for raising the level of public taste." But what if the council were to be appointed by Senator Barry Goldwater?[60]

As an example of the foolish judgments politicians were likely to make about art, Lynes quoted what an Illinois congressman had said about works sent abroad under State Department auspices:

The movement of modern art is a revolution against the conventional and natural things of life as expressed in art. . . . Institutions that have been venerated through the ages are ridiculed. . . . Without exceptions, the paintings in the State Department's group that portray a person make him or her unnatural. The skin is not reproduced as it would be naturally, but as a sullen ashen gray. Features of the face are always depressed and melancholy.[61]

Administrators, Lynes pointed out, would have to decide what is art and what is not and would have to draw a line between "popular" and "serious" arts. They would find it far easier to defend before a congressional committee (which, he said, respects market values) the considerable expense of a symphony orchestra or a Shakespearean repertory company than the small expense of a recital of the works of John Cage or performances of the nihilist theater of Samuel Beckett. It could be expected therefore that funds would be granted to the states, which in turn would give them to cultural institutions such as orchestras. On these grounds, Lynes commended the creation of an arts council to "the conservatives and to those who want to keep art what is called 'safe.' " He did not commend it, however, to "those who believe that the function of art is to push back the horizons of truth and experience and discovery."[62]

The art critic of the *New York Times*, John Canaday, took a similar position, although in less dogmatic language:

In a nation idealistically determined to make all good things available to all good people, a national arts program might be forced into the service of exactly the mass audience most likely to corrupt it. . . . The contradiction of a vast popular audience seeking the rewards that are essentially aristocratic makes one wonder where an art created by and for the few belongs in the program of a government of the people, by the people, and for the people.[63]

Writing a month before the passage of the 1965 act, the critic Stanley Kauffmann saw a danger that subsidies would go to the artistically unworthy: "Does the bill envision a grant to a brothel barrel-house pianist? Why not subsidize more bowling alleys or hobby groups." Declaring that his own view was "elitist" ("it seems culturally suicidal to adhere to any but the most cruelly rigorous standard"), Kauffmann raised some rude questions: "*Can* our art—at its best —be brought to a wider audience? Why, in fact, do they want it? Is the obviously increased demand anything more than what has been well described as culture-vulturism?" What was really wanted, he concluded, was a sense of community: "The burned mattresses that now hang on museum walls, the random-playing radios on the concert stage in lieu of an orchestra, the black humor and sexual savagery of our novelists, are all cries for relationship, spasms of unrequited love." Without community, culture would not grow and society would have no need of it. Kauffmann did not oppose the bill, however. Government subsidy was becoming inevitable. Therefore the bill could "be welcomed, if only as a necessary first step."[64]

In the discussions leading to the passage of the law no one asked whether the anticipated benefits—an increase of national prestige, the advancement of civilization, relief of the cultural crisis—were properly the concern of government. It was simply assumed that, if an end were worthy, the government ought to pursue it.

CHAPTER

3

Administering the Law

> In my lifetime here [at the National En-
> dowment for the Arts], at the end of four
> years, I want a clear policy developed on
> where we're going with the arts in this
> country, and I want a government en-
> dorsement for it.
> —Livingston L. Biddle, Jr.
> *Detroit News Magazine,*
> February 26, 1978

IN the National Foundation on the Arts and the Humanities
Act, Congress had declared its purpose "to develop and promote a broadly conceived national policy of support for the
humanities and the arts. . . ."[1] In view of this intention, one
might have expected that the first endeavor of the National
Foundation for the Arts would have been to translate these
purposes into a set of plans and policies. Such action would
have involved deciding the relative importance to be accorded the several authorities that it had been given, the
most efficient distribution of resources among the various
arts, the terms on which conflicting goals could best be com-

63

promised, and above all, the kinds of aesthetic experience that would best serve the public interest.

One might also have expected that after settling such large questions as these, the NEA would have decided what specific activities—programs—would be the most suitable means of attaining its ends. For example, would its limited resources be more efficiently used by supporting existing cultural institutions or by establishing new ones? Would it be better to make grants to institutions or to individuals? How could the geographical distribution of cultural resources best be improved? Then once the programs were in operation, the NEA would have systematically evaluated the results. What unforeseen obstacles had turned up? Did any program cost more than it was worth?

The NEA did settle down to a set of activities called programs, but they were not created by a process that could be called planning. Fourteen years after passage of the act, W. McNeil Lowry, who had been head of the Ford Foundation arts program and had been much consulted when the act was before Congress, complained to a House subcommittee that "statements of federal policy in the arts are no more precise, and often less so, than they were in the original legislation."[2] Congress, he said, had a right to expect the NEA to have established priorities that could at least be debated; instead, its program categories had proliferated with no apparent strategy. Although Lowry did not make the point, the NEA had not evaluated any of its programs since its inception.

Yet the NEA acted in the normal, even the prescribed, manner of a public agency, which tends, more so than any other organization, to do what is most likely to contribute to its survival and growth. The time horizon cannot extend much beyond the next year's budget and appropriations process: it is critical to fare well with both the Office of Management and Budget (whose final decisions may depend upon someone close to the president) and with the relevant subcommittee of the House Committee on Appropriations (and above all its chairman), and to have devoted supporters—and no opponents—on other congressional committees. With this dependence there is no need for planning and program evaluation. Quite the contrary, planning, if done seriously, is bound to raise questions that threaten the interests whose support is critical; program evaluation never shows that an agency is accomplishing all that it claims to be accomplishing, and sometimes it suggests that it is not accomplishing much of anything.

Even before the NEA's inception President Johnson made it clear that he did not intend to have any planning. Meeting with Chairman Roger Stevens and the celebrities he had appointed to the National Council on the Arts (including Leonard Bernstein, Isaac Stern, Gregory Peck, David Smith, René D'Harnoncourt, and David Brinkley), the president told them in April 1965 that "he expected action from them with a minimum of meetings and discussions."[3]

After their meeting with the president, the members decided that the council should be "an action body and not merely an advisory one"; as such, it "could take any reasonable step not expressly prohibited by law."[4] To begin with, the members unanimously passed resolutions endorsing some thirty ideas gathered from the Heckscher report and other sources: outstanding artists should be honored annually, federal agencies should set aside one percent of their building costs for the purchase of art, the television industry should be prodded to carry more programs on the arts, urban renewal projects should provide studios for artists, and so on. With one dissent, they endorsed the president's position on the pending bill to create arts and humanities endowments.

By June the council members agreed that they should make some general policy proposals. With respect to the visual arts, they concluded that there were two immediate tasks: to call attention to the artist and his problem (undefined) and to educate (also undefined) the next generation.

On signing the 1965 act three months later, President

65

Johnson, reading from a statement prepared by Stevens, declared that the NEA would create a national theater, a national ballet company, a national opera company, and a national film institute. It would also commission symphonies and provide residencies in schools and universities for "great artists."

Stevens was appointed chairman of the NEA. In this capacity he had exclusive authority to approve grants; the council's function was now purely advisory. With $4.5 million in program funds for the remainder of the fiscal year, far too little to launch any of the projects that the president had listed, Stevens began making grants: for example, $500,000 to establish laboratory theater companies; $350,000 for the American Ballet Theater's national tours; $250,000 for the production of no more than ten plays; and $100,000 for a revolving fund to provide housing for artists. Large sums were to go to individuals: $375,000 for sabbaticals for teaching artists, $100,000 for awards to ten choreographers, and another $100,000 for awards to fifty-eight composers. Promising graduates of art schools were to have $80,000 to enable them to broaden their experience.

The list baffled and dismayed some arts advocates. It reflected, they thought, Stevens's concern with emergency situations (a ballet company was stranded in St. Louis), his knowledge of the theater and his ignorance of other cultural forms, and pressure on him from the White House to make a splash. The worst of it, these critics thought, was that the NEA was missing its chance to attract support from the core elements of the cultural world—symphony orchestras, for example—that were its natural constituency, by concentrating support on Stevens's pet projects, some of which were eccentric or even bizarre. By making bad grant decisions, it was cutting itself off from opportunities for future growth.[5]

A bureaucracy was necessary to recommend and administer grants. Stevens asked his friends and acquaintances in the art world for the names of people upon whom he could rely.

He appointed Henry Geldzahler to head the NEA's Visual Arts Program. A New Yorker in his late twenties, Geldzahler had recently left graduate study at the Fogg Museum to help launch the new gallery of contemporary art at the Metropolitan Museum of Art; he was not the choice to expect from Stevens, a man Stanley Kauffmann had said was "of irreproachably bourgeois taste."[6] An ardent admirer of experimental and advanced art, Geldzahler was just what Stevens was looking for. "I wanted something to happen in the goddam place," he said some years later. "Henry appealed to me for four reasons: he was under thirty, avant-garde, bright, and had a good background," which referred to his work at the Metropolitan. Being part politician, Stevens recognized the need to give what he called sociological and Sunday painters their due. The proper business of the NEA, however, was to support "real" art, by which Stevens meant the kind approved of by the "big-name" artists whom Geldzahler admired and who had given him his standing in the art world. Meeting his director of visual arts for the first time, Stevens told him, "I know nothing about art. You are my man as long as you do a good job."[7]

In the next two years Geldzahler initiated some of what were to be the NEA's principal permanent programs for the visual arts: direct grants to individual artists ($5,000 at first; in fiscal 1982, $12,500 to established artists and $4,000 to emerging artists), grants to museums for the purchase of works by living American artists ($20,000 at first; in fiscal 1982, from $5,000 to $20,000), and, at the suggestion of sculptor David Smith (a member of the National Council on the Arts), the commissioning of works—mostly sculptures—for public places.

In setting up his programs, Geldzahler kept one eye on what he deemed good art and the other on political reality. An overwhelming majority of "good" artists lived in New York City. There would have been howls in Congress, however, if an overwhelming proportion of the grants had gone to New Yorkers. Accordingly, Geldzahler set up regional panels of "experts" to discover worthy candidates in other parts of the country, which worked well at the beginning; there were, he said later, "some gorgeous feathers to be plucked in unlikely places."[8]

Museums could be depended upon to buy "real" art with their grants, but their acquisitions were mostly from New York artists, which created problems of political geography. Geldzahler tried to soften this by writing letters offering formal congratulations to the congressmen representing the districts in which the artists were born—and hence could take pride in the artists who were the recipients of these grants, even though these artists had moved to urban artistic centers. Happily, the museums themselves were rather widely scattered among congressional districts.

In its first annual report (made jointly with the National Council on the Arts), the NEA pledged its allegiance to the arts advocates' creed:

We are at a moment in American life when choices must be made. We must now decide what kind of society we wish to pass on to our children. The decisions we make today, difficult as they may be, are going to form the basis of the new society that is to follow.

What is it we wish to pass on? Are we again to exalt affluence as the sole essence of the good life? Let us offer our young people more than well-intentioned promises and vague assurances of a better tomorrow. These young men and women want to know what we are about and what we are made of. If we fail them, history will not be kind, nor will they.

The NEA was vague as to what it proposed to give the young men and women of America. It had not yet decided what, given its limited resources (far less than the operating budgets of dozens of cultural institutions), it could or should do. It was obliged to deal in generalities:

We need to make our open spaces beautiful again. We must create an environment in which our youth will be encouraged to pursue the discipline and craft of the arts. We must not only support our artistic institutions, both national and local, but we must also make the arts part of our daily life so that they become an essential aspect of our existence.

The blandness of the language concealed the size of the claim that Chairman Stevens was staking out for the agency. The time had come, the report said, to make the arts "a desirable as well as practical career possibility for our young people." "We should provide," it said, "equal opportunity for the actor as well as the physicist, for the poet as well as the biochemist, for the sculptor as well as the mathematician."[9] This implied that the forces of supply and demand should be set aside for artists. But how could this be done? Why should career opportunities for artists be "equal"—whatever it might mean—to those of scientists? Why not of, say, baseball players? Stevens and his associates never addressed these matters; the pressing task was to get the NEA under way and create enthusiasm for it.

State arts agencies could help muster public support. When the NEA was created Michigan and New York already had such agencies, and almost twenty-five other states, anticipating a flow of federal grants, were in the process of setting them up. The NEA made $25,000 grants to the states to hasten this process, and by the spring of 1967 almost all had arts agencies. As long as Stevens remained chairman, the NEA also made a practice of creating organizations that, since they owed their existence to the NEA, would support it with an enthusiasm not expected from well-endowed, established institutions.[10]

Stevens's initiatives surprised and alarmed some members of Congress. Halfway through NEA's second fiscal year the House voted overwhelmingly to renew its authorization for one year rather than the expected two, to cut its budget authorization to a mere $11.2 million, and to revoke its authority to make grants to individuals. Eventually, the House yielded to the Senate on all points, but it had been a close call. Many congressmen were annoyed and a few were out-raged by one or another of the NEA's undertakings. Setting up a fund to buy theater tickets in bulk for resale (at a loss) in order to keep unpopular plays from closing (a means pre-sumably of giving actors equal opportunity with physicists and biochemists) did not make sense to some lawmakers; neither did giving promising art students "graduation pres-ents" of several thousand dollars. Other congressmen ques-tioned the appropriateness of underwriting a housing project for artists in New York City.

The election of Richard Nixon in 1968 gave the arts advo-cates further cause for apprehension. He was a conservative and also—it was generally assumed—a Philistine. What many overlooked was that, whatever else he might be, Nixon was also a professional politician. He knew that all over the country leading Republicans were mainstays of museums, symphony orchestra associations, and other cultural institu-tions; he knew that, whereas a Democrat could take the world of artists and art-lovers pretty much for granted, a Republican would have to exert himself merely to overcome the pre-sumption that he was an enemy of art and culture. Whether from these considerations or out of loyalty to Eisenhower's program, Nixon had endorsed the idea of an arts council when he ran for president in 1960. And again in 1968 the Republi-can party platform called for federal aid to the arts.

Needing a link to constituencies that were not naturally his, President Nixon chose as counselor his friend and former law partner, Leonard Garment, a liberal with many ties to the art world (he was, among other things, an accomplished jazz clarinetist). With Garment in the White House, the NEA would be closer to the president than ever.

One of Garment's first tasks was to find a successor to Stevens, whose term expired in March. R. Philip Hanes, a Republican member of the National Council for the Arts, asked Michael Straight, a friend of both Stevens and Gar-ment, to do what he could to get Stevens reappointed; it was obvious, however, that the former chairman of the Finance Committee of the Democratic National Committee could not hold a high position in a Republican administration. Garment, who did not know that President Kennedy had wanted to appoint Straight chairman of his Advisory Commission on the Arts, favored his appointment to the chairmanship. Nixon, who attached no importance to the revelations that Straight had made to the FBI a few years before, was willing to appoint him, and Straight himself thought that the passage of time had removed the basis for his earlier refusal to serve. Now, however, he believed that his record as a leading Democrat disqualified him; as chairman he would not get the cooperation he would need from party-minded Republicans in the White House and in Congress. Garment and he searched for a Republican who would accept the post, work hard at it, and have the support of Pell, Thompson, and other key figures in Congress. Eventually, they settled upon Nancy Hanks, who as president of the Associated Councils on the Arts had helped secure passage of the 1965 act. She had worked for Nelson Rockefeller when he was undersecretary of the Department of Health, Education, and Welfare; helped prepare the so-called Belmont report on the needs of museums for the American Association of Museums; and then had served as staff director of the Rockefeller Brothers Fund's Panel on the Performing Arts.

The appointment of a "Rockefeller Republican" did not please some of the president's associates. He nevertheless appointed her, and she, at Garment's suggestion, made Straight her deputy. In announcing her appointment, the president took occasion to say that she had chosen a person of "equal stature" as her deputy. In order to give greater prestige and weight to the deputy chairmanship, Senator Jacob Javits of New York offered to introduce a bill amending the act. Straight discouraged him, however, on the ground that the chairman should have full freedom to hire or fire the principal subordinate.

In December 1969 the president astonished the arts world by asking Congress to double the appropriations of both endowments. It would be, Garment had prodded Nixon, "a quintessentially presidential thing to do," and—a point that appealed to Nixon—it would come as a "real surprise."[11]

The obvious obstacles in the way of planning no longer existed. The departures of President Johnson and Roger Stevens ended pressure to "get the show on the road," and as a result somewhat allayed congressional concern about what the agency would do next. The National Council on the Arts was in a purely supportive role. The NEA had money enough to do something worthwhile (in fiscal 1970 it had had only a little more than $8 million), and it was likely that its appropriations would be further increased (in the next five years they were increased to almost $75 million). Nancy Hanks, the former research director for the Rockefellers; Michael Straight, the former editor; and Leonard Garment, the gifted and sympathetic mentor who had the ear of the president, were a combination that would surely produce what the act called for—a broadly conceived policy.

Shortly before taking office, Straight listed some basic questions in an article for *The New Republic:*

The President and the Congress agreed, five years ago, that the arts should have public support. But how much support should be given, and in what ways? Should the program concentrate upon the performing arts, whose problems, due to rising costs, were most acute? Or should equal emphasis be given to the fine arts, to landscape architecture and other related endeavors? Should federal aid go to individuals or only to institutions? Should it be a long-term program, to raise the general level of cultural awareness? Or should it set out instead to rescue orchestras, repertory companies and dance groups from foundering?

These questions, he wrote, were subordinate to another (which had never been publicly discussed): "The central question for the Endowment has been and still is: [W]hy should all of our taxpayers support activities that only a small minority of taxpayers enjoy?" There was only one persuasive answer: "[T]he arts hold out the promise of enrichment for the great majority of citizens, and public funding is a means of bringing that promise into being." Thus, the NEA could justify its existence only by bringing art to the masses; however, "Public support for the arts," wrote Straight, "may benefit the majority of Americans within a generation or two."[12] That benefiting the majority in this way was a proper function of government he seems to have taken for granted.

This view of the NEA's mission implied sharp changes, which soon occurred. The NEA ceased meeting "emergencies," making up the deficits of arts organizations, and creating new organizations that would depend upon it for survival. Instead, it supported projects to widen the range of services offered by existing organizations (e.g., museums, organizations serving low-income people and ethnic minorities, local groups devoted to crafts, folk arts, and jazz, and towns and cities concerned with design); it would bring the fine and the applied arts closer together (e.g., by providing advisers to improve federal architecture, landscaping, graphics, and interior design); and, finally, it would put artists of all kinds in schoolrooms not to teach specific skills but to develop the aesthetic sensibilities of children.[13]

Straight, however, seems to have had very little to do with making any of these changes. Nancy Hanks made most policy decisions on her own. "She never sat down to discuss large questions of policy with me or with any of her subordinates," Straight later said. "She had a positive distaste for stating broad principles, except for platitudinous ones like 'We must preserve our heritage.' She never conceptualized anything. Instead she operated intuitively and pragmatically." Decisions about the kind of art to be supported were almost always made by the various program directors. As

73

deputy chairman, Straight says, "I never knew just what I was expected to do or how far my authority extended."[14]

A reporter who covered the NEA at this time recalled:

Nancy thought of the agency as if it were a family. For some time she ran it like a Mom and Pop store. Then it got too big for that. Michael could have run the administrative side, but he was not disposed to. He may have been disappointed at finding himself playing second-fiddle; probably he had assumed that she would be Chairman in name and that he would really run the show. Anyway, he preferred the role of agency spokesman to that of administrator. When Nancy saw that the thing was getting away from her she tried to deal with the problem by bringing in people to do the administrative work. Michael thought these efforts undermined his position as Deputy. The program directors, meanwhile, laid claim to a great deal of independence.[15]

Leonard Garment did not offer policy advice, but he intervened vigorously and effectively when Nancy Hanks or Michael Straight asked for his help. They did so when it was necessary to appeal decisions of the Office of Management and Budget on appropriations ceilings, to fight off efforts of the White House patronage office or the Republican National Committee to foist unsuitable appointments on the agency, and—very rarely—when the NEA was caught in a political bind (for example, when the American Film Institute planned to bring *Milhous,* a documentary produced by Michelangelo Antonioni that was highly critical of President Nixon, to the institute's theater).

Nancy Hanks had a feel for political reality and did not need much help with Congress. She dealt mostly with eight or ten members—committee chairmen, House and Senate leaders (House Minority Leader Gerald Ford was one), and one or two others—on whose interest and goodwill she could depend. Important decisions were cleared with them. For example, Miss Hanks met at least twice in the corridors of the House with Minority Leader Gerald Ford to see how far he would go in support of higher appropriations authorizations; it was he who effectively set the ceilings by saying that he could not carry his party with him beyond some agreed-upon figure. Miss Hanks saw to it that the constituencies of the key congressional figures were not neglected in the distribution of grants. It was rare that one of the leaders took the initiative to offer advice, and when congressmen asked favors for particular constituents, she was usually unyielding.[16]

The NEA's policy changes accorded well with the fundamental political reality of congressmen supporting an agency that served some of their constituents. By taking credit for what federal agencies did for a specific group of constituents, an incumbent had a big advantage over a challenger. Agencies commonly helped in this by proposing new benefits and finding groups of constituents to demand and be grateful for them. It was common practice for agencies to create or foster interest groups that would work for their greater glory. This had to be done with circumspection, for the Office of Management and Budget, as well as an agency's opponents in Congress, could make trouble if it went beyond what were considered reasonable limits.

The NEA, however, had an unusually great degree of freedom to build constituencies; Congress had declared its purpose "to develop and promote a broadly conceived national policy." Nancy Hanks read this as an order to create a national constituency for federal support of the arts and, incidentally, for the NEA itself.[17] Thus, she did not hesitate to make grants for lobbying activities that other agencies would have supported covertly, if at all. The NEA subsidized the publications of numerous arts organizations; one, *Museum News*, produced a special how-to-do-it issue on influencing federal legislation: "We believe . . . that this issue will help you make your own Washington Connection," the issue stated.[18] The agency also issued its own bulletins and pamphlets, among them "Building a Local Base for Federal Arts Support" and "Artists and Schools," which urged congres-

75

sional action to provide space on income-tax forms for voluntary tax-deductible donations to support the arts in education, a measure it estimated might yield $1.7 billion annually.[19] For a time it published a newsletter to keep arts advocates informed of pending legislation, but pressure from the Office of Management and Budget forced a change into the monthly *Cultural Post,* which was devoted mainly to NEA affairs. When the Office of Management and Budget required that subscriptions be paid for, circulation dropped sharply.[20]

In 1974 an NEA grant enabled the National Assembly of State Arts Agencies to establish a Washington office as liaison between federal agencies and Congress. Almost from the beginning, the NEA had passed 20 percent of its annual appropriation on to the state arts agencies. When this grant was made, the state agencies, many of which were now also receiving more than token amounts from state legislatures, had become a strong and growing political force.

From its inception the NEA relied heavily upon panels of "outside experts" to review grant applications and to make recommendations on them. The composition of the panels changed somewhat from year to year. Formally, the chairman made all appointments; the actual procedure varied from panel to panel, but recommendations usually originated with program heads after consultation with their art constituencies; sometimes, however, panelists were proposed by members of existing panels. Straight reviewed the recommendations, generally adding a few names in order to "aerate" the panel, as he put it. Nancy Hanks's approval was pro forma. In later years the procedure was essentially the same.

The panel system helped to insulate the NEA from criticism. It could choose panelists who would not get far "out of line." At the same time, it could disarm critics by saying that decisions about art were made not by officials but by representatives of the art world, for panel recommendations concerning grant applications were always accepted, and those concerning other matters were almost always accepted. The system failed, however, to disarm critics of the cash awards program for individual artists. Some congressmen thought it outrageous that the NEA did not audit the artists' use of the money they were given. By contrast, Geldzahler thought it ridiculous even to think of auditing an artist's use of his grant money. Other congressmen were upset by the kind of art that the NEA favored. As much as anything else, awarding grants to individual artists had turned the House against the NEA in February 1969. Congressman John Ashbrook of Ohio had charged (what was undoubtedly true) that the NEA was rewarding avant-garde artists and discouraging traditional ones; that, he said, "is the exact same [thing as] government censorship."[21]

When Nancy Hanks replaced Roger Stevens in March 1969, Geldzahler resigned to allow her freedom to choose his successor. Straight, among others, advised her to end the program of grants to individual artists, which would now be easy with Geldzahler out of the picture. He maintained that art judgments could not be made fairly (comparing apples to pears was more plausible than comparing avant-garde to traditional art or, for that matter, one avant-garde work to another); moreover, the benefit to the few who got awards was problematic (what *did* they do with the money?), while the discouragement to the thousands who did not get them was indisputable. The proper role of the government, Straight thought, was to raise the general level of aesthetic awareness in the nation, not to pick and choose among artists. Senator Pell, who did not conceal his strong distaste for modern art, led Miss Hanks to believe that the NEA would have fewer critics in Congress if Geldzahler were replaced.[22]

Miss Hanks did replace Geldzahler, but she continued the program of grants to individual artists without reducing its emphasis on the innovative or, some would say, the extreme. As the new head of the Visual Arts Program, Brian O'Doherty, an artist who worked under the name of Patrick Ireland and a former critic for the *New York Times,* was as much committed as Geldzahler to experimental art. When O'Doherty was transferred to another program in 1981, his successor, James Melchert, a professor at the University of California, continued the policy of favoring artists who were, in his words, "involved in radical research into the nature of art."[23]

The Art in Public Places program Geldzahler had initiated also created public relations problems for the NEA (see chapter 7), but Miss Hanks was firm in her support of it, too. Some people wondered why she jeopardized the NEA's standing with programs that were certain to produce frequent uproars in the press and in Congress. The reason, perhaps, was that, like any agency head, she was willing to pay a high price to retain the respect and goodwill of that large part of the art world that regarded controversial programs as being the primary justification for the agency's existence. Not being an art "expert" herself, Miss Hanks was obliged to rely on the judgments of others who were. Unless she supported her professional advisers, the art world would soon cease to take her and the NEA seriously, and any outside interference would ruin the NEA.

It took great political skill to keep the support of Congress without losing that of the art world. The balancing act entailed costs, and these at times seemed excessive to some. Straight, for example, thought that Nancy Hanks was unduly concerned about New York opinion. "In its determination to keep abreast of every passing fad," he wrote while deputy chairman, "the Endowment has, through its awards, funded activities which I can only characterize as frivolous." His essential point of criticism of the visual arts programs, he said later, was that, while they appeared to support advanced elements in the visual arts world, they were—precisely because they moved with its predominant forces and trends— highly conservative:

Except for minor expenditures on "alternative spaces" for the exhibition of art works, the visual arts programs accepted the visual arts world as they found it. The values of this world, being based on scarcity, are wholly inimical to the idea, which should be basic for the Endowment, of bringing the best art to people, not in museums they can visit now and then, but in their homes.[24]

When the Carter administration took office, it was not taken for granted, as it is in the case of most appointments, that Nancy Hanks would be replaced. Some thought that the NEA, like the National Science Foundation, should be kept above politics. On the other hand, although almost all of Miss Hanks's associates were Democrats, she herself was a Republican, and thus, even though she was respected as an energetic administrator who got along well with the key figures in Congress, there were Democrats who thought her job should go to a Democrat.

The possibility that she might be reappointed was eliminated, however, when widespread opposition to her became manifest among the state and local arts councils. These had been made effectively independent of the NEA by the state legislatures, which now gave them more of the total money they received than the NEA did, and by Congress, which, acting contrary to Miss Hanks's recommendation, in 1973 made mandatory the allocation to the states of 20 percent of the NEA's appropriation.

Objections to Miss Hanks varied from state to state. Some state agency officials said she set unreasonable criteria for approval of state plans (the law required NEA approval of state plans as a condition of assistance), and tensions between some program directors and some state officials led to criticism of her. There was a jurisdictional fight over the Artists-in-School Program. But perhaps the most general complaint was that the NEA ignored requests from states and localities to participate in the formulation of programs that they administered while issuing unworkable guidelines.

She had responded by appointing a chairman and a director of a state arts council to each of her advisory panels. This attempt at appeasement did not satisfy the state agencies; in September 1977 they dramatized their discontent by asking Congress to take back funds that had been appropriated and allocated. Nancy Hanks, they charged, was trying to make the state and local agencies appendages of the NEA.

When it became known that the Carter administration intended to replace the chairmen of both endowments, there was alarm in New York City. "A specter is haunting the arts," wrote Hilton Kramer, the chief art critic of the *New York Times*. [25] There had occurred, he said, an "unholy meeting of minds" between Senator Pell and the White House, which had resulted in a memorandum to the search committee for a new humanities chairman, advising the committee to pay less attention to the "Ivy League, academic and scholarly establishments" and saying that the new chairman "should probably be familiar with organized labor, ethnic organizations, community and junior college organizations, and principal educational broadcasters, as well as more familiar nonacademic humanities groups like major research libraries."

It was fair to assume that the search committee for the NEA chairman was given similar instructions, but in fact this was not the case. The appointment went to Livingston Biddle, a Princeton graduate, Pell's old friend and legislative assistant. Biddle, who had played a part in drafting the 1965 bill and in the maneuvers leading to its passage, was supported vigorously by the chairman of the National Assembly of State Arts Agencies and by most of the state arts agencies. [26]

"It looks like a clean sweep for the anti-'elitist' forces," Kramer wrote of Biddle's appointment. [27] "Elitists" were those who, fearing what Russell Lynes had called "creeping mediocrity," [28] wanted government support only for work that met the highest standards of excellence. "Anti-elitists" —or more commonly, "populists"—defined art much more inclusively, found works or performances of little or no artistic merit nevertheless worthwhile on extra-aesthetic ("public service") grounds, and were willing to accept a considerable lowering of standards in order to bring art to the people.

Some so-called populists thought that the elitist-populist distinction concealed the real issue, which they perceived as being an effort by a small closed circle of self-appointed cultural arbiters to monopolize affairs. Pell, for example, was irked when federally appointed chairmen of state humanities agencies decided to reappoint themselves. He was further irked by their failure to do what would get popular support for the cause to which his own prestige was so closely tied.

The alarm over the possibility that the NEA would take a populist direction was surprising: that had always been the thrust of Nancy Hanks's administration. Whether because she agreed with Straight that the NEA could justify its existence only by bringing the arts to the masses or because she wanted to enlarge and strengthen her organization, Miss Hanks supported not only "real" art but also whatever could be made to pass for art. She had put a ceiling of $155,000 on grants to large organizations and made it a cardinal principle to distribute grants widely. She had encouraged the proliferation of outreach programs to meet the demand, or needs, of groups that were "neglected." A resolution passed in 1973 by the National Council on the Arts, if not on her initiative, certainly with her approval, was undiluted populism: "The arts are a right, not a privilege . . . no citizen should be deprived of the beauty and insights into the human experience that only the arts can impart."[29]

All this was well known to those who raised the fuss about populism. Kramer, for example, acknowledged that a great deal of money had always been wasted on programs that had no other claim to existence than political necessity. "Everyone in the field affected knows this to be true," he wrote, "but it is politically convenient never to speak of it openly."[30] Presumably, he meant that during Miss Hanks's administration elitists like himself had kept quiet about the waste of money on bad art and nonart for fear of jeopardizing an enterprise that they thought supported enough good art to justify its existence. With Biddle in charge, Kramer apparently thought, the movement in the populist direction would leave nothing worth saving.

Biddle, who took office at the end of November 1977, displayed the wisdom of Solomon when the press pushed him to take a stand on the elitism-versus-populism issue. He favored, he said, "a balanced equation—I'd say a 50–50 division of resources—so that large institutions are allowed to develop further, and arts-outreach programs in the cities and communities can be advanced."[31]

Like others before him, Biddle talked much of the NEA's "catalytic" function, suggesting that the mere presence of the NEA somehow activated forces that would otherwise remain inert. Actually, NEA officials had always labored hard to stir up interest in the arts and to establish organizations that would promote and support the arts and the NEA. Nancy Hanks and Livingston Biddle both thought advocacy to be one of the agency's most important functions. Advocacy, however, was not the same as funding. Some of the programs that critics considered populist—Special Constituencies, for example—involved much advocacy but little funding.

Despite NEA's ever-expanding interest in activities that elitists considered at best marginal to its proper mission, there was remarkably little change over the years in the share of the budget that went to the various programs. This was documented by James Backas, a former executive director of the American Arts Alliance, in response to a *New York Times* editorial that charged the NEA with spending less and less on solid programs like "grants to artists, writers, and composers" and support of "leading cultural institutions" and more and more on politically inspired programs such as Expansion Arts.[32] Backas compared the NEA's spending in fiscal 1978 (Biddle's first year in office) and in 1981 by "clusters" of programs. (See table 3.1.)

TABLE 3.1

Comparison of NEA Spending by Clusters of Programs, Fiscal Years 1978 and 1981 (in millions of dollars) *

Program	1978	1981
Cluster 1		
Dance	$ 6.9	$ 9.0
Museums	11.5	13.0
Music	10.3	16.2
Opera/Musical Theater	3.9	6.2
Theater	6.2	10.7
Literature	3.7	4.8
Visual Arts	4.9	7.4
Media Arts	8.2	12.4
Cluster Total	55.6 (72.7%)	79.7 (74.7%)
Cluster 2		
Education	5.1	5.0
Design	3.9	5.2
Expansion Arts	7.2	8.6
Folk Arts	1.9	3.0
Special Projects	3.3	5.7
Special Constituencies	—	.4
Cluster Total	21.4 (28%)	27.9 (26%)
Cluster 3		
Research	.5	1.2
Evaluation	.2	.3
Partnership Coordination	—	.6
International Fellows	—	.4
Cluster Total	.7 (1%)	2.5 (2%)
Total Regular Program Funds	$ 77.7	$ 110.1

*The total percentages are of regular program funds: they therefore exclude the 20 percent of appropriations mandated by Congress to go to the states as well as administration costs. Challenge grants, most of which were awarded to major art institutions in both years, are also excluded.
Source: Adapted from James Backas, "Guest Column," in Fraser Barron, *Government & the Arts* (Washington, D.C., January 1981), p. 8.

President Carter intended to expand the government's place in the world of art. Promotion of the arts was a White House interest, which was reflected by the energy and enthusiasm for the arts of Joan Mondale, the wife of Vice-

President Walter Mondale. A former docent and the author of a children's book on art, Mrs. Mondale was "knowledgeable" without being an "expert." She became honorary chairman of the Federal Council on the Arts and the Humanities, a body composed of the chairmen of the two endowments and twelve other high government officials who had been authorized under the 1965 act to coordinate agency activities; the council, which had hitherto been almost entirely inactive, held a public meeting—its first—in June 1978 with Mrs. Mondale at the head of the table and Joseph Duffey, its real chairman, seated beside her on the left. With a staff of six, she used the council to prod agencies having "cultural programs"—the Veterans Administration, for example—into greater activity. Having no formal authority, she could not, like Nelson Rockefeller, August Heckscher, and Leonard Garment, write official reports. However, her access to the White House was greater than theirs, for her husband was a dependable backer. Cabinet agencies now found it expedient to have staff advisers on the arts.

In the first months of the Carter administration, Mrs. Mondale presided over an informal "Tuesday Morning Club," consisting of her friend Mary Ann Tighe (a member of the Hirschhorn Museum's staff until her elevation to arts adviser to the Office of the Vice-President), her executive assistant, a member of the Presidential Personnel Office, a deputy counsel to the vice-president, and two other White House staff members. The club's discussions soon led to the conclusion that a comprehensive plan for government action was needed to raise the cultural life of the nation. As a first step, conferences of cultural leaders would be called in every state. The conferees would study papers prepared by task forces of specialists, hold discussions, and make recommendations. Then there would be held a White House conference to formulate agreement for a program of action, which would be presented to the president and then, by him, to Congress.

A joint resolution authorizing the president to call a White House conference on the arts was introduced in Congress early in 1977 and reported with amendments a year later.[33] Its principal sponsors were the chairmen of the legislative subcommittees that dealt with the arts, Senator Pell, and Representative John Brademas, a Democrat from Indiana and a former Rhodes scholar, who had taken Frank Thompson's place as the principal arts advocate in the House. (Thompson, although still an activist on behalf of the arts, had moved on to another committee.)

Unfortunately, now that the key pieces of legislation were in place, the importance of the legislative committees was much diminished, and the appropriations committees were now more important. Because appropriations bills originated in the House, its subcommittee on the Interior Department and Related Agencies, headed by Sidney R. Yates, a Democrat, who had long held a safe seat in a "lakefront liberal" district of Chicago, was the most important. Although Yates probably knew and cared as much about the arts as anyone in Congress (he attended the symphony, the opera, and the theater and collected on a modest scale contemporary paintings and sculpture), he had been more or less ignored by the arts advocates, who had lavished their attention on Pell and Brademas.

Embarrassment was not confined to the Tuesday Morning Club when Yates served notice that he would not permit the NEA to support a White House Conference from its appropriations. On the recommendation of the Office of Management and Budget, President Carter had said there would be no conference, and then, after conferring with the vice-president, he had changed his mind; now he was obliged to reverse himself yet again.

Yates was not opposed to cultural planning, but his patience had been tried by the NEA's failure to respond to his efforts to get it to plan. When Nancy Hanks and her assistants first came before him, he had asked questions that they could not answer; the information, they promised, would be supplied, but very little was. When she appeared the next spring, still without the answers he wanted, Yates showed some exasperation. The following year, he told her, the NEA was to present the committee with a five-year plan.

In 1979 it was Biddle who appeared before Yates and his committee. He brought with him both a "Statement of the National Council on the Arts on the Goals and Basic Policy of the National Endowment" and a draft (which did not become part of the hearing record) of a "General Plan, 1980–1984." Biddle had set up a planning process that would "hold up to the country a vision that will inspire the arts world."[34] To create this vision, he had appointed a deputy chairman for policy and planning (P. David Searles, a management consultant Miss Hanks had brought into the agency), a director of policy development (Philip M. Kadis, a *Washington Star* reporter who covered cultural affairs), and a deputy chairman for programs (Mary Ann Tighe). These three drafted a statement to be approved by a Committee on Policy and Planning created within the National Council on the Arts. The statement was brief and its language very general. "The goal of the Endowment," it said, "is the fostering of professional excellence of the arts in America, to nurture and sustain them, and equally to help create a climate in which they may flourish so they may be experienced and enjoyed by the widest possible public." It went on to list five objects for support: individual creativity, institutional creativity, preservation of our living artistic heritage, making the arts available, and leadership and advocacy on behalf of the arts. The General Plan, 150 pages long, contained discussions of the state of the arts, issues facing the NEA, program priorities, operational planning and implementation, and funding estimates. These matters were treated in the manner of an annual report, the urgency and wisdom of all the agency's actions being taken for granted.

Yates liked the statement, but this did not prevent him

from taking the opportunity to amuse himself and the spectators at a committee hearing. The NEA, he read aloud, would foster "the living heritage to preserve the birthright of present and future generations of Americans by supporting the best of all art forms which reflect the American heritage in its full range of cultural and ethnic diversity. . . ." Yates asked for a fuller explanation:

Ms. Tighe	The finest examples of various art forms ranging from classical ballet . . .
Mr. Yates	In trouble immediately. Can you tell the Committee what the finest example of abstract expression is?
Mr. Biddle	That is why we have the panels, Mr. Chairman.
Mr. Yates	I see.
Mr. Biddle	The best access to the best of quality.
Mr. Yates	How do you know you have the best?
Ms. Tighe	Fortunately, we don't have to take a single example of abstract art. But I think we are saying there are certain works that are of a higher quality than others, when we are talking about the art forms where they might be lost.
Mr. Yates	The highest quality of Rothko, the best art forms of expression.
Ms. Tighe	Again I think there are all kinds of subsets of things under each individual art form. But yet . . .
Mr. Yates	The thing that caught my eye is how you are going to implement that. It's going to be a very tough thing to implement because who is going to say which is the best of all art forms?

Ms. Tighe acknowledged that implementing it would not be easy. Yates then took up a question he found "very intriguing":

Mr. Yates	. . . You propose to make the arts available to insure that all Americans ". . . have a true opportunity to make an informed and educated choice to have the arts of high quality touch their lives so that no person is deprived of access to the arts by reason of geography, of inadequate income, of inadequate education,

of physical and mental handicaps, social or cultural patterns, unresponsive to the various ethnic group needs. . . ." How are you going to carry that out?

Mr. Searles   This is a statement of an idea. I wish we could say in a foreseeable future we would be able to carry that out fully. We certainly feel that we must continually strive towards those ends.

Mr. Biddle   I think, Mr. Chairman, that the two, if I could summarize . . .

Mr. Yates   Let me ask a question at this point. Is this the function of the National Endowment for the Arts?

Mr. Searles   I think it is a function.

Mr. Yates   How does it relate to the government? It is a goal, I suppose. But you are a long way from the goal, I suggest. I don't know whether it is attainable.

When he came to a section on leadership, Yates asked if this was a national policy. (The NEA would provide leadership "through advocacy and cooperation with other governmental agencies, through advocacy with private institutions to stimulate increasing support for the arts from the private sector, through exploration of effective ways in which the arts may be used to desirable social ends, and through enlargement of the public's knowledge, understanding and appreciation of the arts.") Biddle replied that the arts have "desirable social benefits." By way of illustration he told of visiting a place in Houston, Texas, that had been started as a health clinic but, when it was realized that the most important problem was not health but "what you do with the human spirit," had been turned into a small arts program. After this the truancy rate of a school next door dropped from 85 to 15 percent.

Mr. Yates   I wonder whether we should explore truancy. You are going to wind up with something like Vietnam or some other national goal.

Mr. Biddle   I do not think necessarily that the elimination of truancy was the point. The point was that through the arts, young people were becoming interested in education.

Mr. Yates   Perhaps you will find the kind of social ends you want to reach. I had some trouble with that one.[35]

Apparently, Yates was satisfied that the NEA now had a plan; at any rate, he did not refer to the subject again.

The effort to plan had generated irritation and disappointment within the NEA, and when the pressure ceased, so did the planning. The irritation was on the part of the program directors, who felt that planning reduced flexibility, which Kadis defined as the "opportunity to act on whims," and that they had not been given a large enough part in the planning process.[36] The disappointment was mainly on the part of Searles and Kadis, who concluded that the program directors would never view policy from an agency rather than a program perspective or accept direction or guidance.

It would be impossible within the current structure of the NEA to think three or four years ahead or to raise questions that the art world considered settled. Biddle would have had to tear the agency to pieces and rebuild it in order to get serious discussion of alternatives to present practice. Searles left the agency in 1980 for a better job. Kadis requested a transfer to another position because he thought the planning a waste of time and because Biddle, for whom he had a high personal regard, would not take the steps necessary to get the program directors to give up their autonomy.

Donald H. Moore, Searles's successor as deputy chairman for policy and planning, accepted the realities of the situation. In his contribution to the NEA's 1980 annual report he spoke of the need to clarify the endowment's daily operations and its goals.[37] Members of the National Council complained to Biddle that too much time was spent on budgeting and internal management and that the agency was growing "by accretion." Biddle assured them that a sense of vision would soon emerge.[38]

When President Reagan took office, there was reason to expect that he would try to end federal subsidy of the arts.

89

During and immediately after his campaign there were inti-mations that he did not consider their support a proper func-tion of the federal government. Returning to the states the activities that the Constitution reserved for them was an objective close to his heart—even closer, one of his associates said, than budget cuts.[39]

The Reagan administration proposed cutting the NEA budget for fiscal 1982 to $88 million (from $159 million in fiscal 1981).[40] This provoked Congressman Yates to charge that the Reagan administration was bent upon the destruc-tion of both endowments. Aram Bakshian, a White House spokesman, denied this; the intention, he said, was to in-crease voluntary support of the arts and to minimize "the impact of what we've got now, an almost unholy trinity of foundation bureaucrats, government bureaucrats, and cul-ture bureaucrats."[41]

In May 1981 President Reagan appointed a thirty-six-member Presidential Task Force on the Arts and the Humanities. "Our cultural institutions," he announced, "are an essential national resource: they must be kept strong." He was "sympathetic to the very real needs of our cultural or-ganizations" and hoped that in three months the task force would present him with a plan to make better use of existing federal resources and to increase support for the arts and the humanities by the private sector.

Nothing in the charge precluded the task force from recommending the liquidation of the endowments and the complete withdrawal of the federal government from the cultural scene. Yet Reagan's appointments to the task force made it clear that this was not his intention. With perhaps three or four exceptions (myself among them), those ap-pointed had long-standing business or professional commit-ments to the arts; some had been closely associated with the NEA: Roger Stevens, Henry Geldzahler, Nancy Hanks, Charlton Heston (a former member of the National Council on the Arts), and Hannah Gray (president of the University

90

of Chicago and a consultant to both endowments). While accepting the president's insistence on budget cuts, almost all of the members wanted to minimize any reduction of subsidy to the arts.

In view of its size, composition, and limited time to work, it was impossible for the task force to examine any large question in depth. It wasted no time asking what was meant by "the arts" or why government should subsidize them. This, however, did not prevent it from declaring, "There is a clear public purpose in supporting the arts and humanities: the preservation and advancement of America's pluralistic cultural and intellectual heritage, the encouragement of creativity, the stimulation of quality in American education, and the enhancement of our general well-being."[42]

The president accepted the report at a White House lunch attended by leading figures in the areas of culture, corporate patronage, and bureaucracy (the "unholy trinity"). He then announced the appointment of Frank S. M. Hodsoll as the new chairman of the NEA. Hodsoll, a former foreign service officer who had served in the Ford administration, was then deputy assistant to the president. It was highly unlikely that he would have been offered, or would have accepted, the appointment if the administration's intention were to diminish the agency.[43]

CHAPTER

4

Art versus the Museum

I have gloomy visions of a future museum in which the contents of Aladdin's cave will have been removed to the storeroom, and all that will be left will be an authentic lamp from the period of the Arabian Nights with a large diagram beside it, explaining how oil lamps worked, where the wick was inserted and what was the average burning time.
—E. H. Gombrich[1]

VIEWED from every standpoint but one, the American art museum is an astonishing achievement.* A little more than a century ago there were no great works of art to be seen in this country. Now there are a half dozen collections that rival any in the world and at least another dozen that are not far from doing so.

*As used in this chapter, "art museum" refers only to the general museum serving a national or large regional public.

Art versus the Museum

There are about two hundred art museums with operating budgets of $250,000 or more, many of them world-famous, specializing in some form or period of art (e.g., the Museum of Modern Art) or adjuncts of teaching institutions (e.g., the Fogg Art Museum at Harvard) or of business or philanthropic organizations (e.g., the Barnes Foundation in Philadelphia).[2] The range and variety of art museums in the United States are so great that it is almost impossible to deal with them as a single entity. The difficulty is reduced, but by no means eliminated, by concentrating on large, general art museums. They, too, are all different in important respects, but for the present these differences will be overlooked.

Unlike its European counterpart, which is owned and operated by national governments, the American art museum is a not-for-profit corporation that is subsidized by local, state, and national governments (mainly by gifts of land and tax exemptions) but receives most of its support from private sources and is run by a self-perpetuating board of trustees.

The one standpoint from which the museum is not an astonishing achievement is the artistic. If the proper function of an art museum is to collect and display works of art and, beyond that, to make the experience of art more widely and intensely felt, then the art museum has failed.[3] Although it has afforded countless moments of aesthetic enjoyment to countless viewers, it has mainly misrepresented the nature of art, put obstacles in the way of experiencing it, and encouraged the substitution of pecuniary and curiosity values for aesthetic ones. Because it has so long been the principal intermediary between visual art and the public, the art museum must bear much responsibility for widespread confusion about the nature of art.

The achievements and the failures of the art museum are for the most part incidental consequences of the adaptations it has made to changing circumstances in order to maintain itself as an organization and to grow in size and prestige. However incompatible this may be with the avowed purposes of the art museum, which seem to those in charge most likely to ensure its maintenance and growth, there is deep antagonism between organizational concerns and the aesthetic mission.

The art museum was founded soon after the Civil War as part of a long struggle by the Protestant elite, which ran the large cities, to moralize their populations by eliminating vice and inculcating the domestic and civic virtues. (The Metropolitan Museum of Art was founded in 1870, the Boston Museum of Fine Arts in 1870, the Pennsylvania Museum and School of Industrial Arts in 1876, and the Art Institute of Chicago in 1879.) In the early decades of the nineteenth century, the reformers, concentrating on the suppression of vice, especially drunkenness and prostitution, had relied mainly on direct action by preachers and police officers. With the rapid growth of the cities, the futility of these efforts became apparent.

Meanwhile, many of the elite, returning from European tours (it was estimated in 1873 that some 25,000 tourists visited Europe annually), attributed the orderliness of the London and Paris crowds to the civilizing influence of parks, art galleries, and other such amenities. The strategy of the reformers shifted from direct action to environmental improvement. To Frederick Law Olmsted, a trustee of the Metropolitan Museum as well as one of the designers of Central Park, "public parks, gardens, galleries of art and instruction in art, music, athletic sports, and healthful recreations" were all "means of cultivating taste."[4]

In midcentury, David D. Hall has written, American reformers, most of whom were of Puritan ancestry and many of whom were Unitarians, found kindred spirits among English intellectuals who, like most of themselves, were struggling to find a source of "truth" other than by revelation; they thought of themselves as the vanguard of a new cultural system that would replace the authority of the church with universities and that people like themselves would give intellectual and moral leadership to the masses. The problem of the times, these reformers thought, was "the lack of *habits* of discipline"; accordingly, they "sought to impose upon society an ethic of respect for quality, an ethic of deference to 'the best.' "[5] Cultural institutions were a way of doing this.

The nature of art, as it was most often experienced in the nineteenth century, gave plausibility to these expectations. Art was beauty and truth combined. It existed, Emerson said, to make men better.[6] Art reminded men of their common humanity; it drew them closer to one another and to the values that gave their lives meaning. Because it inspired men to honor their heroes and to love their native land, it was also a support of republican institutions.

The founders of art museums were men of modest wealth. In its initial subscription drive (1870–71) the Metropolitan Museum of Art raised only $106,000; of 106 subscribers, one gave $10,000, two gave $5,000, the rest averaged $825 each. "This state of things is very disappointing," the trustees remarked in the museum's second annual report. "[W]hat makes it more surprising and more sad," they said, "is that in a much shorter period than that during which these appeals have been pending here, $210,000 have been raised in Boston." Most of the Metropolitan's twenty-one elective and six ex-officio trustees contributed $1,000 or more to the subscription.[7]

Like Olmsted, the founders believed that what elevated popular taste improved civilization. The purpose of the Metropolitan, its Organizing Committee declared, was to afford "to our whole people free and ample means for innocent and refined enjoyment, and also supplying the best facilities for the cultivation of pure taste in all matters connected with the arts." Inspired by the example of the South Kensington Museum, which Prince Albert had established with leftovers from the Great Exhibition in the Crystal Palace in 1851, the founders attached as much importance to the practical, or applied, arts as to the fine arts: improving the design of locally manufactured products would both have a civilizing effect and enable workmen and manufacturers to compete in world markets. Even in Boston, where the founders put the words "fine arts" in the name of their museum, the object of general cultivation, C. C. Perkins, the principal figure among them, said, was not less important than improvement in industrial art, which would have advantageous action upon trade through the development of systematic technical education.[8] The art museum was also an exercise in civic boosterism. A report to the Metropolitan's Executive Committee quoted James Jackson Jarves, a collector of early Italian paintings: ". . . were one of our towns to own a great museum, visitors would flock thither from all parts of the union in such numbers as would soon repay its outlay."[9]

But even as the foundations of the art museum were being dug, its main purpose was being undercut by the spread of new ideas about the nature of art. The doctrines of Ruskin, for whom beauty, truth, and goodness were all one, were challenged by Walter Pater and other romanticists, for whom art existed "for its own sake" and had nothing to do with truth or morality. In 1871 Perkins declared that art was not the "servant" of morality and religion but their "noble ally," whose beauty served to "stimulate the soul, awaken its highest faculties to life, and thus lead it through the finite to the Infinite."[10] Probably, he wished to avoid offending the remaining Ruskinians (especially Harvard's powerful professor of fine arts, Charles Eliot Norton, Ruskin's great friend and admirer). He meant, however, that the proper function of art was not the moralization of society or the strengthening of the social bond.

Possibly by coincidence, when the conception of art changed, the art museum passed from the hands of the solid citizens who had founded it to those who could fill it with great works of art, the enormously rich. J. P. Morgan, for example, became president of the Metropolitan in 1904. For this new elite the museum was not a means of cultivating the public's taste but of storing and displaying rare and costly objects: a "depository of grandeur," as Nathaniel Burt has put it so well.[11] For the purposes of the founders, plaster casts and copies served in place of originals. "Copies of very important pictures," an early report to the Executive Committee of the Metropolitan said, "painted by artists for their own instruction, may be counted upon as of high value; they are few, but precious. The small costs of reproductions by mechanical processes may be thought to put them within reach of the Museum. . . ."

When the very rich, who were buying the treasures of Europe by the boatload, took control of the art museum, there was no place in it for things that would not contribute to its grandeur or do credit to its possessors. (Morgan once refused to look at an old master priced at $12,000 on the grounds that he did not buy cheap pictures.) Thousands of casts were disposed of; they were of no use when the purpose of the art museum was to accumulate and display what was rare and costly. In Boston a great row displaced the education-minded management along with its casts. The new regime proclaimed as its guiding principle: "Joy, not knowledge."[12]

Having become a depository of grandeur, the art museum required a building of appropriate size and style. One designed specifically for art at the Centennial Exhibition in Philadelphia in 1876 "ushered in a new pomposity," according to Joshua Taylor. "Art was to be celebrated, and with it the people who collected it. For the next fifty years art museums would resemble noble palaces, usually in a kind of seventeenth-century classical style with a heavy French accent." The imposing character of the art museum building "spelled permanence, selectivity, and discreet withdrawal from surrounding urban activity."[13]

By the twentieth century the art museum took little interest in the applied arts. It had long been evident that manufacturers could learn nothing from displays of industrial art. "What use is this rubbish to our manufacturers?" Lord Palmerston had asked when he viewed a collection purchased for the South Kensington Museum.[14] What the ordinary man might learn from viewing common but well-designed objects did not matter to an art museum devoted to the extraordinary. The art museum was widening the gap between fine art and the minor arts. The decorative arts, however, were made welcome under a principle of "joy, not knowledge" because they were the accessories of wealth and power. Applied arts, on the other hand, were of little interest. When it acquired great collections first of decorative and then of fine arts, the Pennsylvania Museum and School of Industrial Arts disposed of most of its exhibits and changed its name to the Philadelphia Museum of Art. The Metropolitan, whose articles of incorporation pledged it to collect and display all "industrial, educative or recreative" arts, did not have an exhibition of industrial art until 1915.[15]

The greater its achievement as a depository of grandeur, the more peripheral the art museum became as an exponent of aesthetic values. Munificent gifts in 1913 from J. P. Morgan, Benjamin Altman, and William R. Riggs made the Metropolitan "the equal of any major museum in Europe," wrote Germain Bazin.[16] In the same year, America was introduced by the Armory Show to a mode of aesthetic experience (the transcendental) that asserted that much of the art museum's contents, including some of its most prized possessions, were not art at all. Within a few years this new mode of aesthetic experience would dominate the art world.

Whether the museum was truly an "art" museum became increasingly open to question. The founders' mode of aesthetic experience (that called ideational in chapter 1) was intellectual as well as sensual: that objects made reference to historical events, to literature and philosophy, and of course to mythology and religion, contributed to their beauty. So long as this was the prevailing mode of aesthetic experience, it was not anomalous to display objects that appealed mainly to the mind along with others that appealed mainly to the eye. When art came to be responded to simply, or mainly, for form and style, much that had been admired, no longer was. Still more objects ceased to be admired when the aesthetic experience became intense, disinterested contemplation; for those who responded in this way, historical associations—that the object was seven hundred years old and had belonged to a famous queen—were irrelevant or, worse, distracting. "There seems to be an impression in America that art is fed on the history of art, and what is found in museums," George Santayana wrote in 1922, "But museums are mausoleums, only dead art is there."[17]

Even for those who experienced art in the ideational mode, much of the art in the museum was, if not "dead," then not "living" either. Objects stripped from the context for which they had been made—taken from an altar and put behind a pane of glass—could not be responded to as the artist had intended. Now and then the art museum tried to put objects back in context by creating galleries or period rooms. This was highly impractical: the room could not be lighted in the manner of the period, precious objects could not be properly protected, labeling was obtrusive, and viewers could not circulate freely. Such efforts were bound to fail, for putting pieces back together physically could not put them back together aesthetically. As André Malraux remarks in *Voices of Silence:*

[E]very work surviving from the past has been deprived of something—to begin with, the setting of its age. The work of sculpture used to lord it in a temple, a street or a reception-room. All these are lost to it. Even if the reception-room is "reconstructed" in a museum, even if the statue has kept its place in the portal of its cathedral, the town which surrounded the reception-room or cathedral has changed. There is no getting round the banal truth that for thirteenth-century man Gothic was "modern," and the Gothic world a present reality, not a phase of history; once we replace faith by love of art, little does it matter if a cathedral chapel is reconstituted in a museum, stone by stone, for we have begun by converting our cathedrals into museums. Could we bring ourselves to feel what the first spectators of an Egyptian statue, or a Romanesque crucifixion, felt, we would make haste to remove them from the Louvre.[18]

The art museum, therefore, could not help but be a mausoleum. And the affinity of the rich for what was rare and costly, while it brought into being great collections of art that remained alive for most viewers, also made the museum a mausoleum for much that could only be called relics. In the United States, the art historian, whether he liked it or not, was often a purchasing agent for rich collectors, for whom it was critical to know whether a painting was the untouched work of a master or a studio piece by one of his assistants. Inevitably, the art museum was staffed and managed by art historians. Many curators, no doubt, were acutely sensitive to aesthetic values, but their training was in the history of art, not art itself, which caused some of them to treat as important what was really historically interesting. In the obituary of Alpheus Hyatt Mayor, a curator of prints at the Metropolitan, was paid this tribute: "He could look at, say, a 17th-century French engraving of a lute player and not only tell you what the lute derived from but the specific compositions made for it in that era."[19]

In the 1920s and 1930s, according to Laurence Coleman, art museums came "to recognize what they owe to history—the duty of portraying the culture of peoples through their arts." About twenty museums acquired large collections of the decorative arts of the past: ceramics, enamels, metal work and glass, textiles and costumes, woodwork, and furniture. Accepting this duty, Coleman remarked, "is to subordinate the history of painting or sculpture to the history of man as revealed through these expressions."[20] It also involved the broadening of collections and the addition of new categories: the arts of Egypt, Greece, Rome, the Near East, the Far East, and Europe in the Middle Ages, the Renaissance, and modern times. "An art museum is usually thought of as a gallery for the display of masterpieces," wrote Francis Henry Taylor, the director of the Metropolitan (which had built a decorative arts wing in 1910 and renamed it the Pierpont Morgan Wing in 1918), "But possibly we should think of it as a visual reference collection of cultural history."[21]

There was practically nothing—certainly nothing precious—that the art museum did not accept as a duty to acquire. The more it acquired, the greater its prestige and, by extension, that of its benefactors, directors, and curators. It soon came to have more than it could ever possibly display. John Coolidge calculated in 1953 that to display all of the Boston Museum's 300,000 prints would require 6,000 galleries—a structure about twenty times the size of the Metropolitan. And the Print Department, of course, was only one of many.[22] These calculations were telling, even taking into account (what Coolidge did not) that prints could be exhibited no more than six weeks a year without being damaged by exposure to light.

It cost the art museum less to accept a gift it did not want than to decline it: storage room could always be found and it was foolish to risk offending a donor who might eventually give something valuable.[23] To be sure, the art museum committed itself morally and, usually legally, to preserve and, often, to display what it was given. The code of ethics of the Association of Art Museum Directors stressed that any deaccessioning of works "should be related to policy rather than to the exigencies of the moment, and funds obtained through disposal *must* be used to replenish the collection." (Emphasis added.)[24] The costs of preserving things lay mostly in the future, and the art museum, like other organizations, did not look far ahead. Having more "priceless treasures" than it could store, let alone display, would justify eventual expansion of building and staff, and the cost would be largely borne by state and local taxpayers in gifts of land, money for buildings (it has been estimated that state and local governments have provided 40 percent of the cost of museum buildings[25]), and tax exemptions. That so many precious objects should be forever buried in some of the most valuable land of the great cities would be inexplicable but for the fact that the museums did not bear the costs.

To many of the rich, collecting was a fascinating game. The art historian gave it the status of a scholarly activity, making it easy for the art museum to join in the game. As E. H. Gombrich has remarked, the idea of a collection implies a built-in need for expansion, something not implied by a treasure house or a shrine.[26] If instead of 300,000 prints the art museum had 600,000, there would still be gaps in its collection. The value of the collection for scholarly purposes depends largely upon its size, the theory being that a developmental process can only be understood by examining every influence that might have affected it. This is presumably the justification for a print collection that includes not only an impression of every plate produced by certain British artists but also "complete runs of trial proofs and 'states.' "[27]

Obviously, collecting can be pushed to the point of absurdity. In fact, the great contributions to art history have not depended upon the completeness of particular collections. Moreover, the art museum, whose collections have never been fully catalogued or described, has never been an important sponsor of scholarship, and some think that it ought not to be.

If the natural alliance between the collector and the curator trained as an art historian has tended to encourage accumulation, it has also tended to subordinate artistic value in order not to jeopardize the integrity of the collection. All too often the art museum preferred filling a gap to collecting good art that did not fit a collection. It has often displayed things that belong together from an historical standpoint even when that has entailed putting them where what is artistically best is hard to find and perhaps even harder to experience as art.

102

The same alliance has tended to value old master paintings according to criteria that are more antiquarian than aesthetic. A painting, George Savage explains, falls in esteem and market value if it is reassigned from a higher to a lower category on the following scale—this "although it is still the same picture and no worse for the change of label":

(1) The untouched work of a master.
(2) Partly by his hand, the remainder the work of pupils or assistants.
(3) Studio-piece, painted in the style of a master by an assistant.
(4) School-piece, painted by an independent artist of lesser stature influenced by the master.
(5) Contemporary replica executed either as a studio-piece, or by another artist.[28]

To the art museum, the collector, and the art historian, a picture belonging to the last category is not art, no matter how great its aesthetic value. Art museums, by the definition of the museum profession, are "institutions with *original* works of art." (Emphasis added.)[29]

Although in the early twentieth century the art museum overflowed with precious and wonderful things and admission was usually free, one could walk almost alone through its miles of galleries. Of the museum-goers, most were upper-class women; working-class people went elsewhere. The art museum, as a "depository of grandeur," had little appeal to the general public.

Of the few voices that called for an art museum that would attract and serve the general public, the most articulate belonged to John Cotton Dana. An enterprising Vermonter who, after a spell as a librarian, became the director of the newly established Newark Museum in 1913, Dana was a populist par excellence. In his opinion, the art museum was in all respects the opposite of what it should be. In four small books published at his own expense, he gave a Veblenesque critique of it: Private collectors had selected and purchased its contents; beguiled by European examples, they had chosen objects not for their beauty or for their use in cultivating good taste, but their rarity, their likeness to those that European museums contained, and their cost. They had bought original paintings, however atrocious, in preference to copies, however excellent. As with racehorses and yachts, he wrote, one of the attractions of "great" paintings, for example, is that only the very rich can have them. "A copy of a great painting, even though it be so perfect that at a distance of a few feet not one person in ten thousand can tell that it is a copy, is looked upon as a dangerous foe of art and as an almost blasphemous tour-de-force."[30]

The rich had housed their collections in buildings made to look like Greek temples or Renaissance palaces; they had placed the buildings in outlying parks that were hard for the working class to reach, and they kept them closed during most of the hours ordinary people were not at work. The collections, Dana acknowledged, "deserved safe-keeping and even a certain veneration," but to do so did not necessitate museums: "The zeal of the rich for the acquisitions of the honorific in art will assure us that ample care and thought and money will be given to these things." That without the art museum the public would not see the collections did not trouble him. He doubted "the assumed beneficial effect of a sight of an Egyptian tomb or a Greek vase" and believed too much emphasis was given to pictures. "The picture assails us everywhere," he wrote. "[W]hat are all these worth to us? Are they to prove altogether helpful or in some degree harmful?"[31]

Dana described a "truly public" art museum as one fully and generously supported by the city government and serving the whole public. In place of rare and costly paintings and decorative objects (". . . the stigmata of civility and not the causes thereof"), it would collect and display the products of men and women of its own time and place—pots and pans, as well as paintings—in order to "discover possibilities of agreeable emotions in the contemplation of common things" and "to bring forth men and women who can produce helpful and pleasure-giving works of art."[32] In the Newark Museum, Dana displayed well-designed objects of everyday use —a roomful of bathtubs on one occasion; on another pottery, which the viewer discovered was bought in local five-and-ten-cent stores. Sometimes he brought artisans to the museum to demonstrate their craft.[33]

Needless to say, Dana's vision of the truly public art museum, which had no place for the collector or the art historian, had no effect on the real art museum, whose trustees and curators were content to serve the few, especially since serving the many would entail sharing control of the art museum with elected officials—politicians. They were mindful, however, that it would be dangerous for the art museum to let its claim to being a public-service institution lapse; it had always depended on state and local government for support and would like to have had more. This was a reason for free admissions. It was also a reason for deliberately inflating the count of those who passed through the turnstiles. (This was the practice of the Metropolitan Museum and of the National Gallery for many years. When the Metropolitan's trustees demanded an accurate count, attendance dropped from over six million to under three million. John Walker stopped the overcounting at the National Gallery when he became its director. This was a foolish move, he wrote in his memoirs, for "my budget deservedly became more difficult to defend.")[34]

The magic word to keep the art museum safely within the realm of the public interest, in spite of (or because of) the public's lack of interest in the museum, was "education." Insofar as it made itself an adjunct to the public schools, or a supplement to them, the art museum could make a claim on state and local governments. J. P. Morgan, as president of the Metropolitan, perceived the possibilities clearly and was characteristically blunt in speaking of them. "The Museum," he said, "is looking for city support and it is good politics as well as good policy to make its relations close with the public school system."[35] There was much reason to doubt that any educational purpose would be served by having teachers escort their classes through the art museum, but from the standpoint of the museum the best (i.e., most public-serving and least troublesome) mode of education was the teacher-conducted class. According to Coleman, it was difficult to find anything else for young children:

How to start the child younger and hold him through adolescence is a very important practical problem. Children under seven—say from four to six—are underaged for what most museums now offer. Specific methods have not been found for them, for a dozen museums are groping for something that will work; meanwhile the little chaps are gathered in and amused with pictures and puzzles. On the other hand, boys and girls in their 'teens are beyond the effective pull of work with children and they drift away. Efforts to reach them are being directed now through the channel of the high school.[36]

During the Great Depression the art museum expanded its educational efforts. It used volunteer docents—generally young women recruited by the Junior League—to give informative talks to groups of visitors as they escorted them from gallery to gallery. It put more—and longer—labels on the objects it displayed; and it offered special classes and lectures. The Department of Education became an important part of its bureaucracy. To the art historian-curators, who considered the art museum a facility for scholars and collectors, these activities were a nuisance at best and an interference with the real purpose of the art museum at worst. "In many cases public education has been placed in a moral quarantine by the rest of the staff," Theodore L. Low reported in a study made for the Committee on Education of the American Association of Museums. "They have not only forced its submission, but they have set it off as a necessary, but isolated, evil."[37] Francis Henry Taylor, the director of the

Metropolitan from 1940 to 1954, complained of the class bias
of the curators "who look down from their Olympian world
of make-believe upon the teaching staff with a contempt that
is as ill-disguised as it is ill-deserved." Directors, who were
often recruited from among curators, were "seldom able to
cast off their early prejudices, and either neglect the [educa-
tion] department entirely or turn it into a three-ring circus."
Americans, Taylor concluded sadly, had thrown away their
opportunity to make the art museum mean something to the
general public: "We have placed art, both literally and
figuratively, on pedestals beyond the reach of the man in the
street." Instead of trying to interpret their collections to the
average person, museums "have deliberately high-hatted
him and called it scholarship."[38]

In the 1960s art-museum educators, although still regarded as a necessary evil and paid less than curators, gained
importance because of the pressures that the "urban crisis"
put upon the art museums. In the large central cities middle-
class whites were fast being replaced by blacks and Puerto
Ricans, most of whom had relatively little education and low
incomes. It was necessary for the art museum to make some
welcoming gestures to those who would be its neighbors for
decades to come. It was necessary also to enlist in the "war
on poverty," an endeavor of the Great Society that was then
getting much attention from the press and the public. In the
late 1960s the NEA offered "wider availability" funds to
encourage institutions to do more for the poor and for members of minority groups. In response to these pressures the
art museum made efforts to bring "underserved" groups to
it and also "to take the museum out" to them. The former
—they were generally called "outreach" efforts—included
tours and visits from community centers and youth groups,
bilingual lectures and other special classes and workshops,
and arrangement of "relevant" exhibits, commonly displays
of African, Native American, Afro-American, or Hispanic
art.[39]

"Taking the museum out" involved displays of art objects (reproductions) in public buildings, parks, and streets; circulation of television programs, videotapes, and prepackaged lectures to schools and other local institutions (the National Gallery of Art had long been sending out recorded lectures with slides); establishment of branch museums stocked with reproductions and recorded lectures (the Smithsonian established a storefront museum in an unused theater building in Anacostia, where it exhibited objects, most of which visitors could handle); and the use of mobile caravans, or artmobiles, to serve confined groups (those in hospitals, detention centers, schools for the handicapped, homes for the aged), inner-city neighborhoods, and isolated rural communities.[40]

In 1968 the NEA began a $90,000 yearly matching grant to the Detroit Institute of Arts "to explore new and innovative ways to break down the traditional walls of museums. . . ." The idea was to show what could be done in a metropolitan area; the inner-city audience was one target. "Project Outreach's" main effort, however, was to create local arts councils in communities remote from Detroit and to make them constituents of the institute. Delegations of about thirty citizens were sent from each of thirteen "Outreach" cities for three-day "Community Leader Seminars" at the institute. On their return, the community leaders were to marshal local forces to put on an exhibition that would attract, teach, and entertain people who had never seen one; to help them, project headquarters sent original works of art from the institute, together with film strips, slide sets keyed with lecture notes, and tour guide material. As a follow-up, the community leaders received bimonthly "Outreach" newsletters and a calendar of events taking place at the institute.[41] A panel that evaluated the project found that it had "only limited success" in involving the inner-city community and "only a limited response" in the host communities, except among those professionally concerned—teachers, clergymen, and artists.[42]

Art versus the Museum

Although some of its methods were new, "outreach" differed from earlier efforts mainly in its purpose. The founders of art museums had wanted to give the underclass moral uplift along with practical training, and Dana had tried to show the average person how to find beauty in ordinary things. Early in the twentieth century some art museums had offered classes for recently arrived immigrants, and in the 1930s there had been weekend talks and courses for workers and "circulating exhibitions." What was different about the "outreach" activities was that their purpose was to offset the alienating effects of racial injustice and urban poverty. In 1971 a committee of the Association of Art Museum Directors declared in a report that "the museum must *initially* involve itself with the community and take *positive* steps to combat social injustices within the scope of its program. . . ." Quoting these words a past president of the association, George Heard Hamilton, professor of art at Williams College, wrote: "One cannot help feeling that for the educator, social justice has a higher museum priority than historical truth or aesthetic quality."[43]

Other fundamental changes were caused by the so-called cultural explosion that became evident in the 1960s. Like other cultural institutions, the art museum had always drawn most of its patrons from among the relatively well educated. Between 1930 and 1960 the population of the United States had grown from 138 million to 183 million, and within this larger population there were proportionally more college graduates: 140,000 in 1930, 477,000 in 1960, and more than a million after 1970.

Demographic changes, however, do not entirely account for the art museum boom of the 1960s. New merchandising methods brought large crowds to the art museum, which opened new sources of income. This, in turn, changed the character of the art museum in important respects.

An accidental discovery set things in motion. In November 1961 the Metropolitan Museum acquired its thirty-second

109

Rembrandt by successfully bidding against the Cleveland Museum for *Aristotle Contemplating the Bust of Homer*. The price —$2.3 million—made headlines everywhere; it was the first time that a painting had sold for more than $1 million. The astonishing price "was a signal heard round the world by industry, millionaires, investment companies, banks, and the ordinary populace alike. It meant that the moment had come to go into art."[44] The response of the public was another and perhaps more significant signal. The Metropolitan's attendance increased by one million—slightly more than 40 percent—in the year following the purchase. Neither of the directors of the museums, James J. Rorimer of the Metropolitan and Sherman Lee of the Cleveland, could be suspected of having staged a publicity stunt. That paying $2.3 million for a work of art would bring a million people to an art museum probably surprised everyone.

It was no accident, however, when in the next year the French government sent the *Mona Lisa* to the United States for a month's stay at the National Gallery and a second month's stay at the Metropolitan. Rorimer explained in an essay in the museum's *Bulletin* that viewing the painting properly would require at least a half-hour's examination and probably more than one visit. As it turned out, some two million people stood in line for hours to get a ten-second glimpse of it; anyone who tried to linger a moment longer was told to keep moving. Essentially the same thing happened again the following year in 1963 when Michelangelo's *Pietà*, insured for an unprecedented $10 million, was moved from St. Peter's Basilica in the Vatican to the New York World's Fair. This time the mob of viewers got a twenty-second glimpse of the statue (from an escalator timed to give them that), which was twenty feet away in a glass case and bathed in blue light.

Accompanying the *Mona Lisa* back to the Louvre, John Walker, the director of the National Gallery, asked himself:

"What was the significance of these endless lines of people who waited for hours for a quick glimpse of a sinisterly smiling lady?"[45] The editors of the *New York Times* had asked similar questions when the Metropolitan had acquired its *Aristotle:* "At what point does the price of any work of art, no matter how great, become unreasonable when it is thought of in terms of other human benefits that the same sum could bestow? Does such a price have more to do with competitive prestige between museums than with the merit of the work itself?" Such questions, however disturbing, were unanswerable, the *Times* concluded, "since the spiritual benefits bestowed by art are intangible, without price if not beyond price, and since art prices must be arbitrary."[46] To Thomas Hoving, Rorimer's successor at the Metropolitan, the significance of the endless lines of waiting people was clear, and questions like those asked in the *Times* editorial were not at all disturbing. The art museum, he and others realized, had stumbled upon a formula for growth.

The formula was simple: a large crowd of museum visitors was ipso facto a large crowd of good customers and of people whose opinions mattered. The crowd was therefore a valuable commodity. The art museum could make money by selling goods and services to the customers and by selling access to the people whose opinions mattered to those who wanted to influence their opinions.

To attract a large crowd, the art museum had to do something out of the ordinary: something its publicity people could describe as marvelous, stupendous, unprecedented. Perhaps the subject could be as well, or better, treated with objects from its permanent collections, supplemented with some borrowings (which was clearly the case with one of the greatest extravaganzas: the King Tut exhibition at the Metropolitan). To get the kind of publicity that would make a "blockbuster," it was essential to have a special exhibition brought from afar. If it proved to have a "Nielsen rating"

111

that made it competitive with other means of reaching essentially the same audience—for example, an educational television program—then corporations and government agencies would pay to be listed as sponsors. Some would do so in the name of social responsibility, others because they wanted to be noticed favorably by the kind of people (disproportionately young professionals) who went to such exhibitions. George Weissman, the chairman of Philip Morris, was quoted as saying:

Our major products give people pleasure—cigarettes, beer, and soft drinks—and to many people that makes us the bad guys. In our art support activities we're viewed as good guys, and that's nice. In addition, the art support program has provided us with many business bonuses—it attracts the best people to work here, it helps to enhance the cultural atmosphere in communities where we work and live, and it shows our people that we're not afraid to try something new and so they shouldn't either. It's just good business, not philanthropy.

Government agencies, too, want advertising. In the late 1960s and the 1970s almost every blockbuster was sponsored by one of the endowments together with Philip Morris, Exxon, IBM, or some other corporation. The higher the projected "Nielsen rating," the easier it was to get sponsors and the higher the price that could be charged them.[47]

By 1980 special exhibitions, most of them of more historical or ethnic than aesthetic interest, were a mainstay of the art museum. Of the many support programs that the NEA offered to art museums, the most popular was one that helped finance the organization of special exhibitions (or the borrowing of existing ones from other museums). In fiscal 1980 nearly $4.5 million of the $11 million set aside for art museums by the NEA went for this purpose. The special exhibition was the one surefire way of attracting crowds. "You don't have to have *all* Andrew Wyeth or King Tut shows," said Robert Cassellman, the associate director of the Boston Museum of Fine Arts, "but you damn well better have *some* of them."[48]

Contributing to the support of the art museum was a sponsor's means of securing the goodwill and remembrance of the culture-loving public. The higher the art museum's "Nielsen rating," the more of these intangibles it could sell. It offered them in graded amounts and prices: a person might be a member (of little prestige, but the price was low, and there were benefits such as free admission) or, by paying more, a life member, a patron, a benefactor, and so on. In 1978 the Japanese government became a Great Benefactor of the Boston Museum of Fine Arts by making a gift of $1.45 million.

The art museum found many things that it could profitably sell to its visitor-customers: admission to a wide range of lectures and courses of instruction (for $30, a member of the Boston Museum could enroll a child between three and five years of age in a six-week course that included a visit to the galleries, storytelling, and instruction in creative movement), museum-sponsored trips abroad, restaurant meals, space for private parties, and—by far the most important—a vast array of goods from its shop or catalogue.[49]

The phenomenal growth of its retail business in the 1970s again raised a question about the purpose of art museums. A former president of the Metropolitan, Roland Redmond, wrote a blistering attack on the practice in a letter to the *New York Times*. In response the museum's vice-president for public affairs, Richard Doherty, asked if Redmond "would have preferred a course that would have brought increased dependence on endowment income in a declining stock market, or on the city in its current financial plight, or would he perhaps have wished to cut public hours at the museum to one or two days a week?"[50]

Although it sold everything else at the highest possible

price, the art museum kept its admission charge low. One day of the week the visitor could pay what—if anything—he pleased, and the regular admission fee was well below what would have maximized income from this source. The Museum of Modern Art, when it turned itself into a giant Picasso show in 1980, did raise its adult admission fee from $2.50 to $4.50 ($2.50 for students and 75 cents for children and the elderly). It did so apologetically, although $4.50 was still cheaper than the price of a movie in Manhattan and there was a brisk resale market in tickets at $20 to $30.

There was method in the seeming madness of low admission charges, however. For one thing, insofar as the art museum made money from selling objects to its visitors, it was advantageous to charge an admission fee that would ensure a large number of visitors. A more important consideration was the art museum's image as a public service and educational institution. Indispensable tax advantages (e.g., exemption from taxation on the income from its shop) depended upon this image, as did the opportunity of selling the benefits of association with itself to Philip Morris, Exxon, the Japanese government, and numerous other public-relations-minded benefactors. The art museum's public-service aura was valuable not only to advertisers but also to philanthropists. If its pricing policies were those of a private enterprise, then the art museum would have no valuable intangible benefits to sell.

By the end of fiscal 1980, the NEA had made matching grants in excess of $100 million to art museums, most of which did not go for support of what art museum professionals considered proper tasks: the collection, preservation, interpretation, and display of art. Instead it went for competing activities that would attract crowds. (It was NEH, not NEA, that was the main support of blockbusters. Ronald Berman has written, in *Culture and Politics,* that NEH helped underwrite the costs of nearly every blockbuster exhibition from 1972 to 1976, including the Soviet, the Chinese, and the

Tutankhamen shows. The agency's enabling legislation gave it authority to promote the *history* of art and culture.) The number and size of art museums continued to grow, but the art museum "crisis" was as real as ever. More money brought larger crowds, which brought more money, which brought larger crowds, and so on.

There was no obvious reason why this could not go on indefinitely. "If you have decent bathrooms, room for parking, and other amenities," Cassellman said, "people will come to the museum just as they do to Disneyland."[51] The art museum had prospered in the past and might do so in the future only by putting its growth as an organization ahead of the purposes that justified its existence and its claim for public support. It was, Bonnie Burnham remarked in *The Art Crisis,* "an entrepreneur of culture as a leisure-time pursuit."[52] As such, it was obliged to do what might be necessary in order to compete successfully for the public's free time.

What it did to attract crowds was not necessarily valueless from a public point of view. Michael Straight may have been right when he said that the great majority of those who attended the blockbuster shows probably benefited a good deal.[53] Crowd-pleasing activities, however, tended to make art museum professionals uncomfortable. In their meetings and publications they lamented that directors were selected for their talents as showmen, that public-relations people were paid more than curators, that the largest part of the staff dealt with membership, publicity, and fund-raising, that permanent collections and the works of living artists were sometimes put aside to make way for special exhibitions of lesser artistic value, that some treasures were allowed to deteriorate by neglect while others were damaged by excessive travel.[54]

"To say that there seems to be a crisis of confidence among museum personnel may be overstating the matter," wrote Tom L. Freudenheim, director of the NEA's Museum Program. "Yet they do seem preoccupied with the daily grind of keeping large institutions running smoothly and financially solvent, while perhaps paying less attention to the reason for museums' existence. In their eagerness to import from abroad, are our great museums forgetting their own incomparable treasures? If a museum's staff does not value their own collections, who will?"[55]

CHAPTER

5

Art versus the Public School

I do not intend to suggest that the cultivation of a sense of the beautiful as revealed to us in art, is equally important
with that of developing all our faculties
by the reading of good and great
books. Such a proposition would be
absurd. . . .

—C. C. Perkins, 1871[1]

ART came into the public schools of the large cities at about
the time the great art museums were built. It was introduced
by much the same people and for much the same reasons.
C. C. Perkins, for example, who was one of the principal
founders of the Boston Museum of Fine Arts, thanked God
that New Englanders were always ready to promote culture
and that they would not refuse to support any educational
scheme, once convinced of its importance. He was promoting
the art museum, but he gave approving mention to a proposal to place casts of sculptures in some of the public

117

schools. He hoped "they will aid in that unconscious education of the young in the appreciation of beauty, which is so desirable as directly affecting the future of art in this country."[2]

As with the art museums, the motives for art education were mixed. Art was a means of moral improvement; it was also good for business. "Not less important than the establishment of museums with a view to general cultivation," Perkins said, "is the opening of schools of design as bearing upon improvement in industrial art."[3] He noted with satisfaction that there was a bill in the legislature to connect design schools with public schools.

By 1860 Horace Mann among others had established the principle of universal, free schooling. The next generation of reformers made the public school, in the words of William Harris, the "great instrumentality to lift all classes of people into a participation in civilized life."[4] By the 1880s and 1890s the uplifting process was thought, in the larger cities at least, to require a place in school curriculum for music, drawing (to develop ability for accurate representation), and art appreciation (the study of art history and the lives of artists). The child learned to draw in the way he learned to write: from a drawing book, copying the pictures, sometimes using tracing paper. Like music, art was taught by special teachers who visited a class briefly each week. Besides overseeing drawing, the art teacher displayed pictures it was believed every child should know, explained their "stories," and gave the painters' vital statistics.

Soon after the end of the century, when universities established schools of education, there were professors of art instruction, who developed and expounded ideas of what to teach and how to teach it. At the same time, "scientific psychology" was rapidly developing. The psychology professors were occupied mainly with theories of learning intended to improve the teaching of the three R's and with devising tests and scales to measure learning. As for their influence on art instruction, it was to improve methods of teaching drawing (by 1920 the drawing book had been discarded in favor of an object—say, a flower in a vase—that the teacher put before the class) and to increase the amount of information given about the history of paintings and painters.[5]

A philosopher (and author of *Psychology*) who had a profound effect on the methods of teaching all subjects was John Dewey. "Progressive education" transformed the school in the first half of the century, and as its historian, Lawrence A. Cremin, has written, "began as Progressivism in education: a many-sided effort to use the schools to improve the lives of individuals."[6] For Dewey the school was an "embryonic community" that should both reflect the larger society and, more important, improve it, making it more "worthy, lovely, and harmonious."[7] His influence was clearly evident in Harold Rugg and Ann Shumaker's book *The Child-Centered School*, which Cremin called "the characteristic progressivist work of the twenties."[8] The American school, they wrote, had lived too long under the reign of college entrance requirements, which committed it to a rigid grading system and to criteria of education that emphasized discipline, logical thinking, power of sustained intellectual effort, and the retention of classified knowledge. Education was to become dynamic: "Child activities, not studies and lessons, were to be the core of the curriculum. Life experience, not the acquisition of ready-made subject matter, was to orient teaching."[9]

In the new school creative activities were to be central. According to Rugg and Shumaker, "The child's day in the formal school is exceedingly bookish; it is verbal. . . ." Rhythmic activities with music, dramatics, art, and dance would have a large place in the program of the creative school. "Rhythmic training," they wrote, "is peculiarly adapted to the higher conception of growth. Here the individual realizes his own innate capacities, contributes of his powers to further a group enterprise, exercises team play without building up habits of competing for personal advantage." For this, the traditional sort of art education, even at its best, was "fundamentally wrong."[10]

Art as such was not the focus of interest in the new curriculum: "Rather it is a spirit and technique of original expression. Beginning as play, it finally emerges as art. . . ." Insight into the creative needs of the child, Rugg and Schumaker said, had been delayed in America by the late emergence of the creative artist himself, but interest in the art of primitive peoples had recently changed standards: the vigor and freshness admired in primitive art were now prized in children's art. "So today," they wrote, "an exhibit of the artistic effort of children in the progressive schools resembles in its boldness and originality of treatment, in its frank use of primary colors and its charming lack of accurate proportion or finished technique, the qualities found in a collection of Indian, Negro, Mayan, Egyptian, or Igorot art." In the new school every child was a potential artist, according to the authors, and the task of the school was to draw out his creative power.[11]

Although progressive education had some influence almost everywhere, current art education, generally speaking, resembles the "old" much more than the "new." Art in some form is taught from kindergarten through twelfth grade in almost all public and private schools. In about thirty states its inclusion in the curriculum is required by law. It is normally taught in the elementary grade by the classroom teacher who may be assisted, when the budget allows, by a "specialist." At the secondary school level it is, as a rule, an elective subject (about 10 percent of high schools require some training in music or visual art), and the instruction is given by an art teacher.

Participation in the school orchestra or band, instruction in an instrument, or attending a weekly class, constitutes musical training. In most schools if any attention is paid to theater, it is by way of a school play. In the visual arts, courses on art appreciation and art history are the least enrolled.

Most courses, however, are of the applied sort: instruction in crafts—for example, jewelry making—is the most popular, with painting and sculpture second, and design third.

Art educators agree that insufficient time and resources are allocated to the teaching of art; they disagree, however, on curriculum, justifications, and methods. The traditional treatment of art has received much criticism from art teachers through their professional associations, from a growing number of professors in graduate schools of education who are engaged in research and curriculum development in art education, from administrators of federal and state agencies (especially the NEA and the National Institute of Education), and from arts advocates and educators connected with certain foundations (especially Rockefeller-financed ones). The federal government has spent at least $200 million on research and development projects in the past two decades: some on "basic" research (e.g., the nature of creativity) but most on the development of new curricula and new approaches to the teaching of art.

Despite these efforts, art education has changed little since 1960. In the 1970s the proportion of high school students electing to take art courses increased sharply, a reflection perhaps of the counterculture's devaluation of more disciplined studies. (This perhaps is a minor contributing cause of the decline in average scores on college entrance exams and other tests.) But the nature of art education has not changed significantly in most schools. Partly because it is heavily performance-oriented, it is still regarded as a frill by most parents, teachers, and students. The few careful evaluations that have been made put the value of the whole art education enterprise in doubt. A study of 1,500 students in fifteen institutions in eight states found, for example, that high school and college students had about the same attitude toward art when they left school as when they entered and that there was little relation between their knowledge of art and their attitude.[12] Based on the results of several studies of

121

elementary- and secondary-level students, some of whom had taken aesthetics classes, another investigator concluded: "Evidence of effectiveness is virtually non-existent."[13]

It may be that the school, despite art education—or in some cases because of it—tends to destroy whatever capacity to enjoy art the student has. Charles Silberman, an impressionistic observer, wrote that the schools have an enormous effect upon the students' aesthetic sensibilities, all of it destructive; the schools, he said, teach that "interest in the arts is effeminate or effete, that study of the arts is a frill, and that music, art, beauty and sensitivity bear no relation to any other aspect of the curricula or of life."[14] Whatever the reason, most of what the young learn about art, and about culture in general, they learn outside of the school.

There are many reasons to doubt that the schools can do anything significant to enhance the place of the arts in American culture or that, except in isolated instances, they can give anything that can properly be called art education. Indeed, it is likely that most of what is called art education, insofar as it has any effect, obscures or misrepresents the nature of the aesthetic experience. Like so many others who deal with art, art educators are interested mainly in its extra-aesthetic or incidental uses: they tend to see it as a means of building character, improving the classroom climate by involving students in group activities, motivating or consolidating learning in the more traditional subject areas, and coping with discipline problems.[15]

Of the many errors and confusions upon which the system of art education rests, perhaps the most excusable is the belief that art classes encourage and direct the creativity of a child. As every parent knows, practically all children aged about six to nine enjoy drawing and by it express their feelings and perceptions, often with astonishingly appealing results. Art, it would seem, comes naturally to them, and therefore the school should help their creative impulses unfold. But although there is sometimes a striking resemblance between them, the child's "art" is not art properly speaking: no amount of encouragement will develop it into art or cause the impulses that give rise to it to unfold into an aesthetic sensibility.

In his book *Artful Scribbles,* educational psychologist Howard Gardner, drawing on more than a decade of research done for Harvard's Project Zero, for which he is co-director, provides substantial evidence to support his claim that all children in our culture scribble at an early stage of their development and that the character of their scribbling is quite independent of what goes on outside themselves— including, of course, what teachers say or do.[16] When the child reaches a further stage of development, the character of the scribbling changes, and the nature of the change, which is more or less the same for all children, is influenced not by any process of learning in the usual sense of the word but by events within the child's developing psyche. There is indeed an unfolding process, but it occurs in the same way for all children whether or not they are exposed to art, and it does not develop into anything that can properly be called art. (Even with children who turn out to be artistically gifted, there is a radical discontinuity between the "art" they produce as children and what they produce later.)

It is, no doubt, good to give children crayons, paints, and paper so that they may express their impulses and pass the time happily; to call this art education, however, is highly misleading. Although the loss in other respects might well be regrettable, it is safe to say that if "art" were entirely removed from the elementary schools, there would not be an iota's loss of art, or of art appreciation, in consequence. Some may object on the ground that, even though it is impossible to help the child make art, it *is* possible to introduce him to the aesthetic experience—to give him some sense of how an art object may make one think and feel. Gardner's theories do not bear on this directly. However, it seems reasonable to infer that the conditions of immaturity that prevent the child from producing visual art also prevent him from experiencing it.

It is not until the early teenage years, when cognitive faculties are more fully developed, that the early adolescent has the capacity either to make or, if the conjecture above is correct, to experience what is properly called art. In the great majority of instances, he then ceases to make "art": the exercise and development of the cognitive faculties absorb all his attention and psychic energy. This is true, apparently, not only in American culture but in all highly developed cultures —ones, that is, that depend less on impulse and habit than on knowledge and thinking. By the time the student reaches junior high school he has developed to the point where he is capable of experiencing and, if he is gifted, of making art.

There is no guarantee that a more mature student will gain from art education. There is reason to believe that there is a wide range of innate (inborn) differences in the ability of individuals to respond aesthetically to visual (as well as other nonverbal) stimuli. These differences seem to have been measured very little (of some 2,000 measuring instruments used by psychologists, only five measure visual abilities).[17] But the existence of differences is consistent with, and it would seem implied by, the research findings that suggest that one hemisphere of the brain is primarily concerned with cognitive functions such as speech, reading, and writing, whereas the other is primarily concerned with visual and instinctual functions.[18]

It is not unlikely that a considerable proportion of high school students are naturally nonverbal, nonvisual, or nonmusical to such a degree that, notwithstanding any effort they make to learn and others to teach, they can never reach a level of proficiency that would justify the effort. This level, incidentally, is obviously much higher for verbal skills than for others for the simple reason that a minimal ability to read and write is necessary to earn a living and otherwise get along in modern society. There is, therefore, a compelling case for teaching the three R's to people who are extremely nonverbal and nonmathematical. People who are extremely nonvisual and/or nonmusical present an altogether different challenge. Developing these faculties to the limit set by nature serves no practical purpose: it is entirely possible not only to get along but to be independent and happy without being able to tell one color from another or to carry a tune. "Remember," Lord Chesterfield wrote to his son, "that knowing any language imperfectly, is very little better than not knowing it at all."[19]

Here, again, an objection may be made. Surely no matter how great his lack of natural aptitude for making or experiencing any of the arts, a student can learn a good deal *about* them. As a matter of general cultural awareness he should know that Leonardo da Vinci was a great Renaissance artist who painted *The Last Supper*, just as he should know that Magellan was the first man to sail around the world. This claim, like the claim that children should be given crayons and paper to scribble on, may be justified on extra-aesthetic grounds: something is being learned that will contribute to understanding and enjoyment. Learning about art, however, is entirely different from learning to make or experience it. There is, incidentally, some tension between the two activities. By identifying "art" with famous paintings such as the *Mona Lisa*, the teacher may give the student an incomplete, or even incorrect, impression of the nature of art.

Is it possible, then, for a school to teach aesthetic experience? That the normal child has in some degree a capacity for it is not in question. But as philosopher Michael Oakeshott has stressed, knowledge is of two sorts: there is technical knowledge, which can be formulated as rules or maxims and written down, and there is practical knowledge, which is not susceptible of such formulation, cannot be taught or learned, and can be acquired only from someone who is practicing it.[20] Techniques may be taught in school, and if improved enough through practice to become skills of eye and hand,

125

they may lead to the acquisition of practical knowledge, without which experience of art must be rudimentary. It is unlikely, however, that the art teacher will be of much help in imparting the practical knowledge, for this can only rub off on one who sees it constantly being demonstrated. When Harry S. Broudy wrote that "it is possible for anyone to learn to scan a work of art—in any medium—for its sensory, formal, technical, and expressive properties,"[21] he must have meant that there are some helpful rules on a par, say, with those given in a cookbook for people who have no flair for cooking, but he cannot believe that they will carry one very far. Disciplined instruction is a good beginning. But what the student eventually requires is an apprenticelike attachment to persons who constantly experience things aesthetically.

Such a relationship rarely exists in a high school classroom. For one thing, the inadequacy of the classroom situation—too many students, insufficient time, too much course material—prevents it; for another, and one even harder to overcome, it is rare to be exposed to a teacher imbued with an aesthetic sensibility and who therefore can impart to others what it is to perceive objects aesthetically. Granted that a process of self-selection may tend to bring into the profession people of more than ordinary artistic sensibility, still, the average art teacher does not have much firsthand knowledge of the art experience. How could it be otherwise? The art teacher has had, to be sure, special training (as about one-third of classroom teachers have also) on how to understand and appreciate the arts, aesthetic phenomena, and so on, and how to impart this knowledge to students. But if the argument made here is correct, then the teacher cannot have been taught the one indispensable capacity, namely, how to *experience* art. At best he will have been taught what is in the cookbook, and the tendency of that may—but not necessarily—be to incapacitate him for showing, as opposed to telling, what art and the aesthetic are like.[22]

The never-say-die problem solver may propose to deal with the problem of finding qualified teachers in either of two ways. The first, which is impractical if for no other reason than the numbers involved (there are about 1.3 million elementary school teachers and 86,000 visual art teachers), is to recruit teachers from among people having a marked aesthetic sensitivity (how, in the absence of measuring instruments, are these people to be identified?) and then, by way of training, putting the teachers in apprenticelike associations with artists and others of highly developed aesthetic sensibilities.

The other way is to put practicing artists in the schools. Here, again, formidable practical problems exist. A professional artist does not necessarily respect the aesthetic values associated with his own medium, let alone have any feeling for artistic values in general. Allowing for exceptions, the artist who is serious about his work—supposedly a sine qua non to communicating the aesthetic attitude—will not find the secondary school a stimulating environment, and in any case, he may be temperamentally or otherwise unsuited for the classroom. It may be too much to expect a good artist to be a good teacher also.

The difficult question—what should be considered art?—must be faced in a discussion of the uses and limitations of art education as a means of enhancing public appreciation of art and of enlarging the value placed upon it by the culture. The problems arise, of course, both from the disagreement among highly qualified people as to what has artistic merit and from the rapidly changing nature of art and of the aesthetic experience. It is especially acute with visual art. Should art education endeavor to keep abreast of "advanced" opinion? Ought the schools to teach that art is what relieves deep boredom, that representation is at best irrelevant, that self-mutilation is as valid an art form as painting and sculpture? Since what the art world accepts as art

127

changes radically and unpredictably from one decade to the next, art education, were it successful, would risk preparing the student to enjoy what was, but no longer is, art.

The sad fact is that in the overwhelming majority of cases, even the good student carries very little of what he learns in school into the outside world. If the standards that he acquires in school are much more exacting than those prevailing out of it, will they raise these standards or eventually be displaced by them? Responding to art in a classroom, Brent Wilson observes, is different from experiencing it elsewhere, and there is no evidence that what happens in the classroom leaves the student more responsive to art upon encountering it elsewhere. Even under the most favorable circumstances, Wilson says, the effect of school will be intermittent and weak, while that of the nonschool culture will be continual and strong. Art educators, he concludes, are mistaken in assuming that what they teach can be "tacked onto nearly any currently held lifestyle, when in fact many lifestyles negatively reinforce the behaviors taught in the classroom."[23]

The cultural explosion of the 1950s and 1960s brought with it an explosion of interest in art education. Beginning in 1963 and lasting for about a decade, a federal presence— or, rather, several more or less competing ones—became a conspicuous part of the scene. In his 1963 report August Heckscher observed that until recently the U.S. Office of Education had given little attention to the arts; in 1962 President Kennedy had appointed Francis Keppel, dean of Harvard's Graduate School of Education, commissioner of education. Keppel appointed Kathryn Bloom as head of an arts and humanities branch, and she soon assembled a staff of ambitious innovators—"Kathy Bloom's Mafia" they were sometimes called. With Keppel in a position to deal directly with the president, and Miss Bloom in a position to deal with Keppel (and with his successor, Harold Howe), her influence and that of the branch was great. With the passage of the

1965 Elementary and Secondary Education Act it became greater still, for Title IV of the act provided about $11 million for research in art education over the next five years. The branch supported over two hundred projects, thirty or forty of which were for basic research on "perceptual learning," a concept developed by Gestalt psychologist Rudolf Arnheim and philosopher Nelson Goodman, among others. Art, in this view, was a language—a means of thinking and knowing, as basic to education as the traditional ones.

The stimulus of these and other ideas was felt throughout the world of art education. *The Journal of Aesthetic Education* was founded in 1966; at least half a dozen textbooks and anthologies on the teaching of the arts appeared, established foundations hired art education advisers, and new foundations came into being to support implementation of the new doctrines. By 1970 Miss Bloom and most of her associates had joined foundation staffs, and the Office of Education had all but disappeared from the art-education scene. It was replaced to some degree in 1972 by the creation, within the Department of Health, Education, and Welfare, of the National Institute for Education, which continued to support the several large research programs begun by the arts and humanities branch, spending about $28 million annually in the late 1970s to support research centers and development laboratories.[24] Its seven-point "national policy"[25] reflected Miss Bloom's views: to be considered for support, a program "must be designed to encourage the development in students of aesthetic awareness"; it must "involve all of the students in the school"; it must "integrate all the major art forms into the regular educational program"; and so on.[26]

Much larger sums were spent under Title I of the education act to augment the arts-education activities of the schools. In the first three years of the act, nearly $150 million went for isolated performances and one-day "cultural trips." This was sharply reduced in 1970, when an evaluation showed that these activities had little lasting educational

129

value. Meanwhile, nearly four hundred projects directly or indirectly concerned with the arts received about $80 million between 1965 and 1970 under Title III. This funding was also much reduced after 1970. The Office of Education apparently expected both endowments to fill the gap.[27]

If this was the expectation, it was unrealistic. The NEH had never been interested in elementary and secondary school education, because colleges were its constituency. In its first year the NEA had sent sixty poets to schools in six cities, leading to an Artists-in-Schools (AIS) program, which in the mid-1970s sent 1,750 artists in various fields to about 5,000 schools in fifty states at an annual cost of about $4 million. The NEA insisted that the program was of great value to the schools; its principal purpose, however, was to give employment to artists.

The burst of activity that began in the 1960s had little effect on art education in the classrooms. That the spending of so many millions had had "limited impact," according to a 1977 report by a commission of the National Art Education Association, "is a prime example of how effectively schools resist change from outside."[28] It had, however, changed the situation fundamentally by creating an art-education establishment—a coalition of leaders in art education (most of them influential professors in graduate schools of education), in the world of art advocacy (members of the Rockefeller family were conspicuous here), and in government (especially the Office of Education and the NEA). Junius Eddy, who had served under Kathryn Bloom and then became an adviser to the Ford and Rockefeller foundations, wrote in 1977 that "an Arts Education Movement is indeed emerging within American education; and it is preparing itself—and its non-educational community-based partners—to make tactical and strategic inroads in the vast educational enterprise which deals with the young in our society."[29]

Segments of the establishment, centered in Washington and New York, had labored with much success to establish arts and education constituencies in the states and cities and to propagate in them and through them its doctrine or creed. The "creed" was not subscribed to in its entirety by everyone in the establishment: sharp differences of opinion were not uncommon. There was agreement, however, that traditional art education—that is, what then existed in almost all schools—was in urgent need of fundamental reform and that this should entail the reform not only of art education but of all elementary and secondary education. The schools had successfully resisted change through the 1970s, but the art-education establishment was firmly in place, its techniques for extending its network by partnership arrangements were well developed, and there was reason to believe that its doctrine would appeal to the middle- and upper-middle-class parents whose opinions would ultimately be decisive.

An important and reasonably representative example of the art-education establishment's composition, mode of operation, and doctrine may be found in a profusely illustrated 334-page book published by the Panel on Arts, Education, and Americans in 1977.[30] The panel was organized by the American Council for the Arts in Education with funds from fifteen sources: public agencies (the NEH and the Office of Education were "important early contributors," the introduction said, and the NEA also contributed), corporations, and foundations (the Ford Foundation, the JDR 3rd Fund, the Rockefeller Brothers Fund, and the Rockefeller Foundation). Under the chairmanship of David Rockefeller, Jr., the panel consisted of twenty-five "representatives of the arts, education, mass communications, labor, art patronage, government, and other fields." With the help of a dozen researchers and an even larger number of consultants and "resource persons" (among them Kathryn Bloom and Nancy Hanks) and after interviews with more than three hundred artists, educators, and policymakers, and fifteen days of hearings in four cities, the panel produced in two years what Rockefeller described as "the most comprehensive study of

131

the arts and education ever undertaken."[31] Written in a spritely, anecdotal style and illustrated with more than one hundred photographs, cartoons, and graphs, it was obviously intended to reach and influence a wide audience and to affect policy.

Its central theme was that the arts were among the basic skills without which the process of learning could not take place. Because of the baleful influence of Puritanism, American education exaggerated the importance of words as transmitters of information: ". . . had folk other than those relentless English purifiers and pursuers of holiness managed to dominate two centuries of American thinking, this nation might well be far different today." Properly taught, the arts "more than any other subject awaken the learning pores." The arts being essentially all the same in their nature and values, they should be taught "as a whole," although "no one is quite sure about how to go about teaching the arts as a whole."[32]

The report did not enter into the question of whether sensory skills were in the same category as verbal skills, but it did assert that they were a "means to knowledge"—indeed, to "knowledge of all kinds: of the environment, of the skills of reading, writing, and arithmetic, of ourselves and others."[33] The arts, in short, were a route to any and all cognitive learning. There was, Rockefeller wrote, a crying need "to expand the concept of literacy to include the language of gesture (theatre), image (the visual arts), sound (music), movement (dance), and space (architecture)."[34]

The report stressed extra-aesthetic values not only in what it said about "basic education" but elsewhere as well. It did so, for example, with its very plausible claim that the "play" atmosphere of an art class made students more tractable. "The strongest arts programs in the schools of East Harlem," Rockefeller wrote, "have had such a marked effect in reducing vandalism that guidance counselors in nearby schools are now recommending that their most delinquent students be transferred there."[35]

The panel's recommendations—15 "general" and 101 "specific"—were sweeping.[36] There should be a "coherent national policy" for arts in education. This, Rockefeller said, would "require Americans to revise their posture toward the Protestant work ethic. . . ."[37] The Office of Education should have Cabinet status and be provided with a special adviser for the arts in education. All students should have opportunities for creative participation in a variety of the arts (the nature and extent of which were not indicated). The artists-in-schools idea was warmly supported (seventeen entries in the index referred to it). There should be specially designed programs for the ill, the isolated, and the handicapped.

Leading figures in the art-education establishment were scathing in their criticisms of the panel's report. Ralph A. Smith, a professor of cultural and educational policy at the University of Illinois, described it as the preferences of a "new policy complex" that had come into being in the Washington bureaucracy in the past fifteen years and was now extending its influence into state departments of education through a variety of networks, consortia, coalitions, and leagues. The agenda of the new complex, he said, "is the reform of the whole curriculum and school milieu." Its reforms were the cant notions and "innovations" (really hypotheses) of the 1960s; the writers of the report "got caught in the rage for basics, and construing art as a basic way of knowing was seen as a way of exploiting the movement." Its aesthetic theory, "a loosely differentiated mush of aims," vitiated its educational theory. "Having no theory of art's distinctive functions, art is mobilized to achieve a plethora of outcomes limited only by the authors' ability to think up additional ones." Far from sharing the panel's enthusiasm for the Artists-in-Schools Program, Smith doubted that bringing artists into the schools produced fundamental educational change:

I don't doubt for a moment that African drummers and dancers in leotards can transform the atmosphere of elementary classrooms. The question has to do with the point of it all. Where does it lead? What does it connect with? Where does it fit into a coherent curriculum so dear to the new pedagogues? From Greek drama and African dance to Picasso and World War I to Snoopy and dynamic career education! In such free association, we are asked to believe, lies the significance of the arts for American education. This, we are being told, is what art as a unique way of knowing is all about.[38]

It was dubious, to say the least, Smith concluded, "that art is the potent force for educational change which it is assumed to be." Serious discussion of the relations of art, society, and education is not to be found in the report. From start to finish, it "reflects the deteriorating state of culture."

Laura H. Chapman, a professor of art education at the University of Cincinnati, complained that the panel seemed to value art more as a general stimulus to learning than as a unique and significant opportunity for art experience. Its "case" for elementary art, she said, "seems to hinge primarily on its function as 'positive reinforcement'—not unlike the M&M candies and token money that behavioral psychologists are fond of recommending as a stimulus to learning."[39] She was critical, too, of the report's stress on art making, as opposed to historical, critical, and cultural studies. This derived, she believed, from political and administrative considerations: "Members of the Panel evidently would prefer to redefine the professional field of arts than to alter the existing federal structure for funding the arts." The existing structure, she pointed out, channels grants for creative and performance activities through the NEA to state arts councils; the proposed "partnership" of these with state departments of education would thus link the "new" art education to the NEA.

In Professor Chapman's view, the Artists-in-Schools Program used the schools to solve the unemployment problems of artists. "Why not a city or Chamber of Commerce Artists-in-Residence Program?" she asked; "One suspects, again, that the squeaky in-place machinery is getting grease. . . ." The report's recommendation that the arts be taught "as a whole" was also at bottom political. The "movement" to integrated, interdisciplinary arts programs, Professor Chapman said, "is primarily the result of a need, in distributing federal funds, to treat each of the 'art constituencies' fairly." In 1965, she recalled, art educators with ambitious research and curriculum projects "had the choice of bringing along 'all of the arts' or receiving no federal funds." The government's strategy seemed to be: "Persuade people that the arts are 'a whole.' Support 'package deals' that are organized by almost any handy metaphysical or merchandizing principle. . . ." This, she thought, was a critical threat to arts education. Indeed, the report itself was an attack on the art-education profession. "There emerges—by direct claim, innuendo, and omission—the singular impression that arts educators are hopelessly lost souls whose only salvation is to be found by submitting themselves to The-Mythic-Force-of-the-Artist." A council of professionals, she concluded, should convene at once to produce a more substantial, fair-minded, and comprehensive set of recommendations.[40]

The magnitude of the gap between professional opinion and the enthusiasm of the panel, Professor Chapman remarked, could be measured by (among other things) studying the 1977 report of the National Art Education Association's Commission on Art Education.[41] In important respects the gap was indeed great. In others, however, it was remarkably small.

The Commission on Art Education, consisting of five leading professionals, had consulted several hundred art educators before publishing its 137-page report.[42] Although mainly concerned with the status and prospects of art teachers, whose trade association it was, the philosophical, or ideological, premise of the commission's report had much in common with the panel's. On the practical side, the commis-

sion said that art experience, being as essential as other subjects, should have parity with them; participation in an art
program should be required from kindergarten through high
school; the teaching of art should be done by specialists
trained in colleges meeting the association's standards;
schools should work cooperatively with state, local, and national arts councils and other educational groups "to effect
the broadest base possible for the artistic development of
youth"; the College Entrance Examination Board should develop more imaginative means of assessing high school arts
credits; and there should be continued federal support of arts
education ("the Federal Council on the Arts [should] establish legislation for categorical support . . .").[43]

With regard to the rationale for art education, the commission did not give "the senses" the almost exclusive emphasis
that was given them by the panel. There is, it said, "no single,
adequate, comprehensive and perennial purpose for the
teaching of art." It asserted, however, that inherited cultural
values (Thomistic ones) overemphasized "cognitive" learning (the three R's and science), and it made much of art as
a mode of thinking (art-education programs elicit "thinking
processes that are free from the constraints of logic and
strictly defined rules" and that make a "special contribution
to the development of a form of consciousness that functions
as the basis of knowledge in all fields"). It did not, however,
draw an inference from this in favor of "integrated education." Teaching science through dance, reading through
music, and so forth was "an excellent idea" but "needs to be
more finely developed as a seamless and systematic curriculum for life-long learning." The commission nevertheless
recommended that educators "consider the concept of education through art, among others, as creative rationale for
including and implementing highly interdisciplinary and
technological art programs which not only motivate students
to art, but may lead them through the process of diverse art
media to other areas of inquiry." The time was coming, it

said, when elementary school teachers would need special college and in-service workshop training "to help them 'mainstream' art education into total learning."[44]

Whereas the panel had attached very great importance to art education as a means of maintaining order in the classroom, the commission gave that a subordinate, but not unimportant, place:

There is an abundance of hostility and destructive energy (vandalism) which students manifest toward the schools and society in general. Art educators have an opportunity to make a quantum leap by using their resourceful imagination to change the destructive behavior of today into creative energies for a dynamic and rapidly changing tomorrow.[45]

The difference between the two reports was perhaps greatest on the subject of bringing artists into the schools. "At all levels," the commission declared, "art should be taught by teachers who are trained as art specialists." In addition to knowing a great deal about all of the arts (and much else besides; for example, sociology, anthropology, philosophy), the teacher should have "professional competence" as an artist "and thus be capable of fulfilling the role of the artist/teacher in the classroom."[46]

The commission did not share the panel's enthusiasm for teaching the arts "as a whole." When the arts are combined into one program, it said, "there is always the problem of maintaining the identity and integrity of the disciplines."[47]

Aesthetic education—that is, teaching not the arts but rather how to perceive objects in the aesthetic mode—was almost ignored by the panel. The commission made no more than an approving gesture in that direction: the identification of concepts in philosophical aesthetics had some place in a multidisciplinary art program, it said, but a forced synthesis of the arts into a "super-discipline" is "clearly erroneous."[48]

Art education in the schools, as in the art museum, was brought into being by elite reformers who sought to use art

137

for moral uplift and for the diffusion of useful knowledge. These purposes were made obsolete almost at once by changing opinions as to the nature of art. The elite of wealth and culture and the professionals who were in a symbiotic relationship with them—art historians in one case and art educators in the other—labored to bring their institutions into the service of the new ideas; in the art museum they took up the motto "joy, not knowledge" and in the school, "every child an artist." In both settings the realization of the new ideal was largely frustrated by the unwillingness of the public to accept it. The art museum could find a constituency only by becoming a "depository of grandeur," "a collection of cultural history," and a "mausoleum"; in the school art was obliged to remain a frill taught in the traditional way. After World War II the reformers discovered—indeed brought into being—a powerful ally: the grant-giving federal entrepreneur. The mutuality of interest was not complete, but there now existed an art establishment embracing, along with much else, both art education and the art museum. The changing balance of forces within this establishment would largely determine what might be done in the name of art. But in the schools, as in the art museum, the decisive considerations would be ones of organizational maintenance. "What we believe to be merely the means—the school," wrote Martin Engel, the adviser on the arts and humanities at the National Institute of Education, "are in fact ends in themselves. The real goal of the schools is self-perpetuation, not the individual development of their students. That is the real lesson taught by the schools."[49]

CHAPTER

6

Collectibles versus Art

Respect for the original comes close to
pure snobbery.
—Daniel Boorstin[1]

THROUGHOUT his long public career Nelson Rockefeller
was a leading—some might say *the* leading—arts advocate.
Perhaps as much as anyone, he promoted measures to bring
art to the people at the taxpayers' expense. At the end of his
life, however, he launched another venture to bring art to the
people by investing $3.5 million to sell reproductions of art-
works from his private collection. To begin with there were
ninety-six reproductions for sale at prices from $65 to
$7,500. For $850, for example, one could buy by mail a pho-
tographic copy of Picasso's painting *Girl with Mandolin*, a
work for which Rockefeller had been offered $2 million.*

---

*In art world usage a "copy" is in the same medium as the original
whereas a "reproduction" is in a different one. Here the words will be used
interchangeably.

139

Presumably, the arts advocates with whom Rockefeller had labored so long would have cheered him on and sung his praises even louder than before. Important works of art are accessible only to people who live in or near about a dozen of the largest cities, and then usually only if they join the throngs in the galleries of the major art museums. To be sure, there are several hundred small art museums, but few possess masterpieces, and some have nothing that can compare to any one item in Rockefeller's private collection. Of the more than one hundred college art museums, only a dozen have notable works in any number; even in the best university art departments, teaching is done mainly from slides. Except here and there in the big cities, public buildings contain no art of importance. In schools and libraries across the country there is bad art or none at all. Except for the wealthy, ownership of important originals is out of the question. Some kinds of art objects lend themselves to reproduction better than others. Because Rockefeller did not limit his selection to the kinds that can best be reproduced, the art world might have criticized some relative failures while praising the essential principle of his undertaking: to make his collection accessible, so far as technology-cum-economics allowed, to almost any public institution, and even to many private citizens.

Yet the man who all his life had endeavored to bring art to the public was showered with abuse because of it. "We have entered a new era of hype and shamelessness . . . ," declared Hilton Kramer, the chief art critic of the *New York Times.*[2] Other notables of the art world added their words of vilification. The art world was outraged that Rockefeller had challenged the widespread opinion—one on which much of the art world depends for its bread and butter—that a reproduction cannot possibly have the aesthetic value of an original. Reproductions are sold by the millions every year, of course. Art museums, in particular, sell as many as they can, and theirs, like Rockefeller's, are of a higher quality than most. But the size and quality of the ordinary copy ensures that no one can possibly find in it anything approaching the aesthetic rewards of seeing the original.

The art world objected to Rockefeller's copying business on three grounds. First was the taint of commerce. The project was self-sustaining and even profitable, rather than an act of philanthropy or government largess. Second, Rockefeller offered reproductions of unusually high quality (although not necessarily of higher quality than those offered by some art museums). Third were Rockefeller's name and standing as a collector. If anyone could cause the public to doubt that only an original could be art, it was he. Rockefeller, Kramer wrote, certainly knew the "unbridgeable difference" between a work of art and a reproduction, but "apparently the temptation to cash in on the market for *haut Schlock* has proved irresistible." Kramer could hardly have supposed that Rockefeller, generous and high-minded all his life, had suddenly turned unprincipled. More likely, what so upset Kramer was that Rockefeller had turned traitor to the art world.

The position of the art world is that only bad reproductions are good. "The truth is," Kramer explained, "that these reproductions [he was not referring only to Rockefeller's] have nothing to do with the experience afforded by a genuine work of art. As an educational tool, reproductions serve as aids to memory. At best they are mementos of experience rather than the thing itself." *Time* magazine's critic, Robert Hughes, took the same line. After making the point about memory aids (he specified *cheap* reproductions as being "indispensable" for this purpose), he went on to say that "even the most perfect replication" is "intrinsically dead, like a stuffed trout."[3] Ruth Berenson, writing in the *National Review,* incautiously remarked that often "there is no way even an expert can distinguish *ersatz* from *echt,*" but nevertheless dismissed Rockefeller's reproductions as "high-class fakes."[4]

In a press release about the Rockefeller Collection, the Art

Dealers Association of America asserted: "Although a reproduction is and can only be no more than an imitation of the original, replicas have an undisputed educational value as inexpensive reminders of important works of art. Photographs or other copies of paintings, sculpture or antiquities also have some decorative value, as with a poster which reproduces an important painting." A few months later the association presented its annual award for outstanding achievement in art history to the director of the Fogg Museum at Harvard. The award consisted of $5,000 and a bronze replica of a stabile by Alexander Calder.[5]

Cultural commentators apply a curious double standard to the visual arts and music. People who sneer at a good reproduction of a painting will praise a far inferior recording of a symphony. There is, one would think, a wider gulf between seeing and hearing an opera in an opera house and seeing and hearing it on a television screen than there is between seeing an original work of art and seeing one of Rockefeller's reproductions. Yet the National Endowment for the Arts has won great praise for sponsoring television broadcasts of the Metropolitan Opera. Indeed, bringing "live" opera to millions who would never otherwise be able to see it was widely acclaimed as a cultural achievement. Samuel Lipman wrote that "The medium's present limitations—principally the near-universality of small sets producing wretched sound, but also the more basic lack of three-dimensional visual representation—seem less significant than the possibility television presents of bringing operas in high-level productions to those who have little or no other opportunity to experience them."[6]

Yet imagine the howls from the art world if someone were to propose that state and federal governments, rather than subsidizing the purchase of original works of art for museums and public buildings, support efforts to improve the quality of reproductions, perhaps by research to find better technologies, and to make high-quality ones readily available. Why should public art museums not substitute perfect or near-perfect reproductions for originals, thus drastically reducing the ever-increasing costs of security and conservation?

The fundamental economic fact about art is that works of high quality are scarce in relation to the demand for them. This would be true even if all of the demand came from art lovers whose interest was purely aesthetic. But in fact, demand based on aesthetic considerations is only a trivial part of the total demand for art. Individuals and institutions pay large sums for works of art for reasons that have nothing to do with art as such—two reasons in particular. First, art (or "art") in any form is a "collectible," like wind-up toys, Mickey Mouse souvenirs, stoneware, inkwells, beer cans, and almost everything else. For the rich, valuable art (or "art") is considered more suitable than, say, old toys. An important class of collectors are antiquarians: they attach value to whatever has some association with a famous person or event; they collect relics. It was as relics, not as art, that the Gilbert Stuart paintings of George and Martha Washington were valued at $6 million when purchased a few years ago by the National Portrait Gallery.

The other nonaesthetic interest in the demand for art, and the most important one in setting the price, is the investment interest. The investor views all engravings exactly as he does those on his certificates; he buys what he believes will increase in money value faster than other things that he might buy. (When this happens, it is thanks mainly to collectors and other investors.)

No criticism is intended of those who collect art or anything else, whether for pleasure or for profit. The point is that these nonaesthetic interests in the art market compete with the public interest in making the aesthetic experience of art more widely available and more frequent. The government, acting as proxy for the public as a whole, does not buy art on speculation or as a hedge against inflation. It does occasionally buy relics (the Stuart portraits, for example), but it does so on public-interest grounds different from those on which it usually buys art to stock its museums and decorate its public places.

From a public standpoint, it would be advantageous if the demand for art came only from those whose interest in it was purely aesthetic. In such a world the price of art would be much lower, and the public could afford to enjoy more of it. In reality, the public must compete for art in a market dominated by those whose interests are largely or entirely nonaesthetic. It would be greatly to the advantage of the public (and also of those individuals or institutions whose interest is, like the public one, purely aesthetic) if there were two markets for art: one for art as art and the other for art as a collectible and for investment.

In effect, enterprises that put high-quality reproductions on the market serve precisely this publicly advantageous separation of aesthetic from other values.[7] They make separate commodities of what would otherwise be joint ones: art as an aesthetic experience and art as a collectible or investment. Suppose, by way of illustration, that the joint (aesthetic-cum-collectible-cum-investment) value of a certain work is $3 million. Suppose also that it is possible to buy for $900 a copy of the work that gives the viewer exactly the same aesthetic satisfaction that he would get from the original. On these suppositions, $2,999,100 of the value of the original has nothing to do with art defined as aesthetic experience. A public institution or individual interested only in the aesthetic value of the work could buy the copy instead of the original and have $2,999,100 left over for the purchase of other sources of aesthetic satisfaction.

When there is only one example of a work of art, there is obviously no way to make it widely accessible. By bidding against one another, buyers do not increase the supply of art. They simply raise the price. Public institutions, using taxpayers' money, participate in this process, often bidding against one another for the existing supply. From the public standpoint, it makes more sense to use tax dollars to *increase* the supply and *decrease* the price of art.

The art world will object, saying that a copy, however good, cannot have the artistic value of the original. It is clearly true that most do not. But is it true that they *cannot*? From a purely aesthetic standpoint, it can make no difference when, where, or how a work was produced: all that matters is its quality as art. A priori there is no reason to believe that a copy—even a poor copy—cannot be an even *better* work of art than a very good original. And in fact this is doubtless sometimes the case. Michelangelo, Vasari tells us, "made copies of various old masters, making them look old with smoke and other things so that they could not be distinguished from the originals."[8] It is safe to say that the person imposed upon by one of Michelangelo's fakes was better off aesthetically than he would have been with another's original.

Leaving aside this possibility, it is evident that a copy may be, for most or even all viewers, aesthetically of equal value to the original. Most works of art can be copied "perfectly" from an aesthetic standpoint (meaning so well that differences cannot be shown without the use of sophisticated laboratory methods). The history of forgery makes it all too evident that such reproduction is possible. Moreover, there have been many cases in which experts have mistaken copies for originals for long periods of time. Painters and sculptors now and then have been unable to distinguish their own works from copies. Rodin, for example, made the mistake of suing a dealer who had offered for sale a perfectly authentic work of his.[9] The Metropolitan Museum displayed its three famous terra cotta Etruscan warriors under the label "Fifth Century B.C." for forty years before realizing that they were of modern origin.[10] The National Gallery displayed two "Vermeers" for years before discovering that they were fakes.[11]

In 1976 Cornell's art museum announced that a Corot that had been in the university's possession for a quarter of a century was a copy by one of his students, and a few days later it admitted to doubts about the authenticity of three other paintings, a sculpture, and several woodcut prints. One of the paintings, supposed to have been a Bierstadt, was found to be a lithograph painted over with varnish.[12] The following year the Cleveland Museum of Art declared that a painting for which it had paid between $1 and $2 million was a fake. Upon purchase, the director of the museum, Sherman Lee, had called it "a beautiful, mysterious painting, and of great historical importance." After laboratory tests showed it to be a twentieth-century forgery, it was no longer mysterious or of great historical importance; presumably, it was still beautiful, but that did not matter.[13] According to Oscar White Muscarella, a research fellow at the Metropolitan, hundreds of forgeries are exhibited by museums all over the world. In 1978 he published in *Bibliotheca Mesopotámica* a list of 247 objects or groups of objects from twenty-seven other museums and two great collections, all of which he said were fakes.[14]

It is a notorious fact that all forms of art have been successfully forged time and again. Robert Reisner's bibliography of *Fakes and Forgeries in the Fine Arts* lists 859 references, not including newspaper articles, to forgeries in twenty-two art forms.[15] Every important collection has been taken in on at least a few occasions. The Morgan Library recently exhibited seventy-five works by the so-called Spanish Forger, which it gathered from the collections of (among others) J. P. Morgan, the Metropolitan, the Fogg Museum of Art, the Beinecke Library at Yale, and the Cincinnati Art Museum.[16]

The Metropolitan Museum once found itself inadvertently producing forgeries when it discovered that reproductions of early American glassware in its museum shop were turning up in antique stores for sale as originals. To prevent such embarrassments, the Met now stamps "MMA" on all

146

but the very cheapest reproductions it sells. This device may help prevent copies from being passed off as originals, but the fact that it is necessary illustrates that the distinction is more commercial than aesthetic.

The identification of fakes depends largely on the development of laboratory techniques. Chemistry and physics, not the discerning eye of the art lover, make the difference. Had it not been for the spectrograph that revealed manganese dioxide in black glaze, the Metropolitan's Etruscan warriors might still be on display. And had van Meegeren not seen fit to confess, thereby bringing great numbers of works into the laboratories, the paintings of this supremely gifted forger—who sold six fake Vermeers for about $3 million— would still be giving pleasure to countless museum-goers all over the world.

Van Meegeren confessed in 1945 in order to avoid prosecution for selling art treasures to the Nazis. But he had a hard time convincing the authorities that his beautiful "Vermeers" were not valuable art treasures, but rather worthless fakes. According to W. K. Wimsatt, "The confession was officially accepted, more than two years later, only after the demonstrative painting by van Meegeren of a seventh Vermeer under court supervision and, what was of far more weight, the most rigorous radiographic, spectrographic, and microchemical testing of the forgeries by a large corps of Dutch, Belgian, British, and American technicians."[17]

The cult of the original is of rather recent origin, a product largely of investment and antiquarian interests and of the consequent growth of art history as a scholarly discipline. Moreover, even today it is not always clear what the word means or, indeed, whether it means anything of aesthetic significance. Some cultures—admittedly, ones utterly unlike our own, the ancient Egyptian and the Chinese, for example —made no distinction between originals and copies. Indeed, instructions were generally provided for making copies. The Romans attached very little importance to the difference between an original and a copy. Most Roman sculpture (what is today "original" Roman sculpture) was copied by Greek slaves from Greek originals. The Emperor Hadrian had innumerable copies made of famous statues, which now enrich the art museums of the world.[18]

During the Renaissance, an acknowledged imitation often brought as much as half the price of the original. There was no stigma attached to making or owning copies. The Holy Roman Emperor Rudolf II, in about the year 1600, sent his court painters to copy what was best in Venice and Rome. They did their work so well that experts are still trying to decide which is which.[19] In 1619, Rubens did not hesitate to write to a patron regarding a difficult subject: "I fear I shall have difficulty in finding among my pupils someone who will be capable of executing the work, even if I provide the drawing. In any case, it will be necessary for me to retouch the work with my own hand."[20] "Until we reach modern times," art historian Walter Pach writes, "copies, imitations, and even forgeries were made by men of such talent that the works possess qualities connoisseurs value in themselves."[21]

Many works admired as originals today are not as original as the viewer imagines. The figures in Michelangelo's *Last Judgment* in the Sistine Chapel were originally nude; Pope Paul IV had them clothed. "[W]hat we now admire in the works of the old masters," Etienne Gilson writes, ". . . is chiefly the damage caused to them by the passing of years and centuries." Much of this damage, he adds, is caused by restoration, "one of the surest methods scientifically to substitute new paintings for the old ones."[22]

It has been many years since most sculpture has been "original" in the strict sense, that is, carved by the hand of the artist. The normal practice is for the sculptor to make a model in clay, wax, or some other plastic material, which is then either sent to a foundry to be cast or recreated by workmen on the site where it is to be displayed. The dimensions of the finished work often differ from those of the model. Mechanical processes are used to enlarge or reduce the work, and the resulting artifact is at least slightly different from what the artist conceived. Rodin's marble works, for example, were carved, sometimes in multiples, by assistants using measuring instruments to transpose the proportions from plaster models, and his bronzes were produced by professional foundrymen in editions in which no "original" can be identified.[23] Having ordered, supervised, and approved them for sale, art historian and critic Leo Steinberg writes, the master is legally and morally responsible for them: "But he did not make them."[24] Some sculptors are very particular about the quality of the finished product, but others—among them Henry Moore—sell objects that they have never seen.[25]

The concept "original" must be stretched far to include certain famous and very valuable works, including several of Rodin's best-known works, which were not cast in bronze in his lifetime.[26] Of some 150 works of sculpture that were found in Degas' studio after his death only three had been cast in plaster and only one had been publicly shown; nevertheless, 73 were subsequently cast in bronze and are exhibited as "originals" in the Louvre, the Metropolitan Museum of Art, and elsewhere.[27] The huge Arp tapestry commissioned by the National Gallery was made after his death, from a small sketch, and the towering Picasso sculpture in Chicago was based on a small maquette of his design and never seen by him. Indeed, a court decision refused to stretch the word "original" this far: "The maquette," it ruled in 1970, "was an original work of art; the monumental sculpture was a mere copy."[28]

Prints also usually involve a collaboration between the artist and one or more craftsmen. Hans Holbein merely drew on a wood block, leaving the carving to others.[29] There have always been artists who are very particular about the quality of every print that is "pulled," but there are also some who are willing to leave the judgment to the printer and to sell work that they have never seen. Despite the efforts of organized artists to establish standards, the word "original" now has no definite meaning with reference to a print.[30] Black and white prints and drawings and much other art, especially works in modern styles, can be duplicated perfectly, or almost perfectly, by industrial processes. Other works, especially paintings in the old master style, can be copied perfectly by hand.

If the taboo against copies and reproductions were broken, works perfectly reproduced by industrial processes would be bought at very low per-unit prices by small art museums (including many not now existing for lack of money with which to buy worthwhile works), schools, libraries, and individuals. Works of kinds that do not lend themselves to perfect reproduction by such processes could also be perfectly copied, but at much higher cost. (The supply of first-rate talent for copying was vastly greater when art was also craft. In the contemporary art world, a person who might make a great copyist may never have learned to draw. If, however, the art world offered a respected place for copyists, as it does for restorers, the supply of them would doubtless increase and the price of copies decrease accordingly.)

Perfection, however, is not in all circumstances the appropriate standard. If one is willing to settle for copies that are "excellent" (meaning that no one but an expert can detect a difference with the naked eye), the cost will be less. And if one is willing to have copies that are just "very good" (meaning that an experienced and careful viewer gets almost as much aesthetic satisfaction from them as from an original), the cost will be lower still. A reasonable person must ask in what circumstances the difference between "very good" and "excellent," or between "excellent" and "perfect," is worth the difference in cost.

Some people believe that to accept anything short of perfection is philistinism. This, of course, is nonsense. We live in a world that requires at almost every moment a trade-off of some amount of one good for some amount of another. Aesthetic, and for that matter moral, values are not exempt from this necessity. Once again, the double standard for music and the visual arts is enlightening. Many people would never dream of having a "fake" Rembrandt on their walls, however high its quality, yet own and enjoy record sets of the Beethoven symphonies.

Far from encouraging the widest possible dispersal of art reproductions of as high a quality as is practicable, our current government policy aims to prohibit the making of copies that are not so poor as to be travesties of the originals. Forgery of art works, of course, has always been illegal. The art community, however, wants legal and other restrictions against copies good enough to be *mistaken* for originals. "The more exact the reproduction," write two Stanford professors, "the greater the potential confusion and the consequent devaluing effect."[31] They would require by law that reproductions of paintings, drawings, and fine prints be at least 20 percent larger or smaller than the originals and that they be clearly and indelibly labeled "reproduction." In the case of three-dimensional works, they would require a reduction in size of at least one-quarter. The Art Dealers Association is the most vigorous supporter of laws and "professional standards" to limit the quality of reproductions; the College Art Association of America and the Association of Art Museum Directors are generally its allies. Since most "great" art is now in museums, obviously the museums are in a position to obstruct any large-scale effort to make high-quality copies.

It is sometimes argued that it would be a cultural disaster for perfect reproductions of masterpieces to become dirt cheap. Familiarity would breed contempt. The painting before which one stood awestruck would become invisible. The *Mona Lisa* has been reproduced billions of times in the most preposterous contexts, but the crudeness of the imitations has helped to preserve the charm of the original. Would

even the *Mona Lisa* survive widespread near-perfect reproduction? (In fact, there is a *Mona Lisa* sitting in a bank vault
in New Jersey. The owners believe it is a later version by
Leonardo himself, a claim that cannot be disproved by the
experts. Naturally, the painting's value hinges completely on
this presently unanswerable question.)[32]

Some have suggested that this has also happened to the
great musical classics—that the Beethoven symphonies are
degraded, the aesthetic joys of hearing them reduced, by too
frequent and too casual hearing, however excellent the reproduction. But the purpose of encouraging reproduction of
visual-art masterpieces is not to enable people to see them
often enough to get sick of them, but to enable more people
to see them at all. No one is going to travel around looking
at *Girl with Mandolin* at dozens of different museums. Also, to
the extent that having a copy of a classic in your house is like
having Beethoven's Fifth Symphony playing all the time,
this is already true of those lucky enough to own originals.
Widespread reproduction would merely make both the
pleasures and the possible perils of owning topflight art more
widely available.

Some argue that works of art ought not be reproduced,
because they were created to be confronted by the viewer in
particular circumstances of time and place: to view them out
of this intended context is to see them distorted. But, of
course, almost all *original* works (except modern ones) *are*
seen out of context. And, indeed, the culture having
changed, it is impossible to experience a work from another
time and place as it was intended to be experienced.

Several powerful forces are at work to prevent the separation of artistic from pecuniary values. One consists of the
owners of objects whose financial value would be reduced if
reproductions lost their stigma and became legitimate alternatives to original works. If art museums, which directly and,
even more, indirectly (by virtue of the tax exemptions for
wealthy donors) are among the mainstays of pecuniary val-

ues, were to substitute reproductions for originals, the multibillion-dollar art business would fall into an acute and permanent recession.

Artists themselves, it should be noted, get little from present arrangements. Under American law, once a work leaves their hands, they have no right to share in the profit from future increases in the work's value, and no right to control or profit from reproductions. Artists would have nothing to lose if widespread reproduction slowed the appreciation of their past creations, and possibly something to gain, if—as part of an effort to encourage high-quality reproductions—the law were to assure the creator control over quality and part of the profit.

A second powerful force against acceptance of high-quality reproductions consists of that large part of the art world whose interest in art is historical rather than aesthetic. In the United States, the profession of art historian came into being early in the present century when J. P. Morgan and others of the fabulously rich took to stocking their mansions and museums with the art treasures of Europe. In order for their kind of collecting to be a workable game, there had to be umpires whose authority all players in the game would accept. Bernard Berenson, working with Lord Duveen, was the first and most important of these. Soon every major collection had to have its own expert capable of proving that a work long thought to be minor was really major. Art historians, especially those trained at Harvard, became the curators, and sometimes the directors, of the big art museums. Not surprisingly, in view of what they were trained and paid to do, art historians are often more sensitive to historical than to artistic values. In their eyes the authenticity of a work is of supreme importance.

To a large extent, the art-interested public consists of college graduates who learned from books and courses by art historians. Much of the public has been taught to see art as part of this history of culture, rather than as something to be responded to aesthetically. The professional's respect for the authentic, however inartistic, and his contempt for the inauthentic, however artistic, have all too often been communicated to his students and readers.

Finally, it must be said as a fact of psychology that the aesthetic interest is probably not entirely separable from the pecuniary. "We find things beautiful," Veblen observed, "somewhat in proportion as they are costly."[33] That something is costly associates it in our minds with famous persons and places, with power and glory, with what stirs emotions of respect, reverence, and awe. These emotions may have no proper place in the aesthetic attitudes, but they are likely to be there nonetheless. It would not be unduly cynical to say that many of the thousands who stood in line for a ten-second look at *Aristotle Contemplating the Bust of Homer,* after the Metropolitan Museum paid $2.3 million to acquire it, would as willingly have stood to see the $2.3 million in cash. To the extent that these nonaesthetic feelings are linked with aesthetic ones, the public will not accept a perfect copy (labeled as such) as a perfect substitute for the original. Asked how people would respond to perfect reproductions identified as such, Robert Cassellman, the associate director of the Boston Museum of Fine Arts, said he thought they would accept some as a supplement to a display of originals but without any originals the display would fail for lack of glamour. "What would your wife say," he asked, "if you went home and told her you saw a woman who looks *just like* Elizabeth Taylor? Not what she'd say if you said you'd seen Elizabeth Taylor in person!"

CHAPTER

7

"Fine" versus
"Applied" Art

In a world where the objects of daily use
and adornment were made with practical common sense, the aesthetic sense
would need far less to seek consolation
and repose in works of pure art.
—Roger Fry[1]

WHILE STILL in its first decade, the Museum of Modern Art
(MoMA) commissioned the chairman of the Dartmouth College Art Department, Artemas Packard, "to find out in what
way the Museum can most effectively develop aesthetic values in American life." In his lengthy report, Packard, after
some civilities about the value of art museums in general and
MoMA in particular, proposed that MoMA become something quite different from what it was.[2]

In essence, Packard was suggesting that art be supported
not primarily as a plaything for people of leisure but rather
as a guide and measure for all human activities and a means,

155

accessible to everyone in accordance with his need and capacity, to effect a more satisfactory adjustment to his environment. Most people, he said, were capable of finding aesthetic satisfaction in religion, sports, social intercourse, gardening, business enterprise, and even in tinkering with an automobile, which might be as profound and keen as that derived from looking at pictures. It was questionable whether the highly specialized interest in art, so earnestly cultivated by art museums and other educational institutions, was a help or a hindrance in stimulating aesthetic expression. He lamented the almost complete separation of the fine from the practical arts.

The central art problem of the time, Packard wrote, was not how to reorganize society so that painters and sculptors will be guaranteed greater public support in recognition of their special service to humanity. Rather, it was how to identify art with the main currents of contemporary life. The art world's exaggerated concern for the "fine arts" had left the aesthetic consciousness of the American people desperately befuddled by sentimentality and snobbism, which, in the name of Art, exalted a bad etching hanging in the parlor while ignoring a first-rate saucepan in the kitchen.

Mass production had at least revealed that low cost need not be an impediment to high artistic merit, and homes could be filled with objects as beautiful as those produced in the palmiest age of handicraft art. Here, then, was the great challenge to art education, which was far more important than most efforts to elevate the public taste through the study of the fine arts. The schools had not been able to offset the influence on public taste of the cinema, the radio, the department store, the mail-order catalog, and the popular press. Those who wanted to restore art to its proper place in modern civilization should make their head-on attack here, on the forces that chiefly conditioned public taste—forces that were most vulnerable to what affected the marketability of objects made to satisfy the ordinary requirements of daily life.

Although MoMA had done many things remarkably well, it hardly contributed anything new to the museum idea, according to Packard. By following his suggestion it could establish a department exclusively devoted to the industrial arts, whose chief function would be to support research, prepare exhibitions (*bad* design should be shown alongside of *good*), sponsor competitions for new designs of objects in general use, devise educational programs, and conduct a campaign of propaganda among manufacturers and merchandizers to increase their consciousness of their influence on public taste.

The Craft Origins of Art

The proper function of art has long been thought of as the enhancement of the meaning of all human activities rather than as a means of giving a special pleasure to a highly cultivated few. In the medieval languages of Europe, as in Greek and Latin, the word *art* simply meant making or doing.[3] In the Middle Ages paintings and statues were made by craftsmen who, deferring to the church, illustrated themes from the great books of Christian history in order to instruct an almost entirely illiterate public. Each work was a "page" in a "bible for the people." However beautiful, it existed not to be independently admired but to serve a particular function in the context of a whole, whose purpose was to show the sinner the way to God. It was obvious that the quality of work done by some craftsmen was of a higher order than that of others; no craftsman, however, sought to express himself creatively. To have aspired to be "creative" would have been impious.

Fine art had its beginnings in the individualism and the Neoplatonist humanism of the Italian Renaissance. By the fifteenth century, church adornments were less for "cult value" and more for "exhibition value."[4] The supremely gifted craftsman came to be seen—and to see himself—as possessed of divine (i.e., creative) powers. These few craftsmen were treated by popes and princes as people of consequence, but in general the status of painters and sculptors remained very low. In the reign of Pope Pius II, G. G. Coulton tells us, the painter Paolo Romano was admitted to the Great Hall, but the sculptor of the apostolic palace was "relegated to the second hall with the tailors, cooks, porters, couriers, grooms, sweepers, muleteers, water carriers and so forth."[5] In Elizabethan England, according to J. L. Propert, a court painter "was classed with the lowest servants of the establishment."[6]

"The essence of the Renaissance," wrote Frank Chambers, "was the conception of 'fine art.' "[7] The Renaissance, he wrote,

created the idea of ornament and decoration apart from symbolism, an idea which the Middle Ages, in its sense of practicalities and fondness for allegory, hardly knew. The Renaissance created the idea of style, of a superimposed form, conditioned by the character of the artist and by the age in which he lived. The Renaissance created the idea of the spectator, of the art-lover and connoisseur, for whom art was an intellectual diversion. The Renaissance created the idea of the individual artist, devoting his life to the production of beautiful things. The Renaissance created the idea of the artist's inspiration and inborn talent.[8]

It was not until the French Revolution that the artist became wholly separated from the artisan.[9] Paintings and sculptures were now movable and could be viewed independently of any context. They were made on commission for middle-class as well as aristocratic patrons, and were used for decoration, prestige, and investment. With the establishment of public galleries and museums, the artist ascended a pedestal. In the nineteenth century, the Romantic Movement made him a seer.

The artist now belonged to a world that the ordinary man could not enter. Pierre Joseph Proudhon wrote in 1863:

The artist lives in isolation, his thoughts are solitary . . . he has neither faith nor principles; he is given over to the atheism of his feelings and the anarchy of his ideas. He does not know how to make contact with the public. It is a melee in which nobody knows himself and everybody pulls his own way. How could they produce works with a popular appeal, they who know nothing about the soul of the people?[10]

Art Returns to the Useful

Ruskin and especially his great disciple William Morris were a powerful force working to bring life and art together. The "lesser" arts, Morris wrote, not only please the eye but enable men in general to understand and sympathize with the nobler forms that are produced only by great brains and miraculously gifted hands and would exist if men had no needs except essentially spiritual ones. If—as Morris saw happening—the two forms of art were parted from each other, then the lesser, so-called decorative arts would become trivial, mechanical, unintelligent, and incapable of resisting the changes pressed upon them by fashion or dishonesty. At the same time, the nobler arts would become a mere toy for the cultivated classes "till some will stand by and look at it [great art] as a curious exercise of the intellect, useless when done, though amusing to watch a-doing."[11]

Because the high and the lesser arts belonged together, Morris maintained, the true unit was a building with all its due ornament and furniture. Painting was of little use and sculpture of less, except where they formed a part of architecture:

159

A person with any architectural sense really always looks at any picture or any piece of sculpture from this point of view; even with the most abstract picture he is sure to think, How shall I frame it, and where shall I put it? As for a sculpture, it becomes a mere toy, a tour-de-force, when it is not definitely a part of a building, executed for a certain height from the eye, and to be seen in a certain light. And if this be the case with works of art which can to a certain extent be abstracted from their surroundings, it is, of course, the case *a fortiori* with more subsidiary matters.[12]

These ideas were widely influential. The art nouveau movement, which flared throughout Europe from about 1890 to about 1905, sought to create a visual environment that would alter the character of daily life. In Germany young artists, influenced by Ruskin and Morris, turned from easel painting "to conceive a room, the space it encloses, and all the furniture and objects belonging to it—the most modest part being as important as the whole."[13] In the Soviet Union Alexander Rodchenko and some friends, having decided that painting was "bourgeois romanticism," took up what they called production art: the design of housing, clothing, and other goods for workers. In the fashion of the times they issued a manifesto calling for the "fusion of life, work, and art."[14]

This approach to art found its most lasting and powerful expression in the Bauhaus School. At the outbreak of World War I, one of Morris's most gifted disciples, Henry Van de Velde, a Belgian, was head of the Weimar School of Applied Art in Germany. As an enemy alien, the Germans replaced him and appointed architect Walter Gropius, who reorganized the school and gave it the name Bauhaus.[15] Gropius and his associates had been influenced by Morris and his movement, but like most of their generation, they were entranced with the potentialities of the machine; their designs, whether for spoons, chairs, or office buildings, would represent "solutions" to "problems" of machine-age life. Although influenced by the aesthetics of cubism and by their admiration for the power and beauty of machines, the Bauhaus designers, like Morris before them, placed great value on simplicity. But whereas Morris believed that simplicity of life would beget simplicity of taste, Gropius and those of his school of thought, notably Le Corbusier, saw any deviation from simplicity ("structural and functional efficiency")—anything ornamental—as an irrational departure from the requirements of machine-age life. Bauhaus-designed objects —whether spoons, chairs, office buildings, or even chess pieces—looked like machines or machine products; they were made of metal, and were sharp-edged, highly polished, and cylindrical or hemispherical in form.[16]

These various efforts to turn art to the service of everyday life coalesced in a standard of good design—the "international modern style"—which, ironically, had close kinship to fine art but little to what MoMA's consultant, Packard, called "the major needs of society." For the past half century "good design" has referred to the appearance of useful objects that can be associated with the transcendental (or sometimes the nihilist) mode of aesthetic response: that is, an object—spoon, chair, office building, or whatever—is well designed if it has the visual attributes that *in a work of art* would be responded to with disinterested contemplation (or, if in the nihilist mode, with the kind of "interest" that relieves boredom). Modernist architects, although they claimed to be unconcerned with visual effects (they eliminated ornament in favor of smooth, continuous surfaces, and they made much of function by exposing the structural skeleton) were, without realizing it, adherents of the transcendental aesthetic mode. To the architects who came from Europe after the rise of Hitler, "functionalism meant pure ideology, visualizing self-evident truths."[17] Not surprisingly, the implicit aesthetic prevailed over the explicit commitment to functionalism; as critic Alexander Tzonis has put it, the modernist architecture turned "structural and functional containers into decoration."[18]

There was, of course, a fundamental contradiction in efforts to equate good design with the application of the modernist (i.e., transcendental or nihilist) aesthetic principle to the appearance of objects that existed not to be looked at but to be used. The essential idea of this aesthetic was that what belonged to the realm of ordinary experience could not enter into the aesthetic realm. If this was so, could what belonged to the realm of art be of use in the ordinary world?[19]

Usefulness Is Subordinated to Art

What had begun as an effort to improve the appearance of everyday things became an effort to turn everyday things into art. In this latter effort MoMA played a part even before Packard made his report. In 1934 it held an exhibition of Machine Art: among the 402 objects displayed were many household items—knives, forks, spoons, plates, bowls, lamps, chairs, vacuum cleaners, toasters—as well as industrial units, scientific instruments, and laboratory glass and porcelain. These were identified by maker and price; some were inexpensive—aluminum cake pans, for example, cost from thirty to fifty cents. MoMA's purpose, however, was not to show people how they could add meaning to their lives by buying useful objects that were also pleasing to the eye. Rather, it was to display machine-made products that could be experienced—well, almost—as fine art. "The beauty of machine art," Alfred H. Barr, Jr., wrote in a foreword to the catalog for the exhibition, "is in part the abstract beauty of 'straight lines and circles' made into actual tangible 'surfaces and solids.'" (The quoted words were from Plato's "Philebus.") In an accompanying note, the curator who arranged the exhibition—Philip Johnson, soon to be a famous architect in the international style—explained that all of the objects shown were, although useful, "chosen for their aesthetic quality."

With occasional and partial exceptions, MoMA's Department of Architecture and Design continued in the following decades to treat buildings, chairs, spoons, vacuum cleaners, and the rest as objects to be contemplated aesthetically rather than as things to be used. This was true even of its three exhibitions in the 1940s and 1950s: Useful Objects, Everyday Objects, and Good Design. Most of the objects displayed were unique rather than mass-produced; most cost far more than the ordinary person could afford; no effort was made to explain why a design was "good," and Packard's suggestion that examples of "good" and "bad" design be placed side by side was not acted upon.

In 1955, after a change of personnel, these exhibitions were discontinued because "the material was running pretty thin, and they were big shows that took a lot of time and got on everybody's nerves here, and besides, it had become a sort of shopper's service."[20] The museum has since contented itself with a small permanent display of items that it considers landmarks in the history of design—a few chairs, a record player, some kitchen and tableware, a motorboat propeller, and some other industrial items.

MoMA was not an organization that would discourage the pursuit of "pure" aesthetic satisfaction—induce artistic genius to devote itself to the "practical" arts, and so bring aesthetic values into the everyday life of the ordinary American. On the contrary, it was obliged to cater to a carriage trade of enthusiasts for what was modern. "It requires a certain level of taste, money, and education, *et cetera* to appreciate these things," the curator of the Design Collection, Stuart Johnson, told an interviewer in 1978. There were, he said, a lot of such people in New York; to try to reach beyond this privileged clientele with displays of everyday things would be pointless; worse, it would be "a sort of inverted snobbery."[21]

MoMA was not the only museum unable to show how

good design could give "genuine nourishment to the human spirit." The Cooper-Hewitt Museum of Decorative Arts and Design, an element of the Smithsonian Institution, exhibited objects of everyday use in the spring of 1979. It displayed about a half dozen objects in each of ten categories—coffeemakers, toasters, telephones, cameras, clocks, etc. The intention was not, as MoMA's was, to offer the objects for aesthetic contemplation. Nor was it to show the difference between good and bad design. Rather, it was to explain that consumers often choose things on other than aesthetic grounds. Here, for example, is the statement that accompanied one display:

COFFEEMAKERS AND JUICERS

The preparation of coffee and juice can be achieved by a variety of means, or processes. The choices include a manual or an automatic process, one that requires personal involvement or allows relative detachment. Only after a subjective choice of process does the choice of a coffeemaker or juicer make sense. Further affecting choice is the consumer's attitude toward innovation. A new, highly automatic form of coffee or juice preparation may be valued simply for its newness, or for the fascinating aura of convenience. By contrast, a tried and true process may also be valued for its old-fashionedness and for its aura of familiar ritual.[22]

Ada Louise Huxtable, a critic for the *New York Times,* wrote enthusiastically of this exhibition: "We are beginning to have a much more inclusive view of the art of design. It is a rich field for the study of cultural history and society's self-image."[23]

In displaying applied art as if it were fine art, MoMA did what others had long been doing. The Armory Show of 1913, which introduced modern modes of aesthetic experience to the United States, profoundly influenced designers and manufacturers. No one seems to have been disturbed by the incongruity of taking colors, lines, and forms that (according to modernist aesthetic conceptions) were "art" by virtue of their lack of relation to anything real for use to beautify gas pumps, bathing suits, trains, typefaces, fabrics, and just about everything else.

Sir Kenneth Clark remarked that, as a result of the show, "tachism" (derived from the French word *tache,* "stain," "splotch," "blob") spread to fabrics, the decoration of buildings, and the background of television programs, and became as much an international style as Baroque in the seventeenth century or Gothic in the fourteenth had been. Cubism, however, he went on to explain, remained the style of professional painters and specialized art lovers.[24] And as the unacknowledged aesthetic of the Bauhaus, it had much to do with the sharp outlines and machinelike finish of the towering metal and glass shafts built for offices and apartments, not to mention the similar outlines and finishes of cigarette lighters, pencil sharpeners, coffee tables, and more.

It was predictable that modern design would not suit the taste of the masses. In 1925 José Ortega y Gasset pointed out that the exclusion of everything humanly interesting from modern art was bound to make it unpopular. Presumably, designs that parodied this "dehumanized" art, making the ordinary man's visual environment incomprehensible to him, would also be unpopular.

To be sure, some talented designers had striking success in adapting "good design" in ways that improved sales; the styling of products, usually by streamlining, was not taken seriously by the arbiters of "good design," however. None of the designers who helped manufacturers reach mass markets ever managed to get one of his products displayed by MoMA. When it came to the most important thing that he bought—his house—the average person could not be persuaded to accept even a watered-down version of modernism.

In the Ruskin-Morris era, artist-designers did not doubt that there was a high degree of compatibility between the values of good appearance and of usefulness or efficiency.

Given their aesthetic, this was highly plausible. "A work of art," wrote W. R. Lethaby, a disciple of Morris, "is first of all a well-made thing. It may be a well-made statue or a well-made chair, or a well-made book. . . . Most simply and generally art may be thought of as *the well doing of what needs doing.*"[25] But with the coming of the modernist aesthetic, what had been highly plausible became altogether implausible: a chair designed for disinterested contemplation was unlikely to fit the contours of the body if it could be sat on at all. In an article decrying the "design fallacy"—that is, sacrificing too much functional efficiency for aesthetic values —Paul Goldberger, a critic for the *New York Times,* found chairs of Le Corbusier, Marcel Breuer, and Mies van der Rohe "rather uncomfortable" but "nonetheless so handsome that it can be argued that [they] are worth having around just to look at."[26] Enthusiasm for good design had led to what, by any standard except the aesthetic, was bad design.

By the late 1970s there was growing doubt about the goodness of what had long been "good design." MoMA's 1979 exhibition "Transformations in Modern Architecture" was called wrong-headed by a critic who said that it failed to reflect the current dissatisfaction and dissension among architects and other arbiters of taste.[27] The next year Philip Johnson (who before becoming a famous architect in the international style put together MoMA's 1934 exhibition of machine art) announced in the *New York Times* that " 'Modern,' the style of the last 50 years, taught us that the flat room, the flat glass wall, the flat featureless facades would be universal and that men would live better, cheaper, more moral lives surrounded by such abstract, functional, simple shapes. Today we no longer feel this way."[28]

The failures of modern design have been elaborately described by Peter Blake, an architect and critic who as a young man was also a MoMA curator. In *Form Follows Fiasco,* he explains that the ideal of an architecture of pure, geometric forms did not take into account such mundane facts as weathering and maintenance.[29] Skyscrapers (fifty to one hundred floors), he points out, must have walls ("skins") of the lightest possible weight; to the purists of the modern movement the ideal covering was glass. However, the heat loss (and gain) of glass is ten times that of masonry filled with insulation. Moreover, tall buildings require deep foundations; when pumps are necessary to keep the ground water level down, piles supporting neighboring structures will rot. The technical innovation most closely associated with modern architecture, Blake continues, is reinforced concrete and steel framing. By eliminating the need for all but a few slender and widely spaced supporting columns, open planning of houses and office spaces is made possible. This is aesthetically appealing but, according to Blake, not as practical as it may first appear. In housing, the value of open space depends upon the availability of servants or "enslaved wives" to keep it in order; it is also destructive of family life: children, deprived of their privacy, congregate in public spaces and vandalize them. The rise and fall of the ideal of the Vertical City was dramatically exemplified by the history of the Pruitt-Igoe public housing project in St. Louis, Missouri. Acclaimed by the architectural profession when it was built—it won the American Association of Architects' Award—in twenty years it had been reduced to a shambles by the angry people who lived in it. "The collapse—in a dynamite blast on April 21, 1972—of the first Pruitt-Igoe slab," critic Wolf von Eckhardt wrote, "seems to me to mark the beginning of the end of abstract architecture."[30]

The Invasion of the Crafts

While the embrace of the modernist aesthetic on architecture was loosening, it was tightening on the decorative crafts. Roger Fry wrote that, while there was every reason for works of fine art to be, from the purely sensual point of view, supremely and magnificently ugly, a china pot that existed for use rather than for contemplation had no excuse for being ugly. In the craft enterprise that he himself attempted during World War I, Fry did his best to combine beauty with use. His doctrine, however, which asserted the radical separation of the "supersensual" (the aesthetic experience produced by disinterested contemplation of fine art) from the merely "sensual" (the pleasure of seeing a useful thing that was well made), put the artist and the craftsman in wholly different worlds.

That one of these worlds would invade the other was to be expected, and clearly the craft world, being merely sensual, whereas the other is supersensual, was the more vulnerable. "Invasion," according to sociologist Howard S. Becker, is what happens when members of the art world see a potential for artistic exploitation in the materials and techniques of one of the crafts. He writes:

They see a way to do something that will interest the art world to which they are oriented and to which they respond. They have no interest in the conventional standard of practical utility: their notion of beauty is likely to be very different from and more advanced than that of the craft they are invading and the kind of skill and control that interests them is likely to be very different from that prized by the more traditional practitioner.

The new breed of artists in the craft devise new and aggressively non-utilitarian standards. Only the utilities defined by the art world in which they participate interest them. Art utilities typically include usefulness as objects of aesthetic contemplation, as objects of collection and ostentatious display, and as items of investment and pecuniary gain.

Not only does the invading artist typically devalue craft standards of skill, but, Becker says, he "may deliberately create crudities . . ., either for their shock value or to show their freedom from that particular set of conventional craft constraints." Unlike the craftsman, he takes pains to make each object unique. "No one wants to buy a copy from an artist, only from a craftsman."[31] (Becker's book includes several striking photographs of craft works by "invading" artists.)

Insofar as this invasion produces things that are experienced aesthetically, the gain to art may more than offset the loss to craft: if the teakettle that does not hold water manages—perhaps by virtue of its phallic-shaped spout—to jolt the viewer either into the realm of aesthetic contemplation or briefly out of his chronic boredom, then an aesthetic success will have been achieved. What must be kept in mind is that success in providing aesthetic experience in the modern (transcendental and nihilist) modes is apt to constitute failure to provide it in other modes (ideational and romantic) to which a great many people remain attached. Objects that are at once useful and pleasing to the eye may for all we know help to give meaning to everyday activities and, in this way, to life itself, and by so doing make fine art of less value.

It would be foolish to suppose that the craft world is about to be occupied and subjugated by the invading art world. The incursion already made is not small, however, and governmental and other agencies may use their resources rapidly to enlarge it. Under the headline "Planning a Future for American Crafts," the *New York Times* reported NEA's announcement of a National Crafts Planning Project "to survey the current needs of estimated 40 million craftsmen in the United States." "Craftspeople," the director of the project was quoted as saying, "perform an aesthetic function, but have nonetheless been missing out on opportunities generally available to those in the performing arts, because of a lack of organization and a national focus." Craftsmen (". . . those who invest the work of the hand with energy and spirit") include hobbyists, ethnic groups such as American Indians, and *"university-based artisans, who are in the forefront of the new crafts movement."* (Emphasis added.)[32] A craftsman seeking success may view the displays at the American Crafts Museum (some supported in part by the NEA), read its lavishly illustrated, bimonthly magazine, *American Craft,* or visit one of the markets presented in various parts of the country by its subsidiary, American Craft Enterprises; what he will soon realize is that the objects on display (i.e., those most admired by sophisticated people and therefore most likely to win media attention, get the artists teaching positions in colleges, and enable them to sell their works to collectors) are unique, novel, amusing, and frequently shocking (if possible). Sometimes—but by no means always—they are well made; often they are quite useless. The Craft Museum's exhibition Handmade Furniture, which was launched from New York in 1979 for a two-year tour through the United States and Canada, had among its forty-odd pieces a chair carved and painted to resemble parts of the female torso, a carved umbrella stand containing a wooden umbrella, tables without surface space, desks with drawers too small to hold paper, and much else that claimed attention as art. Marion Muller, a reviewer, found two important elements lacking throughout: taste ("The word has been drummed out of existence in the fine arts . . .") and ornamentation (". . . in our time there exists no urge to decorate lovingly or evocatively").[33]

Sculpture: Art or Monument?

What has been happening in the world of crafts has been happening in the world of public monuments and statues; it, too, has been invaded and seen its usefulness sacrificed to aesthetics. Until about a half century ago, outdoor works in stone and metal were sometimes seen as art, sometimes as memorials, and sometimes—indeed often—as both in combination. In the nineteenth century, statues and monuments were popular; some cities accumulated enormous numbers of them—so many in some instances that public spaces were in danger of being filled.[34] The example of the Washington Monument and Grant's Tomb notwithstanding, sculpture cannot successfully address itself simultaneously to the real world and to the (allegedly) categorically different aesthetic realm. The fifty-foot steel obelisk opposite the United Nations Building may be aesthetically satisfying, but it does not bring to mind Ralph Bunche, whose life and work it celebrates. The giant (twelve-foot) statue of Albert Einstein commissioned by the National Academy of Sciences is, according to the president of the academy, Philip Handler, "symbolic of the contributions of science to our society." The artistic world, however, "is unanimous that this is an enormous piece of kitsch," according to Paul Farman, the organizer of a Smithsonian Institution exhibit on Einstein.[35]

The tension, or incompatibility, between art (that which engenders aesthetic experience) and memorialization (that which keeps remembrances alive) was dramatically demonstrated during the construction of the Vietnam Veterans Memorial. Originally designed as a pair of two black granite walls two hundred feet long meeting to form a V enclosing a sloping plot of ground ("in a sense, a tabula rasa, a blank slate—not a room, not a building, not a plaza, not a park, not a conventional memorial at all," *New York Times* critic Paul Goldberger wrote), it now includes a fifty-foot flagpole and an eight-foot-high, realistic statue of three American fighting men. It was a change that was made at the insistence of veterans organizations and over the protests of its designer and, Goldberger wrote, that "seems intent on converting a superb design into something that speaks of heroism and of absolute moral certainty."[36] Today the normal assumption, one critic writes, is that it is impossible to have a public art in the sense of one that solicits a wide audience and deals with subject matter of recognizable social import: "All we can ever do is put private art in public places."[37]

This "normal assumption" should acknowledge that there currently are many artists who work at creating visually pleasing subway stations, colorful playgrounds, charming small parks, and good-looking "street furniture" (streetlights, parking meters, bus-stop benches). These efforts, however, have nothing in common with what is called "public sculpture." That is indeed "private art": art that has been moved out of the art museum and into a public place—a plaza in a central business district, an airport, a shopping center, a college campus, or a highway border. Like all fine art, it exists to be experienced aesthetically, not to be decorative, and certainly not to convey some symbolic or other message to the members of the public.

Almost all contemporary public sculpture is meant to be responded to in the transcendental or nihilist mode; consequently, it is unintelligible, or bizarre, when viewed by the standards of other modes. Chicago, for example, has a 101-foot-high baseball bat in front of its Social Security Administration building. Hartford has a triangle of thirty-six rocks, some weighing as much as eleven tons, arranged in a grassy plot adjacent to a historical graveyard and church. Grand Rapids has three steel beams bolted together to form a tripod from which an old truck is suspended.[38]

The federal government is principally responsible for the spread of public sculpture. In January 1963 President Kennedy's administrator of the General Services Administration (GSA), Bernard L. Boutin, made it a policy to commission works of art for public buildings at a cost not exceeding one-half of one percent of the construction budget. In the summer of 1966, after a row broke out in Boston over a Robert Motherwell mural installed in the John F. Kennedy Federal Building there, the program was suspended.

President Nixon's first GSA administrator, Arthur F. Sampson, brought it back to life in late 1972 ("The importance of vigorously promoting this program cannot be overstressed," regional officials were told from headquarters), and it flourished for the next two years. Early in 1976 a new GSA administrator, responding to protests from congressmen, taxpayers, and others, stopped the program pending a review. In April 1977 President Carter's appointee gave the program his enthusiastic support, as did Joan Mondale and her circle.[39]

Despite these ups and downs, the director of the program, Donald Thalacker, has remained in this position since 1973. By 1982 the GSA had commissioned 208 works of art at a cost of approximately $6.7 million. Over the years numerous bills authorizing the allocation of some portion of construction costs for the purchase of fine art were introduced in Congress; none ever reached a vote.

Since 1966 the NEA has also been an important supporter of public sculpture. Through its Art in Public Places program, it makes grants ($900,000 in fiscal 1980) to enable cities, universities, not-for-profit private groups, and state arts agencies to commission or purchase works of art for parks, airports, and other public places. The 1978 guidelines describe what the agency hopes the program will achieve:

. . . the work of art will contribute to the public's enjoyment, education, and enlightenment; that it will create a favorable climate for the reception of the arts; that it will stimulate an effective partnership between cities, states, private institutions, the private sector, and the Federal Government; and that a distinguished heritage of public art will be passed on to future generations.

Judged by these criteria, it is a rare piece of public sculpture that can be called a success. In many cities—probably in a large majority (it is impossible to be sure because the NEA has kept no record of public response, not even a clippings file)—the public, meaning those people who received attention from the press and television, greeted the sculptures with hoots of derision and howls of rage.[40] In a few places works were removed because of opposition. As a rule, however, people learned to live with works that had at first irritated or angered them, and some—apparently a relative few almost everywhere—came to like them. Public opinion rarely prevented mayors and city councils from supporting proposals initiated by the city's business or cultural elite to secure works by famous sculptors: politicians find it hard to refuse anything that will cost their constituents nothing (NEA grants were usually matched by private contributions) while adding to the city's prestige. Thus, while he was in Congress, Gerald R. Ford once told the House that when Grand Rapids "purchased what is called 'a Calder' " it was "somewhat shocking to a lot of people." Some years having passed, he could now assure the members "that the Calder in the center of the city, in an urban redevelopment area, has really helped to regenerate a city." It was, he added, "a good investment."[41]

As NEA's program director for visual arts, Brian O'Doherty took a relaxed view of the battles that raged over public sculptures. Indeed, he was rather pleased by them: for the first time in their lives people were having to respond to art. Was this not NEA's very reason for being? His successor, James Melchert, changed the agency's procedures to give local people more of a say in the choice of artists and the nature of the works to be commissioned. In the past the NEA had chosen three nationally known advisers to meet with three local representatives to select the artists; not surprisingly, the views of the national "celebrities" always prevailed. "I didn't think the federal government had any business telling people what kind of art they had to have," Melchert later said. Accordingly, he required that local people take the initiative with a letter proposing a site and giving some account of the kind of work that they thought people would enjoy. Their proposal would then be reviewed by NEA panelists, who would make suggestions. This change of procedure did not make as much difference as Melchert had expected; the locals tended to propose the same celebrated artists whose work the NEA had supported in the past. "Generally the work has been less adventurous," he said, "but relations with the communities have been better."[42]

Melchert's opinion that the federal government had no business telling people what kind of art they had to have was of course (although he seemed not to realize it) heretical. When Mary Miss, a sculptor, met with the National Council on the Arts in November 1980, she said that early public involvement in decisions about art in public places should be solicited in order to ease as much as possible the public's irritation with such art. Without exception those council members who participated in the ensuing discussion disagreed. Public relations, one member said, could not be allowed to stifle an artist's impulses. Another feared that the NEA would "perish of terminal blandness" if it did not employ "risk capital." Artistic freedom, another said, was simply a facet of freedom of speech. The chairman of the Visual Arts Policy Panel thought fear of controversy made some artists less innovative than they would otherwise be; artists and the public alike needed to be convinced of the value of controversy as "a clarifying force."[43]

The other federal agencies sponsoring art in public places —the GSA, the Veterans Administration, and the Department of Transportation—did not take to consulting with local representatives. The reason, Melchert surmised, was that they did not want to spend the considerable sums that consultation costs.

"Good" Design versus the Market

Those who wanted to restore art to its proper place in modern civilization, Packard wrote in his report, should pay particular attention to the forces that affect the marketability of objects of everyday use. In 1974, long after this advice had been forgotten, MoMA launched a major undertaking whose purpose was to make a particular object of everyday use more acceptable to consumers by improving its design. It had in the past held competitions and exhibitions that resulted in some classics of modern design, the most notable, perhaps, being chairs designed by Eero Saarinen and Charles Eames. Although the chairs and other things were widely imitated, no one could suppose that they significantly affected the life of the ordinary man. Now, however, MoMA's curator of design, Emilio Ambasz, proposed something that he thought would: the creation of a taxicab that would efficiently serve the needs of the industry, drivers, and passengers. With grants from the Department of Transportation and the Mobil Oil Corporation, and in close collaboration with the Taxi and Limousine Commission of New York City, he and a staff of consultants drew up a set of design specifications. Automobile companies were invited to build prototype cars based on these specifications. The cars would be exhibited by the museum, with the expected result of a significant improvement of transit in New York and other large cities.

Curiously, in view of MoMA's predilection for treating objects of use as objects of art and in view also of Ambasz's control of the project, the "design solution" turned out to have no explicit visual content. In his introduction to *The Taxi Project,* the catalog published by the museum, Ambasz did not mention visual considerations. "These taxis," he wrote, "specially designed for meeting urban traffic conditions, might considerably improve the quality of life in the urban environment, for they would use less energy, reduce air pollution, and cut traffic congestion, as well as provide safe and comfortable accommodations for passengers and luggage."[44] If he expected the appearance of the taxis to contribute to the quality of life in the city, he did not say so.

The taxicab project was less than successful; no American automobile or engine manufacturer would participate in it. The Urban Mass Transportation Administration came to MoMA's rescue by supporting an open-bid competition to pay two American companies to build vehicles meeting the design specifications. MoMA offered to display prototype cars built by European manufacturers who agreed to mass-produce the cars in the United States "if the market proved satisfactory." Volvo and Volkswagen accepted the invitation, and Alfa-Romeo adopted the specifications, but for a taxi to be sold in Europe. Between June and September 1976 the museum exhibited five prototype cars. In the title of its catalog the museum claimed that these were "realistic solutions" of a design problem. Perhaps they were. But the taxi problem was never solved.

That museums are remarkably ill-suited, as compared to profit-seeking manufacturers operating in a competitive market, to innovate in such matters had been remarked on long before Packard made his enthusiastic recommendations. William Stanley Jevons, a great economist, writing shortly before Queen Victoria laid the cornerstone for the Victoria and Albert Museum, pointed out that from the standpoint of manufacturers the museum's huge collection would be obsolete almost as soon as it was assembled. Technically minded people, he explained, wanted to see *new* things. One had only to saunter down Holborn from Bloomsbury to the Holborn Viaduct to see the newest in machinery, domestic utensils, tools, toys, and the infinite objects of ordinary use. No exhibition—not even, Jevons said, one with the most distinguished patronage—could possibly compete with what was to be seen in the shop windows.[45]

CHAPTER

8

Art versus Welfare

It makes no sense to be ungrateful for
performance and production, or for the
fortunate survival of civic benevolence.
But subsidized events for large audiences tend inevitably to become a kind
of cultural welfare. They are designed for
the largest common denominator, and
frequently translate art into another medium.

—Ronald Berman[1]

AS CHAIRMAN of a panel of the Eisenhower Commission
on National Goals, August Heckscher wrote a chapter for its
1960 report, in which he gave some advice to the federal arts
agency that would certainly come into being before long. In
its support of the arts, he said, the government should be
entirely clear about its purposes. It should not seek to increase employment among impoverished artists, conduct a
welfare program for deprived citizens, or try to win the cold
war by showing that we have more and better art than rival
regimes. Rather "it should seek to encourage art for its own
sake as an expression of what is noblest in the people's lives:

it should seek to create for the public the finest objects to which our culture can attain."[2]

The report acknowledged that where government had entered directly into the field of art the results had often been disheartening: the standards of artists and critics had been ignored, and the tendency had been for an artistic clique to entrench itself. It would be wrong, however, to conclude that anything was better than the intrusion of government; in some fields, no less delicate than art—Heckscher cited the National Institutes of Health and the National Science Foundation—the political system had acted in accordance with the highest and most sophisticated standards.

Twenty years later the NEA had done all of the things that the panel said it should not do: it had subsidized the employment of thousands of artists (by no means all of them impoverished); it had spent many millions to bring arts to people who were "deprived"; and it had supported efforts to use the arts as a weapon in the cold war. At the same time, it had conspicuously failed to do—or even to try to do—what the panel had said was most important: it had been extremely vague about its purposes even when—indeed, especially when—they were more or less contradictory.

The confusion of purpose began in Congress. In the 1965 National Foundation on the Arts and the Humanities Act it set forth a Declaration of Purpose consisting of seven "findings" (that support of the arts and humanities was an appropriate concern of the federal government, and so on); it defined "the arts" with a long list of activities (which was not to be understood as limiting); and it listed the authorities to be exercised by the NEA chairman.*

Just what Congress had intended all this to accomplish, however, was not easily understood. It wanted to increase the quantity and quality of aesthetic experience. But what kind or kinds of aesthetic experience did it have in mind—

---

*The language defining the arts and listing the authorities of the chairman is quoted in chapter 3, note 2.

"revealing the depths of one's being," producing "a loss of the sense of place and bodily consciousness," inducing "an attitude of communion and contemplation," or apprehending "something with pleasure"? Did it also (contrary to the advice of the Eisenhower panel) want to use art to increase employment of impoverished artists, help the deprived, or try to win the cold war?

Congress emphasized that only high-quality art should be supported: the act contained the phrases "professional excellence," "professional standards of authenticity," "artistic and cultural significance," and "significant merit." But in the contemporary visual-art world there are no standards in the sense that there are in, say, the world of baseball. Indeed, what can "professional" mean as applied to artists? Surely Congress did not intend to limit support to those who were well established and widely known. The Senate committee report that accompanied the bill endorsed "the concept that amateur interest in the arts is necessary to their well-being" and that this interest "should be stimulated and encouraged in all possible ways."[3]

Congress wished to promote art of professional quality (but without neglecting amateur efforts) and also to bring art to a wide audience. In listing the authorities of the chairman, the act included support of "workshops that will encourage and develop the appreciation and enjoyment of the arts by our citizens." In the section authorizing grants to the states, it went further: the NEA might aid the states to "furnish *adequate* programs, facilities, and services in the arts to *all the people and communities in each of the several States.*" (Emphasis added.)

There is, of course, an antagonism, if not a contradiction, between the two intentions: to foster art of "professional excellence," and to bring such art to "all the people." If it were not for the determined opposition of the art world, these objectives might in some degree be reconciled by the creation and distribution of perfect, or near-perfect, copies of works of art as proposed in chapter 6. If, however, excellence in visual art is understood to require "original" works, then it is manifestly impossible to make excellence widely available. Apart from this difficulty—or impossibility—there is another; relatively few people respond aesthetically to art of high quality. "The fine arts," the panel cautioned in *Goals for Americans,* were "creations of the few, directed to the comparatively small and specialized audience."

The vague and contradictory language of the 1965 act was evidence of the competence of the politicians who drafted it. Their task was to find terms with which the supporters of the legislation, whose interests were varied and more or less conflicting, could agree. Unless the bill said everything and nothing, it would not have had enough support to pass.

It was a mistake to believe that once the act was passed its purposes would be clarified by its administrators. There is no "technical" procedure for turning general value statements into specific standards and criteria. Moreover, although the administrators had some latitude in interpreting the act, they were obliged to try to do what it said even if what it said was something that could not possibly be done (as in the matter of bringing excellent original art to all people). Finally, the administrators were under pressures similar to those that the legislators had been under: in fact, administration of the act was a continuation of the processes of accommodation and compromise that had brought about its passage. If the NEA was to survive and grow—its one clear purpose—then it could not afford to have a coherent set of well-defined goals: nothing would have brought it to ruin faster. When W. McNeil Lowry complained that after fourteen years the NEA's policies were even vaguer than the legislation, he gave unwitting testimony to the adroitness of its administrators.

The political and bureaucratic processes shaping the NEA were not at all unusual. In the postwar years it became easier to get bills through Congress. Not only have Supreme Court decisions stretched the powers of the federal government, but changes in institutions have contributed to the steady enlargement of the federal agenda. The decline of political parties, for example, and the concurrent growth of single- and public-interest pressure groups (the latter are groups that seek benefits for a public without special advantages to their members, supporters, or activists) have been important factors.[4] In these recent decades it has usually sufficed to have a sprinkling of activist supporters in many congressional districts and no activist opponents or very few. If the key committee chairmen—for example Claiborne Pell in the Senate and Frank Thompson (and later John Brademas) in the House—are keen supporters of a bill and if the White House does not oppose it, its eventual passage is usually assured. Not surprisingly, the "Individual programs," to quote an Advisory Commission on Intergovernmental Relations (ACIR) report, "have been created largely on a hit or miss basis, chiefly reflecting the entrepreneurial activities of policymakers and organized interests."[5]

On the basis of a study of three federal programs (military employment, water and sewage grants, and model cities grants) R. Douglas Arnold concludes that bureaucrats allocate the benefits of their programs "strategically in an effort both to maintain and to expand their supporting coalitions. When it furthers their purposes, they broaden their program's geographic scope and increase the number of shares of benefits so that more congressmen can be brought into their supporting coalitions. When necessary they allocate extra shares of benefits to leaders and to those who are crucial coalition members."[6]

A study by the staff of the ACIR of the expansion of the federal role in seven policy areas (fire protection, public assistance, elementary and secondary education, the environment, unemployment, higher education, and libraries) found that in all areas the process was much the same: a congressional entrepreneur, or issue activist, "played a consistently crucial role" in the initiation of the expansion; there was "a surprising lack of sustained Presidential importance in the policy process," although "even passing White House interest" sometimes gave a potential program enough importance to secure its passage; the significance of interest groups lay "not in their greatly exaggerated abilities to create or successfully advocate brand new policies but rather in the ability of policies to generate new interest groups." Once established, "a group will inevitably work to sustain the policy which gave it life. If policy is primarily 'created' by Congress, to interest groups—the 'offspring' of policy—accrues their 'care and feeding.' "[7]

If the process that established the NEA was fairly typical, then so was the translation of its mandated purposes into "programs." When the Urban Institute studied the way major government programs were evaluated, it found that most of them "lacked adequately defined criteria of program effectiveness." The lack, it said, "stems partially from the fact that the typical federal program has multiple objectives and partially from difficulties in defining objectives in measurable terms, particularly when the authorizing legislation is very general."[8]

In such matters the difference between a public organization and a private or quasi-private one, such as an art museum, is one of degree. By definition, an organization is public insofar as it is subject to control by the public, which is to say by officials, elected or appointed, who are more or less responsive to the political pressures that play upon them. The art museum, because it is run by a self-perpetuating board of trustees, is better able to resist "outside" pressures than an organization that must come before an elected body every year to ask for appropriations. Nevertheless, the art museum, like all organizations, is intent upon surviving and growing and therefore cannot be immune to such pressures. Typically it, too, prefers a gain (however small) in terms of its maintenance needs to one (however large) in terms of its substantive goals. Thus, it invests little in program analysis and planning. Being entirely clear about its purposes would be dangerous for it, too.

In varying degrees, all of the institutions discussed here—the NEA, the art museum, and the public school—have adapted to their maintenance needs and opportunities by subordinating aesthetic to extra-aesthetic values: they have found it advantageous to present as art what is in fact only incidental to it. To be sure, some extra-aesthetic offerings are of great interest; nevertheless, presenting them as art misleads people.

The Redefinition of Art

The NEA's emphasis on building constituencies has made it an active agent in what Ronald Berman, a former chairman of the NEH, has called the "redefinition" of artistic activity. In collaboration with the various arts lobbies, the state arts agencies, and the key congressional committees, the NEA, Berman says, has sanctioned the idea that the primary purpose of the support of art is the distribution of funds. The arts constituency, he writes, "determines finally what the definition of art or of 'the arts' will be. And that constituency has in the most determined way exempted artistic activity from critical standards. Art is whatever is done, whether crafts, hobbies, or simply the display of intentions. It is an ennobled form of middle-class entertainment."[9]

In their own ways, the art museum and the public school were "redefining" art long before the NEA was created. Neither of these institutions could reconcile itself to occupying the very restricted role that would be open to it if it treated art solely, or even mainly, as that which engenders aesthetic experience. Organizational entrepreneurs saw that the potential for growth ("making an impact," etc.) lay elsewhere; for example, in substituting the history of art, or of culture, for aesthetic experience, or in creating a mix that was mostly entertainment or psychotherapy.[10]

Arts institutions have found it advantageous to redefine art because there is relatively little demand for aesthetic experience of the kind that it affords. Basically, few people in our society respond intensely to what art museums, schools, and other authoritative institutions define as good, let alone great, art. If redefining its product to appeal to a larger clientele enables an organization to grow and prosper, then it must probably be expected to do so.

The tendency to subordinate aesthetic to extra-aesthetic values is not, then, an accidental or temporary feature of the situation. It results from the dynamic of organizational life processes. It will not change with a change of administration, and it cannot be reformed by "more enlightened leadership."

If these observations are accepted, then the art lover must view the continuance of the public arts agencies with much apprehension. The prospect is that they will build an ever-larger alliance of interests, whose effect will be to redefine art in ever more inclusive—and less plausible—terms.

Indirect versus Direct Aid

If one assumes that public support of art is desirable, there is much to be said for ending direct support and relying, as was done before 1965, upon tax exemptions and other forms of indirect aid. The indirect-aid system established an astonishing number and variety of arts institutions, many of them of the highest quality, and it still provides far more revenue than direct appropriation. While Americans who ought to have known better were expressing embarrassment at what they supposed was the failure of their government to support the arts, foreigners were viewing the American system of indirect aid with admiration. Lord Lionel Robbins, a distinguished economist who was long a trustee of the Tate and National galleries, has written:

> In the United States you see great galleries and museums, splendid libraries and research centers, all springing from private donation induced by the tax incentives. Here [in Britain] you see the springs of private benefactions virtually dried up by the incidence of penal taxation and all cultural institutions more or less dependent on state initiatives which more often than not are too little and too late. . . . [C]an there be any serious doubt as to which system is preferable?[11]

Indeed, some have serious doubts. The tax-incentive system allows the donor to give what from a public standpoint is the wrong thing to the wrong institution: he may present a children's room to a museum that desperately needs repairs to its roof, or he may bequeath a Rembrandt to an eastern museum that already has many rather than donate the painting to a southern museum that has none. A museum director who does not court prospective donors may lose his job no matter how outstanding his qualities. The public is often unrepresented on the board of trustees of a museum that depends mainly upon tax-exemption incentives to supply income.

These and other disadvantages are more than offset by two great advantages. One, emphasized by Lord Robbins, is that tax incentives yield large amounts of revenues without depending in any direct way upon state initiatives. The other is that the indirect system, being wholly decentralized in its operation, offers no place for an organization, such as the NEA, whose ceaseless effort is to create an ever-larger coalition of interest groups and thus (an inescapable consequence of this) to give a constant impetus to the redefining of art. To be sure, the indirect system also supports organizations that promote extra-aesthetic values at the expense of aesthetic ones. It does not, however, give them special encouragement, let alone make them a politically powerful coalition.

Art versus Welfare

Nelson Rockefeller, August Heckscher, and the others who proposed direct support to supplement the system of indirect support did so in the belief that aesthetic values, especially those of modern art, could be more effectively advanced by a public agency set up for that express purpose. This was a plausible expectation at a time when—so it seemed—almost any problem could be solved by a bureaucracy with the right authority and enough money. Twenty years of experience has shown that the expectation was unrealistic: the NEA has achieved little that was intended and much that was neither intended nor wanted. This, of course, happened with a great many of the government programs that were started at the same time and on the same optimistic —and as it now appears—simplistic assumptions.

What Price Subsidy?

In carrying the principle of private decentralized choice to its logical conclusion, there is much to be said for the elimination of all subsidy, indirect as well as direct, private as well as public. Subject to qualifications to be noted, a compelling case can be made for the use of the market as a means of using resources efficiently, including, of course, those related to art. To waste resources (time, talent, money) where art is concerned is just as foolish as to waste them where sacks of potatoes are concerned. Waste is a needless loss of satisfaction, including, perhaps, aesthetic satisfaction.

Economists can demonstrate rigorously that the operation of a perfect market will lead to an allocation of goods and services that is optimal in the sense that no reallocation could make one person better off without making others worse off. Of course, the perfect market is a heuristic construct: it can never exist in the real world. Many actual markets, however, approximate the ideal reasonably well.

187

Subsidies impair the working of a market. In the absence of subsidy (or other imperfection) the market performs the immensely useful function of discovering not only who wants what but also how much he or she wants it. If Jones pays an admission charge of $5 to see an exhibition of drawings, then it is reasonable to assume that he expects to get at least as much satisfaction from viewing the drawings as from any other use to which he might put his $5. Similarly, it can be assumed that in a competitive market the exhibitor who charges $5 expects to be better off than he would be at any other price. In the absence of market prices, there would be no way of knowing what use of resources would yield the most satisfaction. If, for example, the exhibition were subsidized and admission were free, then the exhibitor might spend $10 worth of resources to afford Jones satisfaction worth only $1 to him.

The market prevents waste in another way as well. Competition calls a halt to inefficient enterprises; it also stimulates the creation of new and more efficient ones. Subsidy, from whatever source, impedes both processes. Imagine a museum so heavily endowed that, even though no one would cross the street to see its displays, it continues decade after decade to occupy a choice site and to fill its storerooms with costly objects. Although it serves no purpose, there is no way to bring it to an end. By contrast, imagine a museum that, because it must live on its earnings, is constantly searching for ways to give viewers what they will pay to see.

Some will object that, if art museums were to raise their admission and other charges enough to cover their costs, their patronage would decline and they would be worse off than before. This is indeed quite possible. Art-museum visitors have been habituated over the years to paying no more than half as much to go to an art museum as to a movie; this is a fact that must be taken into account, and it may be one that will change only slowly. In many instances, too, an art museum, in order to operate without subsidy, would have to eliminate exhibitions and activities that are not popular. Probably, no museum has looked into these matters seriously; what the unsubsidized art museum would be like is a matter of guesswork.[12]

Some will also object that to charge a full admission would be a hardship on the poor. As noted previously, few of the poor are disposed to visit art museums, and efforts to get them there by offering "free days" have had little success. There is no denying, however, that in the absence of subsidies museum visits, like many other good things, would cost more than some people can afford. Insofar as there is a problem of poverty, it should be dealt with by redistributing income rather than by underpricing certain goods.

A third objection carries little or no weight: in the absence of subsidies all museums would have to cater to the same "popular" taste. This is disproved by the existence of the variety of special clienteles served by restaurants, clothing stores, summer resorts, art galleries, and so on. An unsubsidized enterprise will serve any clientele, however esoteric its tastes, that is able and willing to pay for what it gets. Indeed, it is when, because of subsidies or other reasons, the consumer is *not* sovereign that the range of offerings is likely to be restricted.

A plausible argument for subsidy exists when the market fails to take into account all relevant costs and benefits, or—in the extreme—when there is no market. Economists use the term "externalities" to refer to effects accruing to third parties to a transaction. If A gets satisfaction (or dissatisfaction) from the look of his neighbor's house, that is a benefit (or cost) that the market does not take into account but that nevertheless affects welfare. In the logically extreme case, that of a so-called public good, *all* effects are externalities. A pure public good is one that must be supplied to everyone if it is supplied to anyone: clean air is an example. Since no one can be prevented from consuming such a good if he wishes, no one can be made to pay for what he consumes.

Therefore, the market cannot supply a public good and, to the extent that a good involves externalities, it supplies either too little or too much (too little if it is a benefit, too much if it is a cost) to maximize the satisfaction of individuals.

Economists tend to see market failure as justifying government intervention; the idea is that government should supply benefits (or eliminate costs) to correct for market failures. The difficulty is, however, that there is no way of knowing the incidence or magnitude of most external effects arising either from market failures or from government intervention to correct them. How, for example, can those who commission a public sculpture know what will afford the most satisfaction? The work they choose may please a great many people and displease a great many others; there is no possible way of measuring its contribution to welfare.[13]

Except as there are markets, real or simulated, economics has little or nothing to contribute to policy. "A program to preserve the arts for the nation's posterity," Baumol and Bowen observe, "is a case of indiscriminate benefit [a public good] par excellence."[14] But an inference that such a program would increase welfare must rest on the conjecture that, if there were a way of charging for the benefits to posterity, the receipts would not only cover the costs of the program but also return a larger "profit" than any other use to which the resources might be put.

The case for the market assumes that the individual knows what he really wants (i.e., what would contribute most to his welfare in the long run) and also that his wants are of such a nature that their satisfaction would not measurably reduce the welfare of others. A critic might say that if the subject under discussion here were toothpaste, then these assumptions would accord reasonably well with the facts of life in middle-class America. But the subject matter is art and aesthetic experience, and therefore (a critic might assert) they are preposterous: the ordinary person has no idea of what would best serve his welfare, and if matters are left entirely to him, high-grade art and other cultural institutions will very soon starve for lack of patronage.

Lord Robbins, who has devoted his professional life to elaborating the rationale for the use of competitive markets, believes that subsidies are indispensable to the maintenance of cultural institutions. "It is possible, perhaps," he writes, "to conceive of future societies most of whose members were so enlightened as to sustain all such activities unsubsidized, without degradation of standards and the dissipation of what has come down to use from earlier times. But it is simply deceiving ourselves to suppose that this is possible in the present age."[15]

Investment in Improved Tastes

According to Tibor Scitovsky, another eminent economist, the justification for public support of the arts (the *only* one, incidentally) arises from the need to educate people's tastes. They would get more pleasure if they had more educated tastes. Americans, because they suffer from the effects of a puritan tradition, have never learned how to enjoy themselves. A predictable happy ending or a too-simple piece of music, he says, cannot give one as much pleasure as one would get if he learned to enjoy something more complex. An investment (time and effort as well as money, of course) in improving tastes would pay off handsomely in increased pleasure.[16] Although Scitovsky does not say so, it is obvious that if popular tastes were sufficiently raised, then high-grade cultural institutions might flourish without subsidies.

Art lovers will not accept the equating of aesthetic experience with pleasure (Steinberg writes of the "thrill of pain" sometimes produced by a work of modern art),[17] and some may say that increasing pleasure is not necessarily desirable (recall that Collingwood was alarmed by what he deemed an

191

excessive fondness for pleasure in modern society) and, in any case, is not a proper function of government. The case for public support would surely be stronger if it could be shown that the experience of art, whether pleasurable or painful, strengthens faculties that are distinctively human and by so doing contributes to values that are in a sense public.

Scitovsky says nothing about *how* public subsidy would bring about the desired effect. This is a question that those who have read thus far may be reluctant to pass over. In the present context, however, the pertinent question is: If investment in the improvement of tastes will yield handsome returns (whether in pleasure or welfare otherwise defined), will the individual be motivated to make the investment without any subsidy?

The fact is, of course, that everyone *does* make such investments. "The chief thing that the commonsense individual actually wants," writes Frank H. Knight, "is not satisfaction for the wants which he has, but more and *better* wants." The object of a present want is provisional: "it is as much a means to a new want as an end to the old one."[18] This fundamental want for more wants, adds Milton Friedman, "leads to the employment of people to teach music appreciation, art appreciation, etc."[19] Apparently, what needs explaining is why certain "high-yield" wants are not more widely cultivated.

The explanation may be that those who do not acquire such tastes during childhood find it extraordinarily difficult later on to get information both as to the kind and amount of investment necessary to acquire them and as to the amount and kind of satisfaction (pleasure or welfare, in some sense) to be had from them once they have been acquired. Getting information to help decide whether one would enjoy something is never completely costless, and sometimes the costs are high. These considerations may appear to justify subsidy if the costs of getting information are likely to be high enough to deter the individual from making the investment. One may think of such a subsidy as like the giving of a free sample for the purpose of encouraging the individual to become a regular customer.

But why need the samples be free? If a person will gain from the change of taste, then he will be willing to pay for the knowledge that he will gain, and the amount that he will be willing to pay for the knowledge will equal the value he attaches to the expected gain. If the cost of providing such knowledge is less than the value that people attach to it, then entrepreneurs will find it profitable to offer it for sale.

This may sound farfetched. But it is true, a great many able people exert themselves mightily to learn about people's tastes—not just their existing tastes but what may be called their latent, or potential, ones as well—in order to profit by pandering to them.

The argument is sometimes made that profit-seeking entrepreneurs will find it advantageous to pander only, or mostly, to tastes, existing or latent, whose satisfaction will give the individual a quick and sure return from a small investment, and that therefore pandering is best done by not-for-profit or government agencies. Thus, for example, Edward Everett Hale insisted that amusement for the poor be provided by public authority because "unwholesome" (presumably undemanding and therefore unrewarding) amusements would probably be provided if matters were left to "the wretched and unchristian spirit of 'let alone.'"[20] Economists, with some important exceptions, find this argument unconvincing: they expect entrepreneurs to pander to "difficult" tastes (whether wholesome or not) when doing so appears profitable, as it will if—but only if—individuals think that the prospective gains in satisfaction are worth paying for.[21]

The investments most likely to pay off are probably those involving rather small changes in (or development of) existing tastes. Finding that some small initial investment, perhaps one made more or less accidentally, has yielded an increase in satisfaction, the individual is thereby encouraged to make a further investment, and then, if that also yields a satisfactory return, still another. To borrow an image from Kenneth Arrow, who made a similar argument in another context, the individual may be expected to proceed like an explorer in unknown territory who finds it easier to explore areas near those he has already covered.[22]

This reasoning is consistent with the observation of sociologists that movement from one "taste culture" to another —for example, from enjoying the work of Norman Rockwell to enjoying that of Jackson Pollock—is likely to occur (when it occurs at all) from one generation to the next. A "taste culture," according to sociologist Herbert J. Gans, is integrally a part of a particular social world.[23] A person cannot enjoy an aesthetic (or other) experience that is unintelligible in terms of the categories within which his class (or taste) culture allows him to organize his experience. This is why parents' tastes usually remain much the same, although their children's may be altogether different.

CHAPTER

9

Art and the Public Interest

It is curious how the federal government
has gotten so heavily into the health
business. There is no rolling back this
process, nor would I be in favor of that.
But it would be salutary to remind ourselves that the political regime is not instituted for saving life, or prolonging life,
or curing disease; it is instituted to secure
certain kinds of liberties, to make possible a certain decent way of life, to promote justice, and so on.
                              —Dr. Leon Kass[1]

WHEN in 1963 a bill to establish an Arts Advisory Council
came to the floor of the Senate, Strom Thurmond of South
Carolina, after remarking that the American government is
one of limited powers, asked Senator Pell what provisions of
the Constitution authorized the proposed legislation. Pell,
who was in charge of the bill, was apparently taken aback
by the question. He referred first to the patent and copyright

provision, whose purpose is "to promote the Progress of Science and useful Arts." This, he continued, did not authorize public support of art, but nevertheless deserved mention as an indication of the Framers' interest in the arts. He then quoted from the Preamble, which no one had thought conferred any powers upon the government. ("The Preamble," Edward S. Corwin declared in his famous textbook, "is not a part of the Constitution, but 'walks before' it.")[2] Presumably, Pell had had in mind the words "general welfare" as they appear in the statement of the first of the enumerated powers, which authorizes Congress to lay and collect taxes.

The Supreme Court had in 1936 affirmed Congress's longstanding practice of treating this as a separate grant of power, and Pell might have answered the question by pointing out that, despite Madison's assurance that the powers of the nation's government would be "few and defined," it now had indisputable power to provide for whatever Congress found would serve the general welfare.[3] If any senators knew this, they did not see fit to clarify matters. Indeed, one, Lee Metcalf of Montana, congratulated Pell on his "fine constitutional analysis," which he said was "an important contribution."[4]

Very likely Senator Thurmond intended his question as a gesture of protest rather than a request for information. As late as the mid-1950s it had been the practice of congressmen to ask about the constitutionality of any proposed federal activity.[5] By the early 1960s, however, it was usually taken for granted that any bill passed by Congress and signed by the president was a proper exercise of federal, as opposed to state, power. Whether it was also a proper exercise of *governmental* power was rarely if ever considered.

To be sure, the principles of the regime were sometimes violated by the First Congress, whose members included many of the Framers, and more or less by every subsequent Congress and by every president. The tariff legislation of the First Congress, for example, was designed to serve special interests, and President Jefferson ruefully acknowledged that his Louisiana Purchase made of the Constitution "a scrap of paper."[6]

From the mass and scope of recent legislation one is tempted to conclude that most people now think that the national government ought to do just about everything for which there is widespread demand. Survey data contradict this impression, however. Respondents in a 1981 survey made by the Roper organization for the American Enterprise Institute said only three activities were best provided by the federal government (assuring civil rights, 60 percent; protecting the environment, 54 percent; and caring for the poor, 42 percent); less than a quarter thought the other listed activities were best provided by the federal government (highway construction, 23 percent; college and university education, 22 percent; elementary- and high-school education, 17 percent; mass transit, 16 percent; and fostering the arts, 14 percent). Less than 10 percent of those polled thought these activities were best provided for *outside* of any level of government with two exceptions: college and university education, 10 percent; and fostering the arts, 26 percent.[7]

That the political system so often ignores the limits defining the proper sphere of government is evidence of its sensitivity to the pressures of organized minorities, not of a public opinion that rejects the idea of limits. It is not surprising that people who in the role of citizens deplore the unprincipled extension of federal activity also support, in their occupational roles, organizations that press for measures that will be of special benefit to them. In other words, that the principles of the regime are violated does not mean that they do not exist. Those that the Founders established have not been supplanted by others; natural law liberalism, the basis upon which consent was originally given, is the basis upon which it rests today.

It follows, then, that even if government support of the arts contributed significantly to the welfare (pleasure, satisfaction, enjoyment, and so on) of the great majority of individuals, that in itself would not make it a legitimate activity of government. The principles of the American regime require that the individual be left free to pursue his happiness in his own way except as governmental constraints upon him (e.g., taxation for the support of art) are expected to benefit the body politic (i.e., the public viewed as an abstract entity).

As seen in chapter 2, proponents of public support of art have tried to justify it on public-interest grounds. The arguments that were advanced in the hearings and debates that preceded passage of the 1965 National Foundation on the Arts and the Humanities Act are, allowing for minor variations, the same as those that have been made since.

Perhaps it is fair to say that the real reason for the passage of the act and for the making of appropriations year after year was, and is, to benefit special interests, especially the culture industry of New York City and the "humanist" professors who could not compete for grants with their colleagues in the sciences. It is significant, however, that these special interests could best be served—perhaps could *only* be served—from behind the protective cover of a barrage of arguments claiming an advantage to the public; for example, asserting the danger to its well-being from the cultural explosion and the no less frightening one resulting from the imbalance between scientific and humanistic studies.

Curiously, these public-interest claims rested on extra-aesthetic grounds. They asserted that the public would benefit from values that are incidental to art, from values that could be served—doubtless sometimes better served—by altogether different means. The weight of such justifications would be no less if it were known to all concerned that no one would ever make or view a work of art for aesthetic satisfaction.

Probably, the argument that was most effective in getting "the arts" on the political agenda and then treated favorably was that support for the "culture industry" would contribute to prosperity. That it was the *culture* industry was incidental: the justification would have carried the same weight if it had been the widget industry. The essentials were that the industry employed a great many people directly and indirectly, attracted large numbers of tourists, enhanced real-estate values, and brought customers to hotels, restaurants, and expensive shops. All this was understood to give it a claim on public-interest grounds to be fostered by the government.

The argument is altogether without merit when the claim is made at the federal level. From the standpoint of the public it makes no difference where tourists spend their money; attracting them *to* some cities is attracting them *away* from others. If the federal government equally subsidized the efforts of all cities to attract tourists, then the competitive position of the cities would remain as it was. (Admittedly, the matter is somewhat complicated if the tourists are foreigners and certain assumptions are made about balance-of-payments problems.) The argument may have some merit when it proposes that local government provide the subsidies, especially in those instances where the local tax structure is such that the beneficiaries will pay the costs. But even local governments, as Dick Netzer points out, should not justify subsidy of art museums and symphony orchestras "by claiming that it promotes economic development more effectively than would the expenditure of the same amount of money on, say, raising the salaries of principal employees."[8]

Some of the most frequently and earnestly made arguments rested on grounds that are, to put it generously, insubstantial. It was highly implausible (insofar as it had any meaning at all) that "giving official recognition," as by the establishment of an advisory council, would "give status and recognition to the importance of culture in the United States," increase "national prestige," contribute to international understanding and world peace by enabling other na-

199

tions "to discover that America has a soul," and bring the ghettos of the cities into "the mainstream of American culture." What exactly is national prestige? How is it measured? Why should Americans want more of it? (After the Revolutionary War, according to historian Neil Harris, art was seen as a means of convincing skeptical foreigners of the existence of an American nation.[9] By now, it is safe to say, they have been fully convinced.)

Nineteenth-century social reformers thought that art could be used, along with parks, playgrounds, and settlement houses, to prevent social unrest and alleviate social pathologies. "Whatever Central Park might cost," James Jackson Jarves asked in 1864, "is not so much saved from prisons, priests, police and physicians?" He understood art as something that "elevates and refines the popular mind by bringing it in contact with the true and the beautiful."[10] A century later, however, when there was an accumulation of evidence to show that the popular mind was not affected by access to art and when art no longer had anything to do with truth and beauty or even, as many would say, with any aspect of ordinary experience, it was absurd to claim, as did Douglas Dillon, the chairman of both the Metropolitan Museum of Art and the Business Committee for the Arts, that ". . . artistic performances of one sort or another are essential in handling the crisis of our cities."[11]

Another justification of public support (although one that was not used to help establish the NEA) is that the art experience contributes to the relief and rehabilitation of people confined to custodial institutions such as prisons, mental health centers, and homes for the aged. Art therapy usually consists not of viewing art but of carrying on activities that have some outward resemblance to what artists do.[12]

Although art therapy is rapidly gaining the status of a profession (seven colleges give graduate degrees in it, two "professional" journals have been established to cover the field, and the NEA and the Department of Health and

Human Services support artists who work as therapists), the evidence is sparse and shaky that it does more for patients than relieve boredom. "Before we tell people to spend a few million dollars on art instead of tranquilizers," Dr. John H. Knowles, the late president of the Rockefeller Foundation, told a conference on art therapy, "we had better do some serious research to see what the facts are."[13]

Some psychologists hold that self-expression through art is a means of releasing inner tensions, which the American society urgently needs. Mihaly Csikszentmihalyi, chairman of the Committee on Human Development at the University of Chicago, writes that making symbolic information about existence more readily available to people is "one of the major survival tasks of our society."[14] He envisions a federal Department of Symbolic Resources for this purpose.

But what of the justifications that *do* depend upon art being experienced aesthetically? These justifications, however, are also extra-aesthetic in that the values sought are not aesthetic experience as such but rather some change in the social state that is believed to result from it.

It is often taken for granted that the effect of the arts upon society is both profound and benign. This is surely unwarranted. Whatever may have been (or may be) the effect of the arts upon societies other than those of Western Europe, they were not (or are not) mediated by what in the past two centuries has been called aesthetic experience. As pointed out in chapter 1, even the Greeks did not experience what we call art in the manner that we do. Moreover, among those societies whose people do have what can properly be called aesthetic experience, there are striking differences in the manner and degree to which the societies appear to be affected by it. There are also striking differences in the kinds of social effects that seem to be produced by the various arts —say, music as opposed to painting.

Insofar as art, or the arts, has consequences for society, they may be beneficial, injurious, or both. As Jacques Barzun has written, art "can dignify and exalt the civilization that gives it birth and also weaken and destroy it. It can transmit the ideals of a community. It can also detach the individual from the struggles of his age, making loyal citizenship appear to him as futile and perverse as revolutionary action."[15]

The evidence here bearing on these matters is of course far from conclusive. But it strongly suggests that aesthetic experience of visual art has never greatly affected American society, and that the tendency has been, and is, for it to affect it less and less both because of changes in the nature of and the response to art and of the increasing democratization of American life that has caused arts institutions to subordinate aesthetic to other values. Modern art, Kenneth Clark remarks, "has become so hermetic, so removed from the average man's experience, as to be incomprehensible, even to a semi-professional like myself." Our hope lies, he says, in an expanding elite "drawn from every class, and with varying degrees of education, united in a belief that non-material values can be discovered in visible things."[16]

It is possible that, although the size of the art-viewing public has increased substantially in absolute numbers in the past two or three decades, it has increased very little if at all as a proportion of the well-off and well-educated public from which most art viewers are drawn. In addition, art viewing is done more and more for nonaesthetic purposes, especially to learn about art and cultural history; moreover, insofar as art is responded to aesthetically, the response tends more and more to be a private one, having its effects mainly upon the viewer and little upon those he lives among and thus indirectly upon society. Finally, insofar as the experience of art does affect the society, it may sometimes be destructive of the values upon which social well-being depends.

It is arguable that from the standpoint of society art took a wrong turn with the acceptance of the doctrine "art for art's sake." Taken literally, the phrase is of course absurd. But it means that aesthetic values are not to be weighed against other values—moral ones, for example. The view that aesthetic experience is "one of the ultimate values of human life," Harold Osborne tells us, is one of the "revolutionary changes of outlook" characteristic of present-day aesthetics.[17] It is more revolutionary than may at first appear if the nature and variety of these experiences are fully taken into account.

If, as Aristotle and others believed, that which is distinctively human—reason above all, but love of the beautiful as well—is good, then whatever tends to exalt the distinctively human must also be good and whatever tends to debase it must be bad. By this ("prerevolutionary") standard, the aesthetic experience is good, bad, or indifferent as it raises man to his full potential or lowers him to the level of the brutes.

It may seem that if aesthetic experience has nothing to do with Truth or Beauty (the romantic mode) or, indeed, with any aspect of real or "ordinary" experience (the transcendental and nihilist modes) the worst that can be said from a moral standpoint is that it is irrelevant. If it sticks to its principles it cannot exalt or degrade man, attach or detach him from the struggles of his age, for it belongs to a world that is radically separated from the realm of real experience. This is presumably what Robert Rauschenberg means when he says, "It is extremely important that art be unjustifiable."[18] To be justifiable, it would have to exist for some sake other than its own.

This view raises two problems. One is that much art in these modes does not stay within its aesthetic principle: under the pretense of having to jolt the viewer out of his ordinary perceptions, it comments on the real world. When it does so, its message is often that man is unlovely or deformed, that he is subrational, that he is garbage, that he is absurd.

The other problem concerns art in these modes that does stick to aesthetic principle. It implicitly conveys a message, whose tendency is to degrade human things. It says that man and all that concerns him, including art itself, do not matter. What else can be the message, for example, of the work *Abstract Painting*? Ad Reinhardt, who painted it, has described it as follows:

A square (neutral, shapeless) canvas, five feet wide, five feet high, as high as a man, as wide as a man's outstretched arms (not large, not small, sizeless), trisected (no composition) one horizontal form negating one vertical form (formless, no top, no bottom, direction-less), three (more or less) dark (lightless), non-contrasting (color-less) colors, brushwork brushed out to remove brushwork, a mat, flat, free-hand painted surface (glossless, texture-less, non-linear, no hard edge, no soft edge) which does not reflect its surroundings —a pure, abstract, non-objective, timeless, spaceless, changeless, relationless, disinterested painting, an object that is self-conscious (no unconsciousness), ideal, transcendent, aware of nothing but art (absolutely no anti-art).[19]

This book has argued that a justification for government support of art must rest on the inherent rather than the incidental values associated with it—aesthetic experience, that is, rather than values that could be as well or perhaps better secured by other means. If (to use Beardsley's *ad absurdum* example of an incidental use) sculpture were useful as ballast, this would not help to justify a program of support to the arts.

Most of the justifications that have been offered differ from the ballast example in an important way; that is, although sculptures would doubtless make good ballast, art is a quite unsuitable means of serving the public interest in the ways claimed. As mentioned earlier, attracting tourists to one city and away from another does not serve the public interest, and the effectiveness of art in increasing "national prestige," relieving psychic tensions, and so on is extremely dubious. But, to repeat, even if art were as well suited to these uses as sculpture is for use as ballast, these justifications would be irrelevant to the evaluation of a program for the support of art if its purpose is to engender aesthetic experience.

If aesthetic experience contributed significantly to the welfare (however defined) of large numbers of individuals, it would not necessarily follow that it would serve the public interest. Many activities contribute to welfare in this sense without being of concern from a public as opposed to a private standpoint. If, for example, the playing of chess afforded deep satisfaction to almost everyone, probably no one would claim that the playing of chess is therefore in the public interest.

Giving people pleasure has never been considered a proper function of the U.S. government, except as it may be supposed to affect, for good or for ill, aspects of life that are the proper concern of government. Only as an individual's enjoyment of art is correctly perceived by the public as affecting the well-being of the collectivity does it become a matter of public interest.

If it were clear that art significantly affects the quality of society, as opposed to the welfare of individuals, it would not follow that government might properly subsidize it or otherwise intervene in art matters. There are many things that affect society in ways that ennoble or debase men, ways that by common agreement are not the concern of government, either because it is incapable of managing them (e.g., enforcing rules of good manners) or because it is understood that government exists for other purposes.

It may be desirable for the Constitution to spell out in unambiguous detail the proper role of government, but it is impossible for it to do so because there is not, and never has been, general agreement on what that role should be. (If there were such a consensus, it would soon break down in a free society, for people are apt to use their freedom to renege upon their agreements when they think it advantageous, to themselves or to the public, to do so).[20] The role of government in a free society must be a matter of continuous negotiation among members of its public. The American regime rests on the principle that the functions of government are to protect the individual in the exercise of certain inalienable rights and to establish the preconditions for the development of competent citizenry. Some think that the conditions of modern life have made this principle obsolete. It is, however, the principle that has made America what it is, and no one seems likely to propose an alternative that would be generally acceptable.

NOTES

Introduction

1. 89th Congress, Public Law 209. For an account of development of the NEH from 1972–1976 by its then chairman, see Ronald Berman, *Culture and Politics* (Washington, D.C.: University Press of America, 1983).

2. NEA spending by years is given in its *Annual Report, 1980,* p. 366. The estimate of spending by nine major federal departments resulted from an NEA study made in 1978 and was reported in George Gelles, "Public Arts Support and the Federal Presence" (Paper prepared for a conference, Marvin Center, George Washington University, Washington, D.C., June 23–25, 1980).

For an account of federal activities, see *Cultural Directory II: Federal Funds and Services for the Arts and Humanities* (Washington, D.C.: Smithsonian Institution Press, 1980). A listing of grants available from all sources can be found in Virginia P. White, *Grants for the Arts* (New York: Plenum Publishing Company, 1980).

State government appropriations in fiscal 1981 totaled $111,775,084. The amounts are given by state in Annual National Assembly of State Arts Agencies, Survey of State Arts Agencies, *Survey of State Appropriations* (November 5, 1980).

3. On indirect public funding of the arts, see Alan L. Feld, Michael O'Hare, and J. Mark Davidson Schuster, *Patrons Despite Themselves: Taxpayers and Arts Policy* (New York: New York University Press, 1983).

4. Josiah Lee Auspitz, "The True Liberal," *The American Spectator* (December 1982), p. 20.

5. John Locke, *Second Treatise on Civil Government,* ed. Peter Laslett (Cambridge and New York: Cambridge University Press, 1960, first published in 1690). Washington's letter is reproduced in Max Farrand, ed., *Records of the Federal Convention,* vol. 2 (New Haven, Conn.: Yale University Press, 1937), p. 666.

6. Robert Nozick, *Anarchy, State, and Utopia* (New York: Basic Books, 1974), pp. 33, 169.

7. John Rawls, *A Theory of Justice* (Cambridge, Mass.: Harvard University Press, 1971), pp. 282–83, 332.

8. Aristotle, *Nicomachean Ethics,* bk. I, chap. 9.

9. The text is given in Mary Handlin and Oscar Handlin, eds., *The Popular Sources of Political Authority* (Cambridge, Mass.: Harvard University Press, 1966), p. 467.

10. On the townspeople's response, see Robert J. Taylor, "Construction of the Massachusetts Constitution," *Proceedings of the American Antiquarian Society* 90, pt. 2 (October 1980): 330.

11. Excerpts from the state constitutions appear in Paul Eidelberg, *The Philosophy of the American Constitution* (New York: Free Press, 1966), app. 2.

12. Farrand, ed., *Records of the Federal Convention,* vol. 1, p. 605.

13. See the essays in Robert Horowitz, ed., *The Moral Foundations of the American Public,* 2nd ed. (Charlottesville: University Press of Virginia, 1980), esp. that by Joseph Cropsey, p. 87.

14. Auspitz, "True Liberal."

15. Referring to "a very fierce attack" on the proposed Constitution asserting that the power "'to lay and collect taxes, duties, imposts, and excises, to pay the debts, and provide for the common defense and general welfare of the United States' amounts to an unlimited commission to exercise every power which may be alleged to be necessary for the common defense or general welfare, Publius (Madison) in *Federalist* 41 found that "the idea of an enumeration of particulars which neither explain nor qualify the general meaning, and can have no other effect than to confound and mislead, is an absurdity. . . ." After his retirement as president, Madison wrote that the general welfare clause got into the Constitution by accident: "inattention to the phraseology occasioned doubtless by its identity with the harmless character attached to it in the Instrument [the Articles of Confederation] from which it was borrowed." Farrand, *Records of the Federal Convention,* vol. 3, p. 486.

16. *United States v. Butler,* 297 U.S. 1, 66 (1936); in *Buckley v. Valeo,* U.S. 1, 424 (1976), to provide for the general welfare extends to the regulation of the financing of political campaigns. In the same year, the Court found in *National League of Cities v. Usery,* 426 U.S. 833 (1976) that the Tenth Amendment protected states from federal intrusions that might threaten their "separate and independent existence." This decision was in effect overruled in 1983, when in *Equal Employment Opportunity Commission v. Wyoming* (U.S. Supreme Court Reports, 75 O. 2d ed., p. 31) the Court in a 5–4 decision found that an intrusion "less serious" than the one on the *National League of Cities* case and a valid exercise of Congress's powers under the commerce clause. Chief Justice Warren Burger, who wrote the minority opinion, declared that the reserved powers of the states were "turned on their heads" by the decision; for Congress to force the states into a Procrustean national mold, he wrote, "is the antithesis of what the authors of the Constitution contemplated for our federal system" (p. 47).

Notes

The history of federalism is reviewed in two recent Advisory Commission on Intergovernmental Relations (ACIR) publications: George F. Break, "Fiscal Federalism in the United States: The First 200 Years, Evolution and Outlook," *The Future of Federalism in the 1980s* (Washington, D.C.: July 1981), chap. 3, and Cynthia Cates Colella in *An Agenda for American Federalism: Restoring Confidence and Competence* (Washington, D.C.: June 1981), chap. 2.

17. Michael Walzer, *Radical Principles: Reflections of an Unreconstructed Democrat* (New York: Basic Books, 1980), pp. 43, 48.

18. Advisory Commission on Intergovernmental Relations, *A Report to the President for the Transmittal to the Congress* (Washington, D.C.: U.S. Government Printing Office, 1955), p. 123.

19. Advisory Commission on Intergovernmental Relations, *An Agenda for American Federalism: Restoring Confidence and Competence* (Washington, D.C., Commission Report A-86, June 1981), p. 150.

20. Arthur Maass attacks the predominant view in *Congress and the Common Good* (New York: Basic Books, 1983). He differs from the present writer in thinking that political actors generally aim at the common good.

The literature on the concept of public interest is reviewed and evaluated in Barry M. Mitnick, "A Typology of Conceptions of the Public Interest," *Administration and Society* 8, no. 1 (May 1976): 5–28.

21. See Iris Murdoch, *The Fire and the Sun, Why Plato Banished the Artists* (Oxford: Clarendon Press, 1977), and Jean-Jacques Rousseau, *Politics and the Arts, Letter to M. d'Alembert on the Theatre,* trans. Allan Bloom (Glencoe, Ill.: Free Press, 1960).

22. This work, by the artist Alan Sonfist and a research team, is described approvingly by the director of the Visual Arts Program of the NEA in its *Annual Report, 1980,* p. 277.

Chapter 1

1. The selection process was described by the director of the Visual Arts Program to a House appropriations subcommittee in May 1979. See U.S., Congress, *Department of the Interior and Related Agencies Appropriations for 1980, Part II,* 96th Cong., 1st sess., p. 796 et. seq.

2. Michael Straight, *Twigs for an Eagle's Nest* (New York and Berkeley: Devon Press, 1979), p. 130.

3. Ibid., p. 131.

4. Ibid.

5. Joseph Alsop in an important work that appeared when the present book was in process of publication asserts that "the actual *way of seeing* changes with the passage of time." Defining art as what is made by the human hand to please the eye, he conjectures that from the beginning the world has probably known tens of thousands of art traditions. Only five,

however, have involved collecting and some or all of other by-products of art: these "rare" art traditions he describes in systematic detail. Joseph Alsop, *The Rare Art Traditions,* Bollingen Series 35 (New York: Harper & Row, 1982) pp. 23, 30–31.

6. R. G. Collingwood, *The Principles of Art* (London, Oxford, New York: Oxford University Press, 1958), p. 6.

7. Johan Huizinga, *Homo Ludens* (Boston: Beacon Press, 1950), p. 159.

8. Richard L. Anderson, *Art in Primitive Societies* (Englewood Cliffs, N.J.: Prentice-Hall, 1979), pp. 16, 196. See also Alexander Alland, Jr., *The Artistic Animal: An Inquiry into the Biological Roots of Art* (New York: Anchor Press, Doubleday, 1977).

The difficulty, amounting sometimes to an impossibility, of "understanding" the concepts of a culture very different from one's own (and for that matter of attaining perfect communication), may be seen from the account given by the photographer David Attenborough of efforts to communicate with Dogon tribesmen in Africa:

> But what about "beauty"? We had photographs of two different figures of horsemen. Which was the more beautiful, *la plus belle?* The old men looked baffled. As we spoke the question, we realized that it was fraught with possibilities of misunderstanding. What, after all, did we ourselves mean by the word, we who came from Europe where artistic fashions took such violent swings within decades. How could our interpreter translate the word from French to Dogon with any confidence that it meant the same thing to him that it did to us? We tried again. Which was better, *la meilleure?* The old men looked less puzzled. They examined the photographs with care. This one did not show the style of dressing the hair properly. The other figure had details of the horse's harness that perhaps were not carved clearly enough. It was, however, older, and that was important and good. Eventually a judgment was given. The second was better because it was more correct, because it spoke more accurately and eloquently of the ancient truths.

David Attenborough, *The Tribal Eye* (New York: W. W. Norton & Company, 1976), p. 22.

9. Frank P. Chambers, *The History of Taste: An Account of the Revolutions of Art Criticism and Theory in Europe* (New York: Columbia University Press, 1932), p. 270.

Not until the eighteenth century was there general agreement that "art" comprises painting, sculpture, architecture, music, and poetry as an irreducible minimum. Kant, the founder of philosophical aesthetics, included gardening. Other arts are sometimes added; for example, engraving and the decorative arts, the dance, theater, opera, and eloquence and prose literature. "The affinity between the various fine arts," writes the historian of the subject, "is more plausible to the amateur, who feels a comparable kind of enjoyment, than to the artist himself. . . ." Paul Oskar Kristeller, "The

Notes

Modern System of Aesthetics: A Study in the History of Aesthetics," *Journal of the History of Ideas* 12 (1951): 496–527, and 13 (1952): 17–46. The quotation is from vol. 13, p. 44. See also James S. Malek, *The Arts Compared, An Aspect of Eighteenth-Century British Aesthetics* (Detroit: Wayne State University Press, 1974).

10. John Dewey, *Art as Experience* (New York: Capricorn Books, G. P. Putnam's Sons, 1958, originally published in 1934), p. 48.

11. Ibid., p. 5.

12. Ibid., p. 26.

13. Ibid., p. 48.

14. Eliseo Vivas, "The Dignity of Art," *Modern Age* 21, no. 3 (Summer 1977): 245.

15. Ibid., p. 246.

16. Ibid., pp. 244, 247. For a similar account of the nature of art, see Jerome Stolnitz, *Aesthetics and the Philosophy of Art Criticism: A Critical Introduction* (Boston: Houghton Mifflin, 1960). For criticism, see George Dickie, "The Myth of the Aesthetic Attitude," *American Philosophic Quarterly* 1 (1964): 56–65.

17. George Dickie, *Art and the Aesthetic: An Institutional Analysis* (Ithaca, N.Y.: Cornell University Press, 1975), p. 36.

18. Patricia H. Werhane, "Evaluating the Classificatory Process," *Journal of Aesthetics and Art Criticism* 38, no. 3 (Spring 1979): 353.

19. Nelson Goodman, *The Languages of Art* (Indianapolis: Bobbs-Merrill, 1968). See also his essay, "When Is Art?" in *The Arts and Cognition,* ed. David Perkins and Barbara Leondar (Baltimore, Md.: Johns Hopkins University Press, 1977).

20. Goodman, "When Is Art?" p. 17.

21. Ibid., p. 16.

22. Werhane, "Evaluating the Classificatory Process," p. 353.

23. Howard S. Becker, *Art Worlds* (Berkeley: University of California Press, 1982), p. 36.

24. Ibid., p. 155.

25. In an effort to measure the amount of agreement among members of the contemporary art world as to which works are "good" and "bad" and to discover the standards by which the judgments are made, twenty "experts" (dealers, museum directors and curators, collectors, and professors and students) were shown photographs of twenty-six contemporary works (paintings, sculptures, environmental and body art) and were asked to rate them and to explain the basis for the ratings. There was near complete agreement on two or three "excellent" and two or three "very bad" works, but much disagreement on the others. The standards for judgment were mostly clichés ("interesting," "boring," "makes a statement," "powerful," and so on), and different and often opposed standards were frequently applied to the same picture even by judges who agreed on the merit or lack of merit of the work. The findings are not reported in detail here or elsewhere because of methodological deficiencies in the design of the study. (Respondents frequently said that they could not judge the quality of a

work from a photograph, and most of the photographs were of works that were well known to the respondents, which resulted in their tendency to report the general opinion of the art world instead of making independent judgments.) The author is grateful to Mrs. Agnes Gund Saalfield, herself a leading member of the world of contemporary visual art, who did almost all of the interviewing; that the results are of so little value is the author's fault, not hers.

A well-done study that tends to support the opinion that the contemporary art world shares few if any standards is that of Michael Mulkay and Elizabeth Chaplin, "Aesthetics and the Aesthetic Career: A Study of Anomie in Fine-Art Painting," *Sociological Quarterly* 23 (Winter 1982): 117–38.

Tomas Kulka distinguishes artistic (i.e., art-historical) judgments from aesthetic ones and finds that the former may "provide a *rationale* for the judgments of experts which would otherwise have to be regarded as incoherent." Kulka, "The Artistic and the Aesthetic Value of Art," *British Journal of Aesthetics* 21, no. 4 (Autumn 1981): 336. Peter H. Karlen, a practicing art lawyer, writes that "what happens [in courts] is that the party with the most prestigious experts usually prevails . . . the judge throws up his hands and leaves the fate of the art with the jurors. . . ." "It is conceivable," he adds cautiously, "that experts and critics may not be able to comprehend, interpret, or evaluate a contemporary work." Karlen, "Aesthetic Quality and Art Preservation," *The Journal of Aesthetics and Art Criticism* 41, no. 3 (Spring 1983): 316, 318.

26. U.S., Department of Health, Education, and Welfare, *Toward a Social Report* (Washington, D.C.: U.S. Government Printing Office, 1969), p. 74.

27. Vivas, "Dignity of Art," p. 250.

28. Monroe C. Beardsley, "The Aesthetic Problem of Justification," *Journal of Aesthetic Education* 1, no. 2 (Autumn 1966): 33–34.

29. Collingwood, *Principles of Art,* p. 32.

30. Ibid., p. 33.

31. Vivas, "Dignity of Art," p. 248.

32. Ibid.

33. Erwin Panovsky, *Meaning in the Visual Arts* (Garden City, N.Y.: Anchor Books, Doubleday, 1955), p. 14.

34. Charles Francis Adams, ed., *The Works of John Adams,* vol. 5 (Boston: Little, Brown, 1857), p. 111.

35. Quoted by Roger B. Stein, *John Ruskin and Aesthetic Thought in America, 1840–1900* (Cambridge, Mass.: Harvard University Press, 1967), pp. 180–81.

36. Edgar Allan Poe, "The Poetic Principle," *The Complete Poetical Works of Edgar Allan Poe* (New York: Oxford University Press, 1909), p. 222.

37. Walter Pater, *The Renaissance* (New York: Modern Library Edition, first published in 1873), p. 109, and the last sentence of the book. For Oscar Wilde's very similar views see his *Intentions* (London: Unicorn Press, 1945, first published in 1891), and *Essays of Oscar Wilde* (New York: H. S. Nichols, Cosmopolitan Library Edition, n.d.).

Notes

38. The quoted phrase is from Roger Fry, *Vision and Design* (New York: Brentano's, n.d.).

The term "transcendental" is borrowed from Herbert Read, who meant art (especially Etruscan, although he mentions Oriental and Gothic as well), which attempts to express ideas "which are superior to, and not derived from, ordinary experiences or ascertainable fact." Herbert Read, *A Coat of Many Colours* (London: George Routledge and Sons, 1945), pp. 237–38. As used here, the word has nothing to do with the transcendentalism of Emerson or with that of Kant and German Idealism. If it were not for its other associations, "grotesque" as used by Shaftsbury in the following curious passage would serve the present purpose better than "transcendental": "For whatever is capricious and odd is sure to create diversion to those who look no further. And where there is nothing like nature, there is no room for the troublesome part of thought or contemplation. 'Tis the perfection of certain painters to keep so far from nature as possible. To find a likeness in their works is to find the greatest fault imaginable. A natural connection is a slur. A coherence, a design, a meaning is against their purpose and destroys the very spirit and genius of their workmanship." Shaftsbury, *Characteristics,* vol. 2, ed. John M. Robertson (New York: E. P. Dutton, 1900), pp. 159–60. (*Characteristics* was first published in 1711.) On the history of the concept of "disinterestedness" in the philosophy of aesthetics, see Harold Osborne, *The Art of Appreciation* (New York: Oxford University Press, 1970), pp. 27–37.

39. Wassily Kandinsky, *Concerning the Spiritual in Art* (Baltimore, Md.: Monumental Printing Co., 1970, offset reprint), p. 10. According to Kenneth Clark, the first artist to say that he aimed at pure aesthetic responses was Gauguin. Clark quotes a letter in which Gauguin says that he uses subjects borrowed from human life or nature as "pretexts" that "represent nothing real in the vulgar sense of the word; they express no idea directly, but they should make you think as music does, without the aid of ideas or images." Kenneth Clark, *Landscapes into Art* (Boston: Beacon Press, 1961), p. 135.

40. Piet Mondrian, *Plastic Art and Pure Plastic Art* (New York: Wittenborn and Co., 1945), p. 10.

41. Quoted in Tilo Schabert, "A Note on Modernity," *Political Theory* 7, no. 1 (February 1979): 123–37.

42. Karsten Harries, *The Meaning of Modern Art: A Philosophical Interpretation* (Evanston, Ill.: Northwestern University Press, 1968), p. 57.

43. Ibid., p. 65.

44. Joanna Frueh, "Chicago's Emotional Realists," *Artforum* (September 1978): 41.

45. Quoted in Joshua C. Taylor, *America as Art* (Washington, D.C.: Smithsonian Institution Press, 1976), p. 291.

46. Stephen Koch, *Stargazer: Andy Warhol's World and His Films* (New York: Praeger, 1973), p. 39.

47. Robert Horvitz, *Artforum* (May 1976): 24.

48. Fry, *Vision and Design,* p. 30.

49. Curt J. Ducasse, *Art, the Critics and You* (New York: O. Piest, 1944), p. 62.

50. Edgar Wind, *Art and Anarchy* (London: Faber & Faber, 1963), p. 47.

51. Ibid.

52. Wilde, *Intentions,* p. 20.

53. The theory of art as play was introduced by Kant and adopted by Schiller as the center of his theory of aesthetics. See Harold Osborne, *Aesthetics and Art Theory* (New York: E. P. Dutton and Co., 1970), pp. 301–3.

54. José Ortega y Gasset, *The Dehumanization of Art* (Princeton, N.J.: Princeton University Press, 1968, first published in 1925), pp. 48, 50.

55. Fry, *Vision and Design,* p. 25. Cf. George Kubler, *The Shape of Time* (New Haven, Conn.: Yale University Press, 1962), p. 16.

56. Quoted by Roslyn Siegal, *New York Times,* February 21, 1980, p. C3.

57. Ortega y Gasset, *Dehumanization of Art,* pp. 4, 9.

58. Edward Lucie-Smith, in Donald Carroll and Edward Lucie-Smith, *Movements in Modern Art* (New York: Horizon Press, 1973), p. 203. Roy McMullen, *Art, Affluence and Alienation* (London: Pall Mall Press, 1968), p. 168, writes of op and kinetic art: "To attend a large show of their works is to enter the equivalent of an amusement fair, full of people playing with ball machines, laughing at themselves in the distortion mirrors, getting lost in the mazes of light."

59. Leo Steinberg, *Other Criteria: Confrontations with 20th Century Art* (New York: Oxford University Press, 1972), p. 5. According to Schabert, Schlegel thought that ever more novelty would cause ever more boredom: "[A]ssessing the cultural situation of his time, he asserts that even the educated public has ceased to care for the formally perfect construction of artistic creations. Instead, it expects the artist but to display his indulgence in characteristic peculiarities or, more precisely, to reveal the intoxicating effect of that passion. Art in the new age could be moulded in any form or shape, if it would only pander to the passionate love of novelty permeating the souls of modern artists and their followers." Schabert, "Note on Modernity," p. 130.

Chapter 2

1. Lyndon B. Johnson, statement on signing into law the National Foundation for the Arts and the Humanities Act of 1965, September 29, 1965.

The subject matter of this chapter is treated in great detail by Gary O. Larson, National Council coordinator of the NEA, in *The Reluctant Patron: The United States Government and the Arts, 1943–1965* (Philadelphia: University of Pennsylvania Press, 1983). Unfortunately, Larson's work did not appear in time to be used as a source.

2. Quoted by Ralph Purcell, *Government and Art* (Washington, D.C.: Public Affairs Press, 1965), p. 14.

Notes

3. James D. Richardson, ed., *Messages and Papers of the Presidents* (Washington, D.C., 1896, published by authority of Congress), p. 316.

4. Quoted by Lillian B. Miller, *Patrons and Patriotism,* vol. 2 (Chicago and London: University of Chicago Press, 1966), p. 43. This book provides a very detailed account of the politics of the embellishment of the Capitol and congressional buildings.

5. Ibid., p. 48.

6. Ibid., pp. 82–83.

7. Nathaniel Burt, *Palaces for the People: A Social History of the American Art Museum* (Boston: Little, Brown and Company, 1977), pp. 66, 161.

8. To begin with, only 15 percent of individual income was deductible (by 1969 this had been raised to 50 percent for many types of nonprofit organizations). Federal tax immunities of one kind or another have been an important revenue source for museums and other cultural institutions. Because most other countries give direct support to the arts, when countries are listed according to per capita expenditures, the United States is near the bottom. When indirect support is taken into account, it is at or near the top.

9. Richard D. McKinzie, *New Deal for Artists* (Princeton, N.J.: Princeton University Press, 1973), p. 179.

10. Ibid., p. 188.

11. Ibid., p. 152.

12. Ibid., p. 187.

13. Quoted in U.S., Commission of Fine Arts, *Art and Government, Report to the President by the Commission of Fine Arts on Activities of the Federal Government in the Field of Art* (Washington, D.C.: U.S. Government Printing Office, 1953), p. 121.

14. Ibid., p. 29.

15. U.S., Congress, House, Committee on Education and Labor, Special Subcommittee on Arts Foundations and Commissions, *Grants for Fine Arts Programs and Projects* (Washington, D.C.: U.S. Government Printing Office, 1954).

16. Virginia P. White, *Grants for the Arts* (New York: Plenum Publishing Company, 1980), p. 59.

17. William Bragg Ewald, *Eisenhower the President* (Englewood Cliffs, N.J.: Prentice-Hall, 1981), pp. 170–71.

18. Excerpts from Rockefeller's testimony appear in U.S., Congress, House, Committee on Education and Labor, Subcommittee on Special Education, *Federal Advisory on the Arts,* 1959, p. 45.

19. Robert H. Connery and Gerald Benjamin, *Rockefeller of New York* (Ithaca and London: Cornell University Press, 1979), p. 362.

20. *New York Times,* December 15, 1961, p. 40.

21. Interview with August Heckscher, March 16, 1979.

22. Quoted in "The Candidates and the Arts," *Saturday Review of Literature,* October 29, 1960, p. 43.

23. Ibid., p. 44.

24. Quoted in U.S., Congress, Senate, Committee on Labor and Public

Welfare, *Establishing a National Foundation on the Arts and the Humanities,* 89th Cong., 1st sess., S.R. 300, June 8, 1965, p. 12.

25. August Heckscher, *The Public Happiness* (New York: Atheneum, 1962).

26. August Heckscher, "The Quality of American Culture," *Goals for Americans: The Report of the President's Commission on National Goals* (Princeton, N.J.: Prentice-Hall, 1960).

27. August Heckscher, *The Arts and the National Government, Report to the President* (Washington, D.C.: U.S. Government Printing Office, July 11, 1963).

28. Joan Simpson Burns, *The Awkward Embrace* (New York: Knopf, 1975), p. 354.

29. Interview with August Heckscher, March 16, 1979.

30. Michael Straight, *After Long Silence* (New York and London: W. W. Norton and Company, 1983), pp. 316–17.

31. Burns, *Awkward Embrace,* p. 362.

32. U.S., Congress, House, Committee on Education and Labor, *National Foundation on the Arts and the Humanities Act of 1965,* 89th Cong., 1st sess., H.R. 618, July 14, 1965, p. 4.

33. Cited as "somewhat overblown" by Dick Netzer, "The Arts: New York's Best Export Industry," *New York Affairs* 2 (1978): 54.

34. Interview with Roger L. Stevens, May 9, 1981.

35. American Council of Learned Societies, *Report of the Commission on the Humanities* (New York, 1964), p. 4. On the origins of the commission, see Burns, *Awkward Embrace,* p. 229.

36. American Council of Learned Societies, *ACLS Newsletter* (November 1962).

37. An account of the debate is given in Burns, *Awkward Embrace,* pp. 373–76.

38. Rockefeller Panel Report, *The Performing Arts: Problems and Prospects* (New York: McGraw-Hill, 1965).

39. Richard A. Posner, "Theories of Economic Regulation," *Bell Journal of Economics and Management Science* 5 (Autumn 1974): 335–58.

40. *Congressional Record,* House, September 20, 1961, p. 2050.

41. NBC-TV, *The Nation's Future,* February 11, 1961.

42. *Congressional Record,* Senate, August 21, 1964, p. 20279.

43. Ibid., House, August 10, 1964, p. 20648.

44. Ibid., September 15, 1965, p. 23939; see also 1964, p. 20648; 1965, p. 4325; 1968, p. 11308.

45. Ibid., Senate, December 20, 1963, p. 25268.

46. Heckscher, *Goals for Americans,* p. 9.

47. *Congressional Record,* Senate, May 1, 1973, p. 13773.

48. *McCall's* (October 1961).

49. Rockefeller Panel Report, *Performing Arts,* p. 8.

50. *Music Journal* (March 1963).

51. American Council on the Arts, *Carter on the Arts,* 1977, p. 46.

52. *Congressional Record,* Senate, December 20, 1963, p. 25270.

216

Notes

53. Ibid., p. 25266.

54. Ibid.

55. Rockefeller Panel Report, *Performing Arts,* p. 57.

56. *Congressional Record,* House, September 1, 1965, pp. 23937–38.

57. Rockefeller Panel Report, *Performing Arts,* p. 2.

58. Arnold Gingrich, *Business and the Arts, An Answer to Tomorrow* (New York: Paul S. Eriksson, 1969), p. 3.

59. *Congressional Record,* House, February 27, 1968, p. 4325.

60. Russell Lynes, "The Case Against Government Aid to the Arts," *New York Times Magazine,* March 25, 1962.

61. Ibid.

62. Ibid.

63. Quoted in *Vital Issues* 12, no. 4 (December 1962), Center for Information on America, Washington, Connecticut.

64. Stanley Kauffmann, "Can Culture Explode?" *Commentary* 40, no. 2 (August 1965): 19–28.

Chapter 3

1. The authorities (goals) given the chairman of the NEA were listed in Section 5(c) of the act as follows:

> The Chairman, with the advice of the federal Council of the Arts, is authorized to establish and carry out a program of contracts with, or grants-in-aid to, groups or, in appropriate cases, individuals of exceptional talent engaged in or concerned with the arts, for the purpose of enabling them to provide or support in the United States—
>
> (1) productions which have substantial artistic and cultural significance, giving emphasis to American creativity and the maintenance and encouragement of professional excellence;
>
> (2) productions, meeting professional standards or standards of authenticity, irrespective of origin, which are of significant merit and which, without such assistance, would otherwise be unavailable to our citizens in many areas of the country;
>
> (3) projects that will encourage and assist artists and enable them to achieve wider distribution of their works, to work in residence at an educational or cultural institution, or to achieve standards of professional excellence;
>
> (4) workshops that will encourage and develop the appreciation and enjoyment of the arts by our citizens;
>
> (5) other relevant projects, including surveys, research and planning in the arts.

The "arts," as defined in the act, Sec. 3 (20 U.S.C. 952) (b) is as follows:

The term "the arts" includes, but is not limited to, music (instrumental and vocal), dance, drama, folk-art, creative writing, architecture and allied fields, painting, sculpture, photography, graphic and craft arts, industrial design, motion pictures, television, radio, tape and sound recording, the arts related to the presentation, performance, execution, and exhibition of such major art forms, and the study and application of the arts to the human environment.

2. Testimony of W. McNeil Lowry before the Subcommittee on the Department of the Interior and Related Agencies, House Appropriations Committee, April 14, 1979.

3. National Endowment for the Arts, "The History," vol. 1, November 1968.

4. Proceedings of the National Council on the Arts, April 9–10, 1965, p. 4. (Photocopied typescript on file in the NEA.)

5. Michael Straight, *Twigs for an Eagle's Nest* (New York and Berkeley: Devon Press, 1979), pp. 14–15.

6. Stanley Kauffmann, "Can Culture Explode?" *Commentary* 40, no. 2 (August 1965): 19–28.

7. Interview with Roger L. Stevens, May 11, 1981.

8. Interview with Henry Geldzahler, April 30, 1980.

9. National Endowment for the Arts, *Annual Report, 1966.*

10. Straight, *Twigs for an Eagle's Nest,* p. 75.

11. Karl E. Meyer, *The Art Museum: Power, Money, Ethics* (New York: William Morrow and Co., 1979), p. 82. In his account of the development of NEH Harold Berman attributes the White House decision to increase the budgets of both endowments to widespread dissatisfaction with the plans being made by the Bicentennial Commission. The endowments, he says, kidnapped the Bicentennial and kept the ransom. *Culture and Politics,* chap. 4.

12. Michael Straight, "The Arts Go Begging," *The New Republic,* March 22, 1969, p. 14.

13. Interview with Michael Straight, December 7, 1979.

14. Ibid.

15. Interview with Philip M. Kadis, June 16, 1981.

16. Interview with Michael Straight, December 7, 1979.

17. In debate on the 1964 bill creating a National Council, Congressman Johansen had objected to language that seemed to sanction its lobbying:

. . . the very duties outlined for this proposed National Council make it inevitable that the Council, once created, will be the spokesman and the driving force behind the creation of any number of plans and programs using Federal funds and Federal personnel to, in the words of this proposal, "recommend ways to maintain and exercise the cultural resources of the United States," and "to foster artistic and cultural endeavors, both nationally and internationally."

Notes

Congressional Record, House, August 20, 1964, p. 20651. Perhaps because of Johansen's warning, the language he quoted was not included in the 1965 act.

18. American Association of Museums, *Museum News* 54, no. 5 (May/June 1976).

19. "Building a Local Base for Federal Support," NEA *Bulletin,* July 5, 1977; National Endowment for the Arts, "Artists and Schools," October 1977.

20. Proceedings of the National Council on the Arts, November 30–December 2, 1979, p. 19. In 1983 the *Cultural Post* was replaced by a new magazine, *Arts Review,* of larger format, coated stock, and nearly twice as many pages.

21. *Congressional Record,* House, November 11, 1977, p. 12312.

22. Interview with Michael Straight, December 7, 1979.

23. James Melchert, in National Endowment for the Arts, *Annual Report, 1979,* p. 241. His views are elaborated in *Annual Report, 1980,* pp. 277–78.

24. Michael Straight, "Public Funding of the Arts in America," *The Great Ideas Today* (New York: Arno Press, 1977).

25. Hilton Kramer, *New York Times,* October 16, 1977, p. C1.

26. John S. Friedman, *New York Times,* October 16, 1977, p. D36.

27. Kramer, *New York Times,* October 16, 1977, p. D36.

28. Russell Lynes, "The Case Against Government Aid to the Arts," *New York Times Magazine,* March 25, 1962.

29. Resolution adopted by the National Council on the Arts, 1973.

30. Kramer, *New York Times,* October 16, 1977.

31. Leonard, *Detroit News Magazine,* p. 27.

32. *New York Times,* December 15, 1980.

33. U.S., Congress, House, 95th Cong., 2d sess., H. J. Res. 649, Report no. 95–887.

34. Proceedings of the National Council on the Arts, August 8–10, 1980, p. 32.

35. U.S., Congress, House, Subcommittee of the Committee on Appropriations, *Hearings, Department of the Interior and Related Agencies Appropriations for 1980, Part II,* 96th Cong., 1st sess., p. 711.

36. Interview with Philip Kadis, June 16, 1981.

37. National Endowment for the Arts, *Annual Report, 1980,* p. 318.

38. Proceedings of the National Council on the Arts, August 8–10, 1980, pp. 32–33, 37; November 21–22, 1980, p. 37.

39. Robert B. Carleson, quoted in Claude E. Barfield, *Rethinking Federalism* (Washington, D.C.: American Enterprise Institute Studies in Tax Policy, 1981), p. 61.

40. Although the Reagan administration proposed cutting the NEA budget for fiscal 1982 to $88 million, Congress appropriated $143 million; the budget proposal for fiscal 1983 was $101 million and the appropriation again was $143 million. For 1984 the budget proposal was $125 million and the appropriation was $162 million. Hodsoll defended the budget requests in public but was said to have worked behind the scenes for the higher figures.

Addressing a conference sponsored by the Congressional Arts Caucus in

April 1982, Hodsoll said that because small, experimental arts institutions have the most trouble raising money, "There's no question that the NEA should maintain a larger proportion of support for them." For the same reason, he said, individual artists were a second priority of the agency. Other priorities, according to the *New York Times* of April 24, 1982, were long-term financing of "high quality" organizations, arts education, and indigenous American art "not part of the Western European mainstream."

In a feature article in 1983 on changes brought by Hodsoll in the NEA, Robert Pear reported that, unlike previous chairmen, Hodsoll has questioned many grant applications recommended by peer-review panels and ultimately rejected 20 of the 5,727. Some of the projects he reluctantly approved were reminiscent of ones approved by Nancy Hanks in 1974 after Michael Straight, her deputy, declined to approve them (see chapter 1). The *Times* gave an example described in confidential documents provided to council members:

> "Brooklyn Bridge Sound Sculpture," by Bill Fontana. "This project will involve mounting six to eighteen microphones just below the steel grid road surface of the public Bridge to capture the 'singing tones' tones produce by the vibrating metal structure." "Touch Sanitation Show," a public performance event produced by Mierle Laderman Ukeles. The performance includes "the arrival of a barge containing the work gloves of sanitation workers collected from the five boroughs of New York City" and "a large-scale sculpture utilizing sanitation vehicles frozen in gestures of their working day." "Dance of Machines," an interdisciplinary work sponsored by the Snake Theater/Nightfire Division in Sausalito, Calif. Cranes and heavy construction machines will "dance" at a large construction site in a performance featuring video projections and original music.

Hodsoll, according to the *Times* report, said these projects raised the question: "At what point does art end?" It troubled him because there seemed to be "no defined audience" for such works. He approved the grants after being persuaded that the artists had "serious intentions." Robert Pear, "Reagan's Arts Chairman Brings Subtle Changes to the Endowment," *New York Times*, April 10, 1983, p. H1.

41. Aram Bakshian, in *The MacNeil-Lehrer Report* (library #1444, show #6204), April 9, 1981, pp. 2–3.

42. Presidential Task Force on the Arts and the Humanities, *Report to the President* (Washington, D.C.: U.S. Government Printing Office, October 1981), p. 2.

43. When Hodsoll came to select his deputy chairman for programs, the perennial contention between elitists and populists flared up in a struggle between supporters of David W. Rubin, vice-president for concerts at Steinway & Sons, and Hugh Southern, executive director of the Theatre Development Fund, a New York–based organization that encourages theater-

going by providing subsidies. Rubin was the elitist ("It isn't enough to bring thousands of people in if the art they see or hear is less than fine"). Southern, whose supporters included Nancy Hanks, was the populist. Southern got the job. (*New York Times,* April 24, 1982.)

Chapter 4

1. E. H. Gombrich, "The Museum: Past, Present, Future," *Critical Inquiry* 3, no. 3 (Spring 1977): 460.

2. For historical accounts of American art museums, see Nathaniel Burt, *Palaces for the People: A Social History of the American Art Museum* (Boston: Little, Brown and Co., 1977), which contains a good bibliography; and Karl E. Meyer, *The Art Museum: Power, Money, Ethics* (New York: William Morrow and Co., 1979). On the current affairs of art museums, see Sherman E. Lee, ed., *On Understanding Art Museums* (Englewood Cliffs, N.J.: Prentice-Hall, 1975); and Brian O'Doherty, ed., *Museums in Crisis* (New York: George Braziller, 1973).

3. This view of the function of the art museum follows from the assumptions made in previous chapters about the nature of art and the special relevance from a policy standpoint of the aesthetic experience. Other assumptions would of course carry other implications. For example, Karsten Harries has pointed out to the author that the European antecedents of the art museum were the church, whose contents were not perceived as art, and the "cabinet of curiosities," which contained not only precious artifacts but horns of unicorns and the like. Both institutions enabled one to step out of the ordinary world and into one that was different in time and place. Modern man, Harries thinks, needs places where he can get in touch with the extraordinary, and the art museum may help meet the need, one not easily addressed in a democratic society. Letter from Karsten Harries, September 2, 1982.

4. Quoted by David D. Hall, "The Victorian Connection," in *Victorian America,* ed. Daniel W. Howe (Philadelphia: University of Pennsylvania Press, 1976), p. 90. On the strategies of reform, see Paul Boyer, *Urban Masses and Moral Order in America, 1882–1920* (Cambridge, Mass.: Harvard University Press, 1979). See also Helen Lefkowitz Horowitz, *Culture and the City: Cultural Philanthropy in Chicago from the 1880s to 1917* (Lexington: University of Kentucky Press, 1976).

5. Hall, "Victorian Connection."

6. Ralph Waldo Emerson, *Essays: First Series* (Boston: Philips, Samson and Co., 1856), essay 12.

7. Quotes by Calvin Tomkins, *Merchants and Masterpieces* (New York: E. P. Dutton and Company, 1970), pp. 35–36. See also Winifred E. Howe, *A History of the Metropolitan Museum of Art* (New York: Metropolitan Museum of Art, 1931), p. 133.

8. C. C. Perkins, "Art Education in America," *Journal of Social Sciences,* no. 3 (1871): 46, 49.

9. *Report of the Executive of the Metropolitan Museum of Art to the General Committee* (New York: New York Union Printing House, 1870), p. 13.

10. Perkins, "Art Education in America."

11. The phrase "depository of grandeur" is used by Burt, *Palaces for the People,* p. 231.

12. See "The Battle of the Casts," in *Museum of Fine Arts, Boston: A Centennial History,* vol. 1., ed. Walter Muir Whitehead (Cambridge, Mass.: Belknap Press of Harvard University Press, 1970). C. C. Perkins expressed the founders' enthusiasm for casts in "Art Education in America," p. 42.

13. Joshua Taylor, in *On Understanding Art Museums,* ed. Sherman E. Lee (Englewood Cliffs, N.J.: Prentice-Hall, 1975), pp. 41–42.

14. Quoted in John Walker, *Self-Portrait with Donors* (Boston: Little, Brown and Co., 1974), p. 280.

15. Laurence Veil Coleman, *The Museum in America,* vol. 1 (Washington, D.C.: American Association of Museums, 1939), p. 86. Also, W. E. Howe, *A History of the Metropolitan Museum of Art,* vol. 1 (New York: Arno Press, 1946).

16. Germain Bazin, *The Museum Age,* trans. Jane van Luis Cahill (New York: Universe Books, 1967), p. 247.

17. James Bellows, "Marginal Notes on Civilization in the U.S.," in *George Santayana's America,* ed. Bellows (Urbana-Champaign: University of Illinois Press, 1967), p. 171.

18. André Malraux, *The Voices of Silence* (Garden City, N.Y.: Doubleday and Co., 1953), p. 65.

19. *New York Times,* March 1, 1980, p. 26. In an admiring eulogy, Russell Lynes remarked that Mayor "collected not just what was regarded as 'art' but commercial catalogues of furniture and fixtures and clothes, wine labels, cigarette cards and other unlikely printed ephemera." *ARTnews* (Summer 1980): 121.

20. Coleman, *Museum in America,* vol. 1, p. 83.

21. Francis Henry Taylor, *Babel's Tower: The Dilemma of the Modern Museum* (New York: Columbia University Press, 1945), p. 26.

22. John P. Coolidge, "Some Problems of American Art Museums," paper delivered at the Boston Club of Odd Volumes, Boston, Mass., March 18, 1953, p. 13.

23. Here is a reporter's account of a visit by the curator of paintings of the Boston Museum of Fine Arts to two elderly women who had offered to give a painting:

> In the dim lamplight of their Victorian-filled home, Mr. Walsh carefully studied the work, a painting that, he confided later, the museum probably wouldn't buy with its own money and wouldn't hang all of the time.
>
> But it was worth consideration. "Yes, yes, I can see something of David [the eighteenth-century artist] in it," he mused. "The museum

would be pleased to have it," he said. "I'd like to show you how to make a bequest."

Liz Roman Gallese, *Wall Street Journal,* July 23, 1979, p. 1. See also an article by economist J. Michael Montias, "Are Museums Betraying the Public Trust?" *Museum News* 51, no. 9 (May 1973): 25–31.

24. The association's code of ethics appears in *Museum News* 51, no. 9 (May 1973): 49.

25. Daniel M. Fox, *Engines of Culture: Philanthropy in the Art Museums* (Madison: State Historical Society for the Department of History, University of Wisconsin Press, 1963), p. 40.

26. Gombrich, "The Museum," p. 457.

27. Reference to Albert H. Wiggin Collection in the Boston Public Library, in Walter Whitehall, ed., *History of the Boston Public Library* (Cambridge, Mass.: Harvard University Press, 1956), p. 237.

28. George Savage, *Forgeries, Fakes and Reproductions* (New York: Praeger, 1963), p. 218.

29. Lee, ed., *On Understanding Art Museums,* p. 123.

30. John Cotton Dana, *A Plan for a New Museum* (Woodstock, Vt.: Elm Tree Press, 1920), pp. 20–21.

31. Ibid, pp. 34–35.

32. Ibid, p. 33.

33. Richard Grove, *Museum News* (May/June 1978): 39; Frank Kingdon, *John Cotton Dana: A Life* (Newark, N.J.: Public Library and Museum, 1940).

34. Walker, *Self-Portrait with Donors,* p. 305.

35. Fox, *Engines of Culture,* p. 49.

36. Coleman, *Museum in America,* vol. 2, p. 346.

37. Theodore L. Low, *The Museum as a Social Instrument* (New York: Metropolitan Museum of Art for the American Association of Museums, 1942), p. 17.

38. Taylor, *Babel's Tower,* p. 22.

39. The Brooklyn Museum seems to have been the first major museum to concern itself with the inner city. Residents of nearby Bedford-Stuyvesant found hardly anything in it "relevant to their daily lives," according to Henri Ghent; it "seemed to many of them to exalt the trophies of an alien culture." In the fall of 1867, the museum established a Community Gallery to serve Bedford-Stuyvesant. Henri Ghent, "Brooklyn Museum's Community Gallery: Can It Happen Again?" *Art in America* (July–August 1973), p. 19. The outreach programs of several art museums are described in Barbara Y. Newsom and Adele A. Silver, eds., *The Art Museum as Educator* (Berkeley, Los Angeles, London: University of California Press, 1978), chap. 3.

On the failure of young minority students (blacks and Puerto Ricans) to understand what they see in "white elitist" art museums, see Robert Coles, "The Art Museum and the Pressure of Society," *ARTnews* (January 1975): 24–33.

40. See American Association of Art Museums, *Museums: Their New Audience*

(Washington, D.C., 1972); Carol Supplee, "Museums on Wheels," *Museum News* (October 1974); and Emily Harvey and Bernard Friedberg, *A Museum for the People* (New York: Arno Press, 1971).

41. For a brief and uncritical account of the program by its director, see Irwin M. Gross, "Outreach in Michigan," *Museum News* (October 1970): 33–35.

42. National Endowment for the Arts, *Two Years Later . . . A Report on 'Project Outreach' to the National Endowment for the Arts* (Washington, D.C., 1969).

43. George Heard Hamilton, "Education and Scholarship in the American Museum," in *On Understanding Art Museums,* ed. Sherman E. Lee (Englewood Cliffs, N.J.: Prentice-Hall, 1975), p. 126.

44. Bonnie Burnham, *The Art Crisis* (New York: St. Martin's Press, 1975), p. 32.

45. Walker, *Self-Portrait with Donors,* p. 66.

46. *New York Times,* November 18, 1961, p. 22.

47. The analysis here owes much to Robert Raymond Weller, "An Economic Model of the Public Art Museum" (Ph.D. diss., Harvard University, March 1968).

48. Interview with Robert Cassellman, March 22, 1978.

49. The products offered in some one hundred art museum stores are listed in the 173-page *The Shopper's Guide to Museum Stores* (New York: Universal Books, 1977), under the following categories: furniture, miniatures, tableware, desk accessories, stained glass, posters, reproductions, objects and ornaments, toys and games, jewelry, textiles and fashion accessories, needlework, greeting and note cards, calendars, cookbooks, books, and miscellany. Beginning in the 1970s several major museums profited from the sale of cookbooks. *A Culinary Collection from the Metropolitan Museum of Art,* first published for Christmas in 1973, contained recipes "from world-famous millionaire trustees next to those from typists and guards." Kay Groves, "Museum Cookbooks for Fun and Profit," *Museum News* (June 1975).

50. The attack and the reply are quoted by Philip M. Kadis, "Who Should Manage Museums?" *ARTnews* 76, no. 8 (October 1977): 48–49. For an account of the sales practices of art museums and of the debate about them within the art museum world, see Terry Trucco, "The Shopping Boom at Your Local Museum," in ibid., pp. 56–60. See also *Business Week,* October 24, 1977, pp. 135–36.

51. Interview with Robert Cassellman, March 22, 1978.

52. Burnham, *Art Crisis,* p. 235.

53. Michael Straight, conversation with the author, June 1980.

54. David B. Little, "The Misguided Mission: A Disenchanted View of Art Museums Today," *Curator* 10, no. 3 (1967): 221–26. For other criticisms, see Thomas Albright, "The Contemporary Art Museum: 'Irresponsibility Has Become Widespread,' " *ARTnews* (January 1980): 42–47.

55. National Endowment for the Arts, *Annual Report, 1979,* p. 141.

Notes

Chapter 5

1. C. C. Perkins, "Art Education in America," *Journal of Social Sciences*, no. 3 (1871): 40.

2. Ibid., p. 51.

3. Ibid., p. 46.

4. William T. Harris, quoted in Lawrence A. Cremin, *The Transformation of the School* (New York: Knopf, 1961), p. 17. An historical perspective on teaching and research in art in the United States by Geraldine Joncich Clifford can be found in Gerald L. Knieter and Jane Stallings, eds., *The Teaching Process and Arts and Aesthetics* (St. Louis, Mo.: CEMREL, 1979), pp. 11–39.

5. Harold Rugg and Ann Shumaker, *The Child-Centered School* (Yonkers-on-Hudson, N.Y., and Chicago: World Book Co., 1928), chap. 15.

6. Cremin, *Transformation of the School*, p. viii.

7. Quoted in ibid., p. 118.

8. Ibid., p. 183.

9. Rugg and Shumaker, *Child-Centered School*, pp. 35, 37.

10. Ibid., pp. 73, 181, 226.

11. Ibid., pp. 233, 228, 229.

12. Elliott Eisner, paraphrased in National Art Education Association, *Report of the NAEA Commission on Art Education*, Charles M. Dorn, commission chairman (Reston, Va., 1977), p. 124.

13. Brent Wilson, "One View of the Past and Future of Research in Aesthetic Education," *Journal of Aesthetic Education* 8, no. 4 (1974): 60. The research he summarizes is reported in *Studies in Art Education* (Autumn 1966, Fall 1970, and Winter 1972).

14. Charles E. Silberman, *Crisis in the Classroom: The Remaking in American Education* (New York: Random House, 1970).

15. These judgments reflect those of leading figures in the world of art education. For example, Harry S. Broudy writes:

> Tradition, the enhancement of the quality of life, self-development, facilitation of academic performance in basic skills, recreation, and similar "effective" reasons are offered, usually unconvincingly, to administrators. The curriculum itself also follows such justifications and thereby fails to teach, lacks rigor, objures the hardship of discipline and work, and trivializes the arts in the schools. Nevertheless, the forces of advocacy for the arts in education have become increasingly vocal.

Harry S. Broudy, "On Cognition and Emotion in the Arts," in *The Arts, Cognition, and Basic Skills*, ed. Stanley S. Madeja (St. Louis, Mo.: CEMREL, 1978), p. 24. See also Lee S. Shulman's summary of the views of the specialists at a conference on art education in *The Teaching Process and Arts and*

Aesthetics, ed. Gerald L. Knieter and Jane Stallings (St. Louis, Mo.: CEMREL, 1979), p. 24, and Elliott W. Eisner, "What We Don't Know about the Teaching of Art," *Phi Delta Kappa* 61, no. 9 (May 1980).

In Soviet schools all of the arts except dance are taught at an early age (a child begins to learn to draw at four), apparently with considerable success. The overriding objective of Soviet art education, however, in the opinion of C. M. Smith, an American professor of educational policy studies, "is extra-aesthetic, namely, the shaping of the Soviet personality." See her review of Miriam Morton, *The Arts and the Soviet Child* (New York: Free Press, 1972), in *The Journal of Aesthetic Education* 9, no. 1 (January 1975): 111–18.

16. Howard Gardner, *Artful Scribbles: The Significance of Children's Drawings* (New York: Basic Books, 1980). See also Michael D. Day, "Child Art, School Art and the Real World of Art," in *Arts Education and Back to Basics,* ed. Stephen N. Dobbs (Reston, Va.: National Art Education Association, 1979), pp. 115–28.

17. On tests measuring visual abilities, see O. K. Buros, ed., *Mental Measurements Yearbooks* (Highland Park, N.J.: Gryphon Press, 1953 and 1959).

18. Howard Gardner discusses what is known about the functions of the left and right hemispheres of the brain in a chapter he contributed to *The Arts and Cognition,* ed. David Perkins and Barbara Leondar (Baltimore, Md.: Johns Hopkins University Press, 1977), esp. pp. 104–7.

19. *Letters to His Son by the Earl of Chesterfield,* Oliver H. Leigh, ed. (New York: Tudor Publishing Company, n.d.), letter 23, p. 40.

At the age of eighty-four, Bernard Berenson wrote:

> What is the purpose of teaching the young the history of art? Assuming it is the story of man's effort to give visual interpretation and statement to his reaction toward the chaos outside himself, how is it to be taught in a way that will make the young student feel and understand each achievement on its own merit? Whence is to come the orientation and the standard? And are we out for teaching him about art or how to appreciate it? The present approach seems external even when the subject is Picasso. How is it to be done otherwise? Perhaps by Socratic method, by persuading the student to look and try to state what he finds as he looks at a given art.

Bernard Berenson, *Sunset at Twilight* (New York: Brace and World, 1963), p. 89.

20. Michael Oakeshott, *Rationalism in Politics* (New York: Basic Books, 1962), pp. 10–11.

21. Broudy, "On Cognition and Emotion in the Arts," p. 252.

22. "Most teachers," writes the arts adviser to the National Institute of Education, "require massive and intensive doses of introductory experience in fundamentals of aesthetic perception. Simply stated, they need to learn how to look and see, to hear and to feel." Martin Engel, "The Continuing Education of Teachers," *Art Education* (September 1976): 6.

Notes

23. Wilson, "Research in Aesthetic Education," p. 66.

24. Martin Engel, "Some General Considerations Regarding Research in the Arts in Education," *Art Education* 29, no. 3 (April 1976): 16.

25. *Federal Register* 40, no. 126 (June 30, 1975): 27486–91. The seven criteria are reproduced in Madeja, ed., *Arts and Aesthetics*, p. 218.

26. A detailed history of the branch was published by the Office of Education in 1978: Judith Murphy and Lonna Jones, *Research in Arts Education, a Federal Chapter* (Washington, D.C.: Office of Education, n.d.).

27. Martin Engel, "Aesthetic Education, The State of the Art," *Art Education* 28, no. 3 (March 1975): 17.

In May 1980 the art-education coordinator of the new U.S. Department of Education listed some six hundred arts-related projects and activities funded to a total of at least $30 million by forty-five of the department's approximately 150 separate funding programs. Only three of these provided funding specifically for the arts: the Arts Education Program (to support art education in elementary and secondary schools), the Special Arts Projects (for artists-in-residence programs designed to promote intercultural and interracial communication), and the Institute of Museum Services (to support a variety of museums, including art museums). Most of the other department programs neither excluded the arts nor singled them out for special consideration. The largest single program funding the arts in 1979, both in terms of numbers of projects and of dollars, was the state-administered ESEA Title IV-C program, which supported almost three hundred of the six hundred projects with almost $7 million. Programs funded under the Emergency School Aid Act (ESAA) to ease racial tensions in urban areas undergoing court-ordered desegregation accounted for more than $6 million of the $30 million total. The approximately six hundred projects are listed with one-line descriptions in the department's "The Arts and the U.S. Department of Education: A List of Funded Projects and Activities, 1979."

28. National Art Education Association, *Report of the NAEA Commission on Art Education*, p. 31.

29. Junius Eddy, *Arts Education 1977—In Prose and Print, An Overview of Nine Significant Publications Affecting the Arts in American Education*, prepared for the Subcommittee on Education in the Arts and the Humanities of the Federal Interagency Committee on Education (Washington, D.C.: Government Printing Office, September 1977), p. 3.

30. *Coming to Our Senses: The Significance of the Arts for American Education*, Report of the Panel on Arts, Education, and Americans, American Council for the Arts in Education (New York: McGraw-Hill, 1977).

31. *New York Times*, May 22, 1977, p. D16.

32. *Coming to Our Senses*, pp. 9, 6, 131, 142. The views of those associated with the JDR 3rd Fund are set forth in Jerome J. Hausman, ed., *Arts and the Schools* (New York: McGraw-Hill, 1980).

33. *Coming to Our Senses*, p. 142.

34. *New York Times*, May 22, 1977.

35. Ibid.

36. Ibid.

37. National Art Education Association, *Report of the NAEA Commission on Art Education,* pp. 248–63.

38. Ralph A. Smith, "The Naked Piano Player: Or What the Rockefeller Report 'Coming to Our Senses' Really Is," *Art Education* (January 1978): 10–16.

39. Laura M. Chapman, "Coming to Our Senses: Beyond the Rhetoric," *Art Education* (January 1978): 5–9.

40. Ibid., pp. 7, 9.

41. National Art Education Association, *Report of the NAEA Commission on Art Education.*

42. The commission members were: Elliott W. Eisner of Stanford; Albert Hurwitz of the Newton, Mass., public schools; Stanley Madeja of CEMREL; Anne Taylor of the University of New Mexico; and Charles M. Dorn of Purdue University, who served as chairman.

43. National Art Education Association, *Report of the NAEA Commission on Art Education,* p. 14.

44. Ibid., pp. 19, 35, 41, 65, 66.

45. Ibid., p. 75.

46. Ibid., pp. 47, 49.

47. Ibid., p. 55.

48. Ibid., p. 56.

49. Martin Engel, "The Future of Aesthetic Education," *Art Education* (March 1976): 6.

Chapter 6

1. Daniel Boorstin, *The Image* (New York: Atheneum, 1961), p. 126.

2. Hilton Kramer, *New York Times,* December 10, 1978, p. C1.

3. Robert Hughes, *Time,* December 18, 1978.

4. Ruth Berenson, "HIYA, RODIN!" *National Review,* March 16, 1979, p. 373.

5. *Boston Globe,* November 24, 1978.

6. Samuel Lipman, "Music: On the Air," *Commentary* 69, no. 4 (April 1980): 79; see also Michael Straight, *Twigs for an Eagle's Nest* (New York and Berkeley: Devon Press, 1979), pp. 66, 152.

7. There are differences of opinion about this. For the pros and cons, see the collection of essays edited by Denis Dutton, *The Forger's Art: Forgery and the Philosophy of Art* (Berkeley: University of California Press, 1983).

8. Giorgio Vasari, *Lives,* IV, pp. 110–11, quoted by Etienne Gilson, *Painting and Reality* (New York: Pantheon Books, 1957), pp. 79–80.

9. Gilson, *Painting and Reality,* p. 88.

10. Richard Harris, "A Reporter at Large: The Forgery of Art," *The New*

Notes

Yorker, September 16, 1961, p. 114. For an account of some of the Metropolitan Museum of Art's most memorable experiences with forgeries, see Calvin Tomkins, *Merchants and Masterpieces: The Story of the Metropolitan Museum of Art* (New York: E. P. Dutton and Company, 1970), pp. 125–34.

11. *Philadelphia Inquirer,* March 14, 1973.

12. *New York Times,* November 14, 1976, p. 49.

13. Ibid., October 23, 1977, p. C21.

14. Ibid., February 10, 1978, p. B1.

15. Robert Reisner, *Fakes and Forgeries in the Fine Arts* (New York: Special Libraries Association, 1950).

16. *ARTnews,* September 1978, p. 30.

17. W. K. Wimsatt, *The Verbal Icon* (Lexington: University of Kentucky Press, 1967), p. 264.

18. Quoted by Harris, "Reporter at Large," p. 114. Much historical detail is provided by Joseph Alsop who remarks that the historical response to art that always goes with art collecting causes all works of art to be considered as historical documents. Joseph Alsop, *The Rare Art Traditions,* Bollingen Series 35 (New York: Harper & Row, 1982), p. 131.

19. Harris, "Reporter at Large," p. 114.

20. Quoted by Max J. Friedlander, *On Art and Connoisseurship* (London: Bruno Cassirer, 1942), p. 253.

21. Quoted by Harris, "Reporter at Large," p. 114.

22. Gilson, *Painting and Reality,* pp. 96, 97.

23. Kirk Varnedoe, "A Reappraisal of the Rodin Legacy," *Smithsonian* (July 1981): 43. See also Etienne Gilson, *Form and Substance in the Arts* (New York: Charles Scribner's Sons, 1966), p. 86.

24. Leo Steinberg, *Other Criteria: Confrontation with 20th Century Art* (New York: Oxford University Press, 1972), pp. 330–31.

25. Klaus Perls, president of Art Dealers Association of America, quoted by John L. Hess, *New York Times,* February 3, 1968, p. 420.

26. Varnedoe, "Reappraisal of the Rodin Legacy."

27. Fogg Art Museum, *Newsletter,* 14, no. 3 (March 1977): 2.

28. *The Letter Edged in Black Press, Inc. v. Public Building Commission of Chicago,* 320 F. Supp. 1310 (1970).

29. Nelson Goodman, *The Languages of Art* (Indianapolis: Bobbs-Merrill, 1968), p. 119.

30. See Judith Goldman, "The Print's Progress: Problems in a Changing Medium," *ARTnews* (Summer 1976), and Betty Chamberlain in *American Artist* (April 1976): 26 et. seq.

31. Albert Elson and John Merryman, "Art Replicas: A Question of Ethics," *ARTnews* (February 1979): 61. See also their book, *Law, Ethics, and the Visual Arts* (New York: Matthew Bender and Co., 1979).

32. Grace Glueck, *New York Times,* April 23, 1982, p. C1.

33. Thorstein Veblen, *The Theory of the Leisure Class* (New York: Modern Library Edition, 1931), p. 169.

Chapter 7

1. Roger Fry, *Vision and Design* (New York: Brentano's, n.d.), p. 76.

2. Artemas Packard, "A Report on the Development of the Museum of Modern Art" (Typescript, copy on file in Fogg Museum library, Harvard University, Cambridge, Mass., n.d.).

3. Frank P. Chambers, *The History of Taste* (New York: Columbia University Press, 1932), p. 10.

4. Walter Benjamin, "The Work of Art in an Age of Mechanical Reproductions," in *Illuminations*, ed. Hannah Arendt (New York: Schocken Books, 1969). See especially the footnote pp. 244–46.

5. G. G. Coulton, *Art and the Reformation* (New York: Knopf, 1928), app. 7, p. 254.

6. J. L. Propert, quoted by Arthur H. R. Fairchild, "Shakespeare and the Art of Design," *University of Missouri Studies: A Quarterly of Research* 7, no. 1 (January 1, 1937): 101n.

7. Chambers, *History of Taste*, p. 29.

8. Ibid., p. 38.

9. The 1964 edition of the French Academy's dictionary treated "artisan" and "artiste" as equivalent; it was not until the edition of 1762 that "artist" was defined in the modern manner. Jean Gimpel, *The Cult of Art: Against Art and Artists* (New York: Stein & Day, 1969), p. 5.

10. Quoted in ibid., p. 127.

11. *Collected Works of William Morris*, vol. 22 (New York and London: Longman's, Green and Company, 1914), pp. 3–4, 55, 134, 236, 337.

12. Ibid., pp. 359–60.

13. Peter Selz and Mildred Constantine, eds., *Art Nouveau, Art and Design at the Turn of the Century* (New York: Museum of Modern Art, 1959), p. 111.

14. Hugh Adams, *Artforum* (Summer 1979): 29.

15. For an account of the Bauhaus, see Herbert Bayer, Walter Gropius, and Ise Gropius, eds., *Bauhaus, 1919–1928* (New York: Museum of Modern Art, 1938).

16. Gillian Naylor, *The Arts and Crafts Movement* (London: Studio Vista, 1971), p. 108.

17. Sibyl Moholy-Nagy, quoted in Alexander Tzonis, *Towards a Non-Oppressive Environment* (Boston: i Press, 1972), p. 88.

18. Ibid., p. 87.

19. Writing about the installation in the new Michael C. Rockefeller Wing of the Metropolitan Museum of Art ("a huge, abstract space"), the *Times* critic, Paul Goldberger, complains that "these remarkable pieces of primitive art become, in effect, modernist objects." *New York Times*, February 3, 1982, p. C1.

20. Russell Lynes, *Good Old Modern: An Intimate Portrait of the Museum of Modern Art* (New York: Atheneum, 1973), p. 319.

Notes

21. Stuart Johnson, interviewed by Judith Fuhring, March 1978.

22. "Take Your Choice: Contemporary Product Design," Cooper-Hewitt Museum, April 17–May 13, 1979.

23. *New York Times,* April 29, 1979, p. D32.

24. Sir Kenneth Clark, "The Blot . . . and . . . the Diagram," *ARTnews* (December 1962). Reprinted in *The Art World,* ed. Barbaralee Diamondstein (New York: Artnews Books, 1977), p. 318.

25. Quoted by Naylor, *Arts and Crafts Movement,* p. 181.

26. Paul Goldberger, *New York Times,* November 16, 1978, p. C10.

27. Manuela Hoelterhoff, *Wall Street Journal,* April 13, 1979.

28. *New York Times,* December 28, 1978. Evelyn Waugh saw the limitations of the New Architecture very early. Because of the British climate, its triumphs, he wrote in 1937,

> began to assume the melancholy air of a deserted exhibition, almost before the tubular furniture within had become bent and tarnished. It has now become *par excellence* the style of the arterial highroads, the cinema studios, the face-cream factories, the Tube stations of the farthest suburbs, the radio-ridden villas of the Sussex coast.

Evelyn Waugh, *A Little Order* (Boston and Toronto: Little, Brown and Co., 1977), p. 62.

29. Peter Blake, *Form Follows Fiasco: Why Modern Architecture Hasn't Worked* (Boston: Little, Brown and Co., 1977), pp. 32, 33, 79.

30. Wolf von Eckhardt, *Back to the Drawing Board: Planning for Liveable Cities* (New York: New Republic Books, 1978), p. 63.

31. Howard S. Becker, *Art Worlds* (Berkeley: University of California Press, 1982), pp. 278–79.

32. *New York Times,* August 14, 1980.

33. Marion Muller, *The New Leader,* August 13, 1979, pp. 25–26.

34. For a remarkable record of one such city, see Fairmont Park Art Association, *Sculpture of a City: Philadelphia's Treasures in Bronze and Stone* (New York: Walker Publishing Co., 1974).

35. *Wall Street Journal,* March 6, 1979.

36. *New York Times,* October 7, 1982.

37. Amy Goldin, "The Esthetic Ghetto, Some Thoughts about Public Art," *Art in America* (May/June 1974): 32.

38. For photographs and descriptions of public sculptures commissioned by the General Services Administration, see Donald W. Thalacker, *The Place of Art in the World of Architecture* (New York: Chelsea House, 1980). Thalacker, an architect, has been director of the GSA program since 1973. For the projects supported by NEA, see introduction and text by John Beardsley in Andy Leon Harney, ed., *Art in Public Places* (Washington, D.C.: Partners for Livable Places, 1981).

39. Data in this paragraph of the text, except for the last sentence, are taken from Thalacker, *The Place of Art.*

40. The local response to some GSA public sculptures is described by ibid., pp. 70, 83, 180. For an account of a particular incident and some general discussion of the public-relations problem as perceived by GSA, see Jo Ann Lewis, "A Showdown for Hoe-Down," *ARTnews* (Summer 1980): 199–200. Two philosophy professors have argued that public sculpture that "offends the eye" presents moral issues not unlike those presented by pornography: Douglas Stalker and Clark Glymour, "The Malignant Object: Thoughts on Public Sculpture," *The Public Interest*, no. 66 (Winter 1982): 3–21. See also Donald Hawthorne, "Does the Public Want Public Sculpture?" *ARTnews* (May 1982): 56–63.

41. Quoted by Wolf von Eckhardt, "The Malignant Object," *The Public Interest*, no. 66 (Winter 1982): 24.

42. Interview with James Melchert, Washington, D.C., June 16, 1981.

43. National Council on the Arts, Minutes, Meeting of November 21–22, 1980.

44. *The Taxi Project: Realistic Solutions for Today* (New York: Museum of Modern Art, 1976), pp. 16, 18.

45. William Stanley Jevons, *Methods of Social Reform* (New York: A. M. Kelley, 1965, first published in 1883).

Chapter 8

1. Ronald Berman, "Art vs. the Arts," *Commentary* 68 (November 1979): 49.

2. August Heckscher, *Goals for Americans: The Report of the President's Commission on National Goals* (Englewood Cliffs, N.J.: Prentice-Hall, 1960), p. 145. Heckscher was chairman of the panel, which included Alfred Kazin and Eileen Sanden.

3. U.S., Congress, Senate Committee Report, Calendar no. 288, to accompany F–1483, 1965, p. 14.

4. See Jeffrey M. Berry, *Lobbying for the People: The Political Behavior of Public Interest Groups* (Princeton, N.J.: Princeton University Press, 1977), p. 7.

5. Advisory Commission on Intergovernmental Relations, *An Agenda for American Federalism: Restoring Confidence and Competence,* Report A–86 (Washington, D.C.: U.S. Government Printing Office, June 1981), p. 94.

6. R. Douglas Arnold, *Congress and the Bureaucracy* (New Haven and London: Yale University Press, 1979), p. 207.

7. Cynthia Cates Colella, "The Creation, Care and Feeding of Leviathans: Who and What Makes Government Grow," in Advisory Commission on Intergovernmental Relations, *Intergovernment Perspective* 5, no. 4 (Fall 1979).

8. J. S. Whally, *Federal Evaluation of Policy* (Washington, D.C.: Urban Institute, 1970), p. 15.

9. Berman, "Art vs. the Arts," p. 49.

Notes

10. The public library has much in common with the art museum, including a tendency to redefine its mission with a view to survival and growth. A study by the economist Lawrence J. White finds *inter alia:* The library was never a socializing influence for most immigrants; most of the population does not use it in any significant way. Librarians face a dilemma: if they stress worthwhile books, patronage will fall off, but if they do not, the library has no reason for existence as a public service; in fact, most adult users want (and get) mysteries, westerns, best sellers, and hobby books; the library community is primarily middle class; lower-income persons subsidize its use by higher-income persons, and efforts to extend its services to the poor and to minorities have for the most part failed. Nevertheless, librarians are reluctant to charge users for services, to specify operational goals, to measure accomplishments, or to consider ways in which resources might be used more effectively. Beginning about 1960 organized librarians have lobbied strenuously and with much success for state and federal funds: they favor "a national public policy to promote universal library and information services." (These words are from a statement by the 1979 White House Conference on Library and Information Services.) White concludes that "the case for a tax-supported public library . . . is not a strong one." "In the end," he says, "one can only fall back on the notion that library use is a good thing and on the library community's assurance of just how good a thing it is." Lawrence J. White, *The Public Library in the 1980s: The Problems of Choice* (Lexington, Mass.: D.C. Heath and Company, 1983), p. 137.

11. Lord Lionel Robbins, "Unsettled Questions in the Political Economy of the Arts," *The Three Banks Review* (September 1971): 3.

12. An economic analysis of the demand for and supply of art-museum services, together with references to the literature, is given in Werner W. Pommerehne and Bruno S. Frey, "The Museum from an Economic Perspective," *International Social Science Journal* 32, no. 2 (1980): 323–339.

13. Douglas Stalker and Clark Glymour have argued that much, perhaps most, public sculpture creates public "ill-fare" rather than welfare. See Douglas Stalker and Clark Glymour, "The Malignant Object: Thoughts on Public Sculptures," *The Public Interest,* no. 66 (Winter 1982): 3–21.

14. William J. Baumol and William G. Bowen, *Performing Arts: The Economic Dilemma* (New York: Twentieth Century Fund, 1966), p. 385.

15. Lord Lionel Robbins, *Political Economy, Past and Present* (New York: Columbia University Press, 1976), p. 24.

16. Tibor Scitovsky, "What's Wrong with the Arts Is What's Wrong with Society," *American Economic Review* (May 1972): 1–19. These and other ideas are developed in his book *The Joyless Economy* (New York: Oxford University Press, 1976). In the book, Scitovsky remarks on the "dubious rationality" of calculating the return on investment in changing tastes (p. 236) and remarks that changes in lifestyle take a very long time (p. 284).

17. The phenomenon of "pain" in aesthetic "pleasure" is discussed by Marcia M. Eaton, "A Strange Kind of Sadness," *The Journal of Aesthetics and Art Criticism* 41, no. 1 (Fall 1982): 51–63.

18. Frank H. Knight, *The Ethics of Competition* (New York and London: Harper and Brothers, 1935), pp. 22–23.

19. Milton Friedman, *Price Theory* (Chicago: Aldine Publishing Co., 1976), p. 12. The conception of wants as unstable is discarded by George J. Stigler and Gary S. Becker, "De Gustibus Non Est Disputandum," *American Economic Review* 67, no. 2 (March 1977): 76–90.

20. Edward Everett Hale, *Public Amusements for the Poor and Rich* (Boston: Phillips, Samson and Co., 1857), p. 23.

21. The view attributed to most economists was advanced by Milton Friedman in discussions with the author. Frank H. Knight took the opposing view:

> We may observe that business is interested in the fact of change in wants more than in the character of the change, and presumably affects chiefly those changes which can be brought about most easily and cheaply. Our general moral teaching would indicate that it is easier to corrupt human nature than to improve it, and observation of the taste-forming tendencies of modern marketing methods tends perhaps to confirm the view and to substantiate a negative verdict on individualistic activity of this sort.

Knight, *Ethics of Competition*, p. 52n.

De Jouvenel takes a position similar to Knight's. In a productive society, he writes,

> the individual has no incentive to guide the desires of others toward worthier objects that are easier to produce. He must therefore take an interest in the satisfaction (and in the excitation) of the desires of others, but show no interest in their quality. If these desires appear to him badly guided, his attitude in this respect may be described, in flattering terms, as tolerance, but could be described in more accurate terms, as interested complacency.

Bertrand de Jouvenel, "A Better Life in an Affluent Society," *Diogenes* (Spring 1961): 71.

22. Kenneth J. Arrow, *The Limits of Organization* (New York: W. W. Norton, 1974), p. 41.

23. Herbert J. Gans, *Popular Culture and High Culture: An Analysis and Evaluation of Taste* (New York: Basic Books, 1974).

Notes

Chapter 9

1. American Enterprise Institute, *A Conversation with Dr. Leon Kass,* Studies in Health Policy (Washington, D.C.: American Enterprise Institute, November 16, 1978), p. 21.

2. Edward S. Corwin, *The Constitution and What It Means Today,* 14th ed. (Princeton, N.J.: Princeton University Press, 1978), p. 1.

3. See the discussion in the introduction and in notes 14 and 15 of the introduction.

4. *Congressional Record,* Senate, December 20, 1963, pp. 25263, 25268.

5. As late as the mid–1950s, writes William A. Niskanen, an economist who has held several high positions in government (he is currently a member of the Council of Economic Advisers), "There was a general obligation to identify some constitutional basis for new programs. . . . At the present time [1975], the enumerated functions do not even command lip service. The U.S. Constitution, in terms of its effectiveness in constraining the functions of the federal government, is a dead letter." William S. Niskanen, "The Pathology of Politics," in *Capitalism and Freedom: Problems and Prospects,* ed. Richard T. Selden (Charlottesville: University Press of Virginia, 1975), p. 25.

6. Writing of the first Congress, many of whose members had been delegates to the Constitutional Convention, historian E. A. J. Johnson says, "Congress had apparently accepted the idea that government ought properly to lend its assistance to any occupational group large enough and important enough in the national economy to deserve congressional recognition." To which he adds, "Legislative procedure, as contrasted with economic or political theory, simply assumed that the machinery of government ought to be employed to aid importuning interests." E. A. J. Johnson, *The Foundations of American Economic Freedom* (Minneapolis: University of Minnesota Press, 1973), p. 260.

7. *Public Opinion* 5, no. 1 (February/March 1982): 29.

8. Dick Netzer, *The Subsidized Muse* (New York: Cambridge University Press, 1978), pp. 33–34. The absence of a *national* interest in fostering a local industry did not prevent the NEA from supporting research to show the local "economic impact" of the arts. See, for example, David Cwi and Katherine Lyall, *Economic Impacts of Arts and Cultural Institutions: A Model for Assessment and a Case Study in Baltimore,* National Endowment for the Arts, Research Report no. 6 (Baltimore, Md.: Center for Metropolitan Planning and Research, Johns Hopkins University, October 1977). In this case NEA may have gotten more than it bargained for: the authors caution the reader against inferring that (a) support for the arts, as an economic development strategy, is to be preferred over other uses of public or private dollars, (b) the economic effects identified would not have occurred if the institutions examined had not existed, and (c) economic effects are or ought to be important determinants of public policy toward the arts (pp. 3–4).

Business leaders who urge support for the arts usually make all of these inferences. See, for example, W. M. Krome George, "Why Does Business Support the Arts?" (Remarks before the Economic Club of Detroit, October 22, 1979). George is the chairman and chief executive officer of the Aluminum Company of America and chairman of the Business Committee for the Arts.

9. Neil Harris, *The Artist in American Society: The Formative Years, 1790–1860* (New York: George Braziller, 1966), p. 20.

10. James Jackson Jarves, *The Art Idea,* ed. Benjamin Rowland, Jr. (Cambridge, Mass.: Belknap Press of Harvard University Press, 1960), p. 248.

11. Douglas Dillon, quoted in Arnold Gingerich, *Business and the Arts* (New York: Paul S. Erikson, 1969), p. 49.

12. For more on art therapy, see *The American Journal of Art Therapy* and *Art Psychotherapy.* Also see Elinor Ulman and Claire A. Levy, eds., *Art Therapy Viewpoints* (New York: Schocken Books, 1980).

13. Quoted in *RF* 3, no. 3 (May 1977): 8. For an account of the conference, see the Rockefeller Foundation, "The Healing Role of the Arts," *Working Papers* (New York, July 1978).

14. Mihaly Csikszentmihalyi, "Phylogenetic and Ontogenetic Functions of Artistic Cognition," in *The Arts, Cognition, and Basic Skills,* ed. Stanley S. Madeja (St. Louis, Mo.: CEMREL, 1978), pp. 121, 124, 125.

15. Jacques Barzun, *The Use and Abuse of Art* (Princeton, N.J.: Princeton University Press, 1974), p. 17.

16. Kenneth Clark, *Moments of Vision* (New York: Harper and Row, 1981), p. 80.

17. Harold Osborne, *Aesthetics and Art Theory* (New York: E. P. Dutton and Co., 1970), p. 294.

18. Quoted by Joshua C. Taylor, *America as Art* (Washington, D.C.: Smithsonian Publication, 1976), p. 290.

19. Quoted by T. J. Clark, "Clement Greenberg's Theory of Art," *Critical Inquiry* 9, no. 1 (September 1982): 155n.

20. The point is developed in E. C. Banfield, "Federalism and the Dilemma of Popular Government," in *How Federal Is the Constitution?* ed. Robert A. Goldwin and William A. Schambra (Washington, D.C.: American Enterprise Institute, 1984).

INDEX

AIS Program, *see* Artists-in-School Program
Abstract Painting, 204
Acconci, Vito, 25
Adams, John, 9, 29
Adams, John Quincy, 40–41
Advisory Commission on Intergovernmental Relations (ACIR), 13, 182–83
Aesthetic experience, 6, 16–17, 77, 143–45, 153–54, 160–62, 168–69, 172, 179–80, 184–85, 190–92, 201–5; and children, 73, 121–22, 125–26, 132, 137–38, 194; definition, 21, 24; nature of, 28–29, 33–37, 98–99
Aesthetic values, 29, 103, 132, 155–56, 163, 165–66, 184, 186, 202–3
Ambasz, Emilio, 176
American Association of Museums, 106
American Council for the Arts in Education, 131
American Crafts Museum, 169–70
Anarchy, State, and Utopia, 8–9
Anderson, Richard L., 22
Applied arts, 23, 31–32, 35, 73, 97–98, 118, 160–67, 175–77
Architecture, 73, 159–61, 166–67; *see also* Public buildings
Aristotle, 9, 203
Aristotle Contemplating the Bust of Homer, 110, 111, 154
Arlt, Gustave O., 53
Arnheim, Rudolf, 129
Arnold, R. Douglas, 182

Arp, Jean, 149
Arrow, Kenneth, 194
Art, 6–7, 34, 37, 147–48 (*see also* Applied arts; Decorative arts; Fine arts; Forgeries; Reproductions); appeal, 35–36; as play, 34–35; cognitive content, 33–34; definitions, 15–16, 21–26, 80–81, 127–28, 179, 184–85; economic aspects, 113, 143–45, 152–53, 189–91 (*see also* Art museums, finance; Federal spending; Taxation); nature of, 93, 95, 96; role of, 27–32, 155–56, 157–62
Art as Experience, 22–23
Art Commission (1860), 41
Art Crisis, The, 115
Art criticism, 61–62, 111–13, 140–42, 146, 148–49, 164, 166, 171
Art Dealers Association of America, 141–42, 151
Art education, 15, 65, 76, 118–19, 138, 140, 141, 142, 156
Art historians, 16, 100, 102, 103, 138, 153
Art history, 17, 22, 29n, 95–97, 102–3, 118, 157–62, 165–66
Art in Public Places program, 78, 173
Art Institute of Chicago, 26, 94
Art museums, 3, 58, 92–93, 117–18, 137–38, 140, 153, 158–59 (*see also* Exhibitions; specific museums); acquisitions, 68, 100–105, 116, 142–43; admission charge, 59, 105, 113, 114, 188–89; attendance,

Art museums *(continued)*
36, 100, 103, 105, 109, 110–11, 115, 154, 188–89, 202; educational function, 105–9, 113, 114, 157; finances, 93, 95, 98, 104, 107, 112, 114, 185–91; purpose, 93–100, 113, 183–84
Art therapy, 15–16, 185, 200–201
Artful Scribbles, 123
Artists, 33–34, 41, 65, 99, 118, 153, 158–59, 171–72, 175, 179; as teachers, 73, 127, 137 *(see also* Artists-in-School Program); grants to, 19–20, 66, 67–68, 69–70, 77, 82, 201; technical skill, 37, 157, 165–66, 168–69
Artists-in-School (AIS) Program, 79–80, 130, 133–35
Arts agencies, 4, 5–7; *see also* Art museums; National Endowment for the Arts; Public schools; State arts agencies
Arts Commission (1963), 49–50
Arts institutions, 25, 58
Arts policy, 84–85, 129, 133, 135, 151, 174–75 *(see also* National Endowment for the Arts, policy); history, 40–50
Ashbrook, John, 77
Associated Councils on the Arts, 71
Association of Art Museum Directors, 101, 109, 151
Auspitz, Josiah Lee, 8, 10–11

Backas, James, 82
Bakshian, Aram, 90
Barr, Alfred H., Jr., 162
Barzun, Jacques, 201–2
Bauhaus School, 160–61, 165
Bazin, Germain, 98
Beardsley, Monroe C., 28, 204
Beauty, 33, 161, 168, 203
Becker, Howard S., 26, 168–69
Berenson, Bernard, 153
Berenson, Ruth, 141
Berman, Ronald, 114–15, 178, 184
Bibliotheca Mesopotámica, 146
Biddle, George, 43, 44

Biddle, Livingston L., Jr., 53, 63, 80, 82, 86, 87, 88, 89
Blake, Peter, 166–67
Bloom, Kathryn, 128, 129, 130, 131
Boorstin, Daniel, 139
Boston Museum of Fine Arts, 94, 96, 97, 101, 113, 117, 154
Boutin, Bernard L., 172
Brademas, John, 85, 182
Braque, Georges, 33
Breuer, Marcel, 166
Brewster, Kingman, 56
Broudy, Harry S., 126
Bruce, Edward, 43
Buchanan, James, 41
Budget, *see* National Endowment for the Arts, appropriations
Bundy, McGeorge, 45
Burnham, Bonnie, 115
Burt, Nathaniel, 97

Cahill, Holger, 43
Calder, Alexander, 142, 174
Canaday, John, 61–62
Carey, Hugh, 60
Carter, Jimmy, 57–58, 79, 80, 83, 84, 85, 173
Cassellman, Robert, 113, 115, 154
Chambers, Frank, 158
Chapman, Laura H., 134–35
Chicago, Illinois, 149, 172
Child-Centered School, The, 119
Children: and art, 121–25, 129–30; *see also* Aesthetic experience, and children; Art education
Cincinnati Art Museum, 146
Clark, Sir Kenneth, 165, 202
Cleveland Museum of Art, 110, 146
Coffee, John M., 43
Coleman, Laurence, 100, 106
Collections, *see* Art museums, acquisitions
College Art Association of America, 151
Collingwood, R. G., 21, 25, 28, 191–92
Commission on Art Education, 135–37

Index

Commission on Fine Arts, 44
Commission on Intergovernmental Relations, 13
Committee on Government and Art, 44
Congress, 43, 49, 69–70, 74–75, 78, 179–80, 196 (*see also* House of Representatives; Senate); powers, 11–12, 40–41
Constitution, 8, 10, 11–12, 40, 42, 90, 195–96, 197, 205; *see also* State constitutions
Coolidge, John, 101
Cooper-Hewitt Museum of Decorative Arts and Design, 164
Copies, *see* Forgeries; Prints; Reproductions
Corcoran Gallery, 42
Cornell University: art museum, 146
Coulton, G. G., 158
Crafts, 73, 105, 157–59, 167–70
Creativity, 121, 122–23, 157; *see also* Originality, in art
Cremin, Lawrence A., 119
Csikszentmihalyi, Mihaly, 201
Culture and Politics, 114–15

Dana, John Cotton, 103–5, 109
Decorative arts, 35, 98, 100–101
Degas, Hilaire, 33, 149
Dehumanization of Art, The, 34–35
Department of Health and Human Services, 200–201
Department of Health, Education, and Welfare (HEW), 45, 46, 120
Department of Transportation, 175, 176
Department of the Treasury: Section of Fine Arts, 43, 44–45
Detroit Institute of Arts, 108
Dewey, John, 22–23, 26, 27, 119
Dickie, George, 24–25, 26
Dillon, Douglas, 200
Discourses, 30
Doherty, Richard, 113
Ducasse, Curt, 33
Duchamp, Marcel, 20
Duffey, Joseph 84

Eames, Charles, 176
Eddy, Junius, 130
Education, 110–20; *see also* Art education; Art museums, educational function; Public schools
Eisenhower, Dwight, 44–45, 46, 55, 70
Eisenhower Commission on National Goals, 48, 56, 178–79, 180, 181
Elementary and Secondary Education Act, 129
Engel, Martin, 138
Exhibitions, 26, 29, 98, 107–15, 157–58, 162–66, 169–71, 176–77, 189
Expansion Arts (program), 82

Fakes and Forgeries in the Fine Arts, 146
Farman, Paul, 171
Federal Art Project, 43–44
Federal Council on the Arts and the Humanities, 84
Federal spending, 5; *see also* Grants; Public funding of the arts; Public funding of the humanities; State appropriations; Subsidies
Fine arts, 23, 35, 73, 98, 158, 161, 168, 181; *see also* Sculpture
Fine Arts, Section on, *see* Department of the Treasury, Section on Fine Arts
Fogg Art Museum, 93, 142, 146
Ford, Gerald R., 57, 74–75, 174
Forgeries, 145–47, 148
Form Follows Fiasco, 166–67
Fortas, Abe, 50
Foundations, 52, 93, 121, 129, 131
Freudenheim, Tom L., 115–16
Friedman, Milton, 192
Fry, Roger, 33, 155, 167–68

GSA, *see* General Services Administration
Galbraith, John Kenneth, 55
Gans, Herbert J., 194

Gardner, Howard, 123
Garment, Leonard, 70, 71, 72, 74, 84
Geldzahler, Henry, 67–68, 77, 90
"General Plan, 1980–1984," 86
General Services Administration (GSA), 172–73, 175
Gifts, 4, 58, 93, 98, 101–2
Gilson, Etienne, 148
Girl With Mandolin, 139, 152
Goals for Americans, 48–49, 65, 128, 181
Goldberg, Arthur, 47, 55
Goldberger, Paul, 166, 171
Gombrich, E. H., 92, 102
Goodman, Nelson, 25–26, 27, 129
Goodwin, Richard, 49, 50, 51
Government (*see also* Congress; State government; Supreme Court): functions, 8–14, 46, 59–60, 73, 77, 90, 182–83, 197–98, 205–6; powers, 5, 11–13, 181–82, 195–97
Government buildings, *see* Public buildings
Grand Rapids, Michigan, 172, 174
Grant applications, 18–21, 76–77
Grant-in-aid programs, 13, 73, 82; *see also* specific programs
Grants, 4, 53, 69, 81–82, 138; *see also* Artists, grants to; Matching grants; Publications, grants for
Gray, Hannah, 90–91
Great Depression, 42, 106
Gropius, Walter, 160–61

HEW, *see* Department of Health, Education, and Welfare
Hale, Edward Everett, 193
Hall, David D., 94
Halle, Katherine, 48
Hamilton, George Heard, 109
Handler, Philip, 171
Hanes, R. Philip, 70
Hanks, Nancy, 18, 21, 71–81, 82, 85–86, 90, 131
Harding, Warren, 42
Harries, Karsten, 31–32
Harris, Neil, 200
Harris, William, 118
Hartford, Connecticut, 172

Harvard University, 93, 142
Heckscher, August, 48–49, 50, 56, 57, 84, 178–79, 187
Heckscher report, *see Goals for Americans*
Heston, Charlton, 90
Hodsoll, Frank S. M., 91
Holbein, Hans, 149
Hopkins, Harry, 43
House of Representatives, 46, 48, 64, 77, 85; Committee on Education and Labor, 45, 54; Select Subcommittee on Education, 51
Hoving, Thomas, 111
Howe, Harold, 128
Hughes, Robert, 141
Huizinga, Johan, 22
Humanities, 52–54, 80, 81, 90–91, 129; *see also* National Endowment for the Humanities
Humphrey, Hubert, 58
Huxtable, Ada Louise, 164

Industrial arts, *see* Applied arts
Interest groups, 14, 55, 75, 82, 182, 186, 198
Internal Revenue Code, 42, 58
Ireland, Patrick (pseud.), *see* O'Doherty, Brian

Jackson, Andrew, 41
Jarves, James Jackson, 96, 200
Javits, Jacob, 56, 71
Jefferson, Thomas, 40, 41, 197
Jevons, William Stanley, 177
Johnson, Lyndon B., 38, 50, 51, 54, 57, 65–66, 72
Johnson, Philip, 162–63
Johnson, Stuart, 163
Journal of Aesthetic Education, The, 129

Kadis, Philip M., 86, 89
Kandinsky, Wassily, 31

240

Index

Kass, Leon, 195
Kauffmann, Stanley, 62, 67
Keeney, Barnaby C., 52, 53
Kennedy, John F., 47, 48, 49, 56, 57, 59, 60, 71, 128, 172
Keppel, Francis, 58, 128–29
Kestenbaum commission, *see* Commission on Intergovernmental Relations
Knight, Frank H., 192
Knowles, John H., 201
Kramer, Hilton, 80, 81–82, 140, 141

Languages of Art, 25–26
Last Judgment, 148
Last Supper, The, 125
Le Corbusier, 161, 166
Lee, Sherman, 110, 146
Lehman, Herbert, 46
Lethaby, W. R., 166
Library of Congress, 48
Lindsay, John, 49, 55
Lipman, Samuel, 142
Locke, John, 8
Low, Theodore L., 106
Lowry, W. McNeil, 64, 181
Luce, Clare Booth, 57
Lucie-Smith, Edward, 36
Lynes, Russell, 60–61, 80

MoMA, *see* Museum of Modern Art
McKinzie, Richard, 43–44
Madison, James, 10, 11, 14, 40, 196
Malraux, André, 99–100
Mann, Horace, 118
Manzoni, Piero, 20
Massachusetts, 9–10
Matching grants, 47, 108, 114, 174
Mayor, Alpheus Hyatt, 100
Melchert, James, 78, 174–75
Metcalf, Lee, 196
Metropolitan Museum of Art, 97, 100, 105, 113, 146–47; acquisitions, 109–10, 111, 154; exhibitions, 98, 145, 149; history, 94, 95, 96–97, 101

Michelangelo, 16, 110, 145, 148
Michigan, 47
Mies van der Rohe, Ludwig, 166
Miss, Mary, 175
Mona Lisa, 110–11, 151–52
Mondale, Joan, 83–84, 173
Mondrian, Piet, 31
Moore, Donald H., 89
Moore, Henry, 33
Morgan, J. P., 96, 97, 98, 105, 146, 153
Morgan Library, 146
Morris, William, 159, 160, 161, 165, 166
Motherwell, Robert, 172
Muscarella, Oscar White, 146
Museum of Modern Art (MoMA), 93, 114, 155, 157, 162–64, 165, 166, 175–77
Museum News, 75–76
Museum Program, 115–16
Museums, 23, 73, 177; *see also* Art museums

NEA, *see* National Endowment for the Arts
NEH, *see* National Endowment for the Humanities
National Art Education Association, 130, 135
National Arts and Cultural Development Act, 50
National Assembly of State Arts Agencies, 76, 80
National Collection, 42
National Commission of the Humanities, 52–53
National Commission on Fine Arts (1910), 42
National Council on the Arts, 18, 50, 65, 68, 72, 81, 86, 89, 175
National Crafts Planning Project, 169–70
National Endowment for the Arts (NEA), 3, 20, 121, 142, 184 (*see also* Grant-in-aid programs); annual reports, 68–69, 89; appropriations, 38, 39*n*, 54, 64, 69–70, 72, 74–75, 82, 90, 91 (*see also* State appropria-

241

National Endowment for the Arts (NEA) *(continued)* tions); creation, 38, 51–54, 183, 187, 200; criticism of, 76–77, 78, 80–82, 179; policy, 63–66, 68–69, 73–75, 82, 86–89, 173, 179, 181, 183

National Endowment for the Humanities (NEH), 4, 130

National Foundation on the Arts and Humanities Act, 4, 63, 65–66, 179; benefits, 54–60; criticism, 60–62; passage, 38–39, 54, 71, 80, 180–81, 195–96, 198

National Gallery of Art, 42, 48, 105, 108, 110–11, 145, 149

National Institute of Education, 121, 138

National Portrait Gallery, 143

National Review, 141

Natural law liberalism, 8, 10, 12, 197

Netzer, Dick, 199

New Deal, 11, 42–44

New Republic, The, 72

New York City, 51–52, 55, 59, 67–68, 70, 78, 130, 132–33, 163, 170, 198

New York State, 47, 49

New York Times, 61, 78, 80, 82, 111, 113, 140, 164, 166, 169, 171

Newark Museum, 103–4, 105

Nixon, Richard, 47–48, 57, 70, 71, 72

Norton, Charles Eliot, 96

Nozick, Robert, 8–9

Oakeshott, Michael, 125

O'Doherty, Brian, 20, 77–78, 174

Office of Education, 53, 128, 129–30, 133

Office of Management and Budget, 64, 74, 75, 76, 85

Oldenberg, Claes, 26

Olmsted, Frederick Law, 94, 95

Originality: in art, 36–37

Ortega y Gasset, José, 34–36, 165

Osborne, Harold, 203

Pach, Walter, 148

Packard, Artemas, 155–57, 161, 162, 175, 177

Paintings, 33–34, 103, 104, 158, 159–60; *see also* specific paintings

Palmerston, Henry, Viscount, 98

Panel on Arts, Education, and Americans, 131–35, 137

Panofsky, Erwin, 29

Pater, Walter, 30, 96

Pell, Claiborne, 51, 53–54, 56–57, 71, 77, 80–81, 85, 182, 195–96

Pennsylvania Museum and School of Industrial Arts, *see* Philadelphia Museum of Art

Pepper, Claude, 43

Perkins, C. C., 96, 117–18

Philadelphia Museum of Art, 94, 98

Picasso, Pablo, 114, 139, 149

Pietà, 16, 110

Plato, 16, 162

Poe, Edgar Allan, 30

"Poetic Principle, The," 30

Pollock, Jackson, 194

Poor, 59–60, 107, 189

Posner, Richard, 55

Powell, Adam Clayton, 56, 59

Presidential Task Force on the Arts and the Humanities, 90–91

Prints, 149–50

Programs, *see* Grant-in-aid programs

Project Outreach, 108–9

Propert, J. L., 158

Proudhon, Pierre Joseph, 159

Public buildings, 41, 73; art commissioned for, 42, 43, 48, 117–18, 142, 172–75

Public funding of the arts, 4–7, 14, 20, 72–73, 91, 129–30, 134, 136, 184, 185–87, 204; *see also* Grant-in-aid programs; National Endowment for the Arts, appropriations

Public funding of the humanities, 52–53, 91, 129

Public interest, 5, 11, 13, 14–15, 16, 55, 143–44, 198, 204

Public schools, 3–4, 10, 117–18, 184; *see also* Education

Public welfare, 14–15, 178–79, 189–90, 197–98

Publications, 129; grants for, 75–76

Index

*Radical Principles: Reflections of an Un-
    reconstructed Democrat,* 13
Rauschenberg, Robert, 203
Rawls, John, 9
Reagan, Ronald, 89–90, 91
Redmond, Roland, 113
Reinhardt, Ad, 204
Reisner, Robert, 146
Rembrandt, 33
Reproductions, 97, 139–45, 152,
    180–81
Reynolds, Sir Joshua, 30
Robbins, Lord Lionel, 185–86, 191
Rockefeller, David, 59–60
Rockefeller, David, Jr., 131–32
Rockefeller, John D. III, 58
Rockfeller, Nelson, 45–46, 47, 71,
    84, 139–42, 187
Rockefeller Fund Panel, 54–55, 57,
    59
Rockwell, Norman, 194
Rodchenko, Alexander, 160
Rodin, François Auguste, 145, 149
Romano, Paolo, 158
Roosevelt, Franklin, 43, 44
Rorimer, James J., 110, 111
Rousseau, Jean-Jacques, 16
Rubens, Peter Paul, 148
Rubin, Leonard, 3
Rugg, Harold, 119–20
Ruskin, John, 30, 96, 159, 160, 165

Saarinen, Eero, 176
St. Louis, Missouri, 167
Sampson, Arthur F., 172
Santayana, George, 99
Savage, George, 103
Schlegel, Friedrich von, 31
Schlesinger, Arthur, Jr., 49
Scitovsky, Tibor, 191
Sculpture, 23, 33, 117–18, 148–49,
    158, 159–60, 170–75, 204
Searles, P. David, 86, 88, 89
Senate, 54, 180; Subcommittee on
    Arts and Humanities, 51
Serpentine Gallery, 36
Shumaker, Ann, 119–20
Silberman, Charles, 122

Sirovich, William I., 43
Smith, David, 67
Smith, H. Alexander, 46
Smith, Howard, 49
Smith, Ralph A., 133–34
Smithsonian Institution, 42, 48, 164,
    171
South Kensington Museum, 98
Special interests, *see* Interest groups
State appropriations, 69, 76, 79–80,
    180
State arts agencies, 47, 69, 76, 79–80,
    134; *see also* National Assembly of
    State Arts Agencies
State constitutions, 9–10, 14
State government: powers of, 11–12,
    90
State legislatures, 76, 79
Steinberg, Leo, 36–37, 149, 191
Stevens, Roger L., 50, 52–53, 65–67,
    69–70, 72, 77, 90
Straight, Michael, 18–20, 49–50, 70–
    74, 77, 78–79, 81, 115
Stuart, Gilbert, 143, 144
Subsidies, 4–8, 47–48, 58, 59, 142,
    187–94, 199, 205; *see also* Grants
Supreme Court, 11–12, 181, 196

Tax exemptions, 4, 42, 58, 93, 102,
    114, 152–53, 186
Taxation, 9, 42, 48, 76, 186, 198, 199;
    see also Internal Revenue Code
Taylor, Francis Henry, 101, 106–7
Taylor, Joshua, 97
Thalacker, Donald, 173
Theory of Justice, A, 9
Thinker, The, 33
Thompson, Frank, 45, 51, 53, 71, 85,
    182
Thurmond, Strom, 195–96
Tighe, Mary Ann, 84, 86, 87
Time magazine, 141
Tolstoy, Leo, 18
Truman, Harry, 44
Tutankhamen exhibition, 111–12,
    115
Twigs for an Eagle's Nest, 19–20
Tzonis, Alexander, 161

van Meegeren, Han, 147
Vasari, Giorgio, 145
Veblen, Thorstein, 154
Velde, Henry Van de, 160
Vermont, 14
Victoria and Albert Museum, 177
Vinci, Leonardo da, 125
Visual Arts Policy Panel, 175
Visual Arts Program, 20, 67, 77–79, 174
Viva, Eliseo, 24, 26, 27, 28–29
Voices of Silence, 99–100
von Eckhardt, Wolf, 167

Washington, George, 8, 40
Washington, George (painting), 143
Washington, Martha (painting), 143
Weissman, George, 112
What Is Art?, 18
Wilde, Oscar, 30, 34
Wilson, Brent, 128
Wilson, James 10
Wimsatt, W. K., 147
Wind, Edgar, 33–34
Winged Victory, 28
Works Progress Administration (WPA), 43
Wyeth, Andrew, 112

Walker, John, 105, 110–11
Walton, William, 49
Walzer, Michael, 13
Warhol, Andy, 32

Yale University: Beinecke Library, 146
Yates, Sidney R., 85–89, 90